QUINCY JONES

QUINCY JONES

His Life in Music

CLARENCE BERNARD HENRY

University Press of Mississippi / *Jackson*

www.upress.state.ms.us

The University Press of Mississippi is a member
of the Association of American University Presses.

Copyright © 2013 by University Press of Mississippi
All rights reserved
Manufactured in the United States of America

First printing 2013
∞
Library of Congress Cataloging-in-Publication Data

Henry, Clarence Bernard.
  Quincy Jones : his life in music / Clarence Bernard Henry.
    pages cm. — (American made music series)
  Includes bibliographical references and index.
  ISBN 978-1-61703-861-7 (cloth : alk. paper) —
  ISBN 978-1-61703-862-4 (ebook) 1. Jones, Quincy, 1933–
2. Jazz musicians—United States—Biography. I. Title.
  ML419.J7H46 2013
  781.64092—dc23
  [B]   2013009232

British Library Cataloging-in-Publication Data available

To Rita Henry, my loving mother

CONTENTS

ACKNOWLEDGMENTS

The writing of this book has taken several years and on many occasions I doubted whether I possessed a work ethic strong enough to complete such a complex project. But in achieving specific goals in life, I learned the value of persistence. My endurance for completing this book was very much invigorated by my faith and religious beliefs, especially when I often focused on a Biblical verse found in the New Testament that states, "I can do everything through him [Christ] who gives me strength" (Philippians 4:13, New International Version). By regularly recalling this verse I was constantly influenced to complete this book that focuses on the life and career of such a distinguished American musician as Quincy Jones.

Several organizations and people assisted me in compiling massive amounts of information on Jones. My research, materials, and information were enhanced through the assistance of many librarians, archivists, and professional staffs of the New York Public Library for the Performing Arts, Bibliothèque Nationale de France (National Library of France), the British Library, Kungligabiblioteket (National Library of Sweden), Seattle Public Library, the Lionel Hampton Library Collection, International Jazz Collections, the University of Idaho, and the University of California, Los Angeles Performing Arts Special Collections Folios of Printed Music Scores. To these organizations and staff members I am truly grateful for several years of diligent assistance.

Family members and friends also encouraged my research and writing. I would like to thank my sisters, Agnes Ingram, Toni Henry, Cheryl Keyes, and my brother, Walter Bruce Henry, for all their prayers and support throughout the years. I would also like to thank Sanford P. Dumain, Esq., for all his assistance through the years and all my friends at Milberg LLP. I deeply acknowledge my mentors and friends, including Jacqueline Cogdell DjeDje, Steven Loza, Cheryl Keyes, Larry Mallett, and Sherrie Tucker for their support throughout the years. I am also extremely grateful to all the book editors, the University Press of Mississippi, peer reviewers, Dr. Henry Louis Gates Jr. of Harvard University, and Shaun Lee of Quincy Jones Productions. Finally to all aspiring musicians, readers, and connoisseurs of music, I hope that the contents of this book may serve as an impetus to excel and achieve many professional types of goals.

INTRODUCTION

This book focuses on the musical experiences and career of Quincy Jones, a musician of legendary status in producing some of the most important recordings in American popular music history. Even now his creativity continues to evolve in different directions. But more than this, Jones epitomizes a positive ideology by overcoming many challenges in his life to achieve the highest status in the entertainment industry.

For several years I pondered whether I possessed the ability to write a book that focused on Jones's career. Part of the inspiration that has brought this project to fruition is Jones himself. During the course of this project, many interesting things were discovered about Jones's life that greatly influence my own understanding of the value of persistence and determination as significant factors in achieving many types of goals in life.

I had two questions that in mind when I began my research for this book several years ago: Who is Quincy Jones? Why is he such an important icon in American popular music history? I must admit that I was not completely familiar with his musical experiences, career, and extensive body of work. Like many people I was familiar with Jones's work on Michael Jackson's *Thriller*, the best selling album of all time, and the recording of the song "We Are the World." In the process of preparing a scholarly paper (presented in 2004 at a conference on American music) that focused on his early life in the Pacific Northwest, I began to better comprehend how this man has vastly contributed to innovation in American popular music on many levels.

In answering the two questions that I have presented, Quincy Jones is one of the most prolific musicians, composers, arrangers, bandleader/conductors, producers, and business entrepreneurs in popular music. His musical experiences and career are just as complex as the American popular music lexicon itself. In the popular music industry his colleagues, friends, and fans know him by many names—Dr. Jones, Mr. Jones, Quincy, Quince, "Q," and even "the Dude." But it is in his musical innovation that he is most regarded as a prominent figure.

Consumers often agree that Jones's music is powerful, aesthetically pleasing, and comprised of rich melodies, rhythms, dynamics, and textures. Many of his works are enmeshed with the influences of jazz, blues, gospel, classical, and many other styles.

From his extensive body of work it seems as though Jones has never approached any challenge with a negative attitude; I believe this has propelled him into a successful career. As a composer and arranger, he has constantly embraced change and new trends in popular music, approaching composition and arrangement as forms of expression in which his tools are similar to palettes of paint in which an artist may have many options to select from to create an artistic work. It seems as though it was destiny for Jones to discover music (and vice versa) as a vital source of inspiration for his life and chosen profession.

Jones has continually embraced the idea of reinvention by associating himself with some of the most innovative popular music performers. He has often used musical expression as a source of empowerment, not only for his own aspirations but also to inspire new generations of musicians.

In an interview around the time of his forty-first birthday, Jones commented about his interest in African American history:

> I'm so curious about everything, I've been digging back into history—not just back in the American thing, but all the way to Haiti and Trinidad and further back to the Berbers and the Moors. . . . Working on this evolution story is like going back to school. A professor at the University of Massachusetts told me I ought to take all this information I'm gathering and write it up as a thesis to get a degree. Man, I don't know what I'd do with a degree.[1]

Over the years Jones has been a major proponent and contributor to education and African and African American Studies projects. He has participated in many professional/educational symposiums and conferences. This includes his work at Harvard University with the Africana multimedia project in conjunction with the W. E. B.

Du Bois Institute of African and African American Studies with Professor Henry Louis Gates Jr. and other prominent scholars and departments.

Jones has wholeheartedly continued to be a major advocate for the appreciation, history, and importance of African American music. In many ways Jones is a representative example of the significant role African American musicians have played in the development of American popular music. Popular music styles innovated by African Americans that have become iconic in the popular music industry include blues, jazz, rock 'n' roll, rap, and gospel. In many ways these styles relate back to ancestral roots of an African musical heritage that in time became integrated with other musical styles and artistic influences in American society.

Scholarship on the significance of African and African American music production is well developed. For example, Amiri Baraka (formerly known as LeRoi Jones) who presented one of the first analytical studies of African Americans in *Blues People* (2002[1963]), observes that traditions such as jazz and blues emerged as a result of the struggles and experiences of African Americans within American society.[2] Houston Baker (1984) further elaborates on African American music by theorizing that expressive traditions such as blues comprise a productive transit, coded language, synthesis, and an amalgam of creative ideology. Noted music scholar Samuel A. Floyd Jr. describes African American music and artistic production as powerful sources that inform the sacred and secular aspects of the African/African American experience.[3] Christopher Small (1998[1987]) describes African American involvement with music in a theoretical model described as *musicking*. This involves not only performing or composing but also listening and even dancing to music. All those involved in a musical performance can be thought of as musicking.[4] This can include members of an audience.

Olly Wilson examines the African American musical experience within an interesting paradigm using theoretical notions from W. E. B. Du Bois's book *The Souls of Black Folk* (1903), which presents the idea of the African American experience involving double consciousness: two souls, two thoughts, and two ideals that evolved directly from the African heritage and the African American experience in American society. In this way styles such as spirituals, rural blues, gospel music, urban blues, jazz, and soul music stem from this dual tradition.[5] In her analysis of rap and hip hop culture, Tricia Rose (1994) suggests that African American music (and culture) in American society has always had bifocal elements that speak to African American and white audiences.[6]

African American music also reflects bifocal elements, valorization, and significance through literary and vernacular traditions (e.g., ballads, sermons, poetic rhythmic forms, stories, and dance) that greatly signify the African American cultural experience in American society.[7] During the Harlem Renaissance that coincided with the Jazz Age of the 1920s and 1930s, Harlem social clubs became popular with African Americans and whites showcasing the talents of dancers such as Josephine Baker and blues singers such as Bessie Smith and Billie Holiday and bandleaders such as Duke Ellington.[8] In African American literature there often has been a valorization of African American music, particularly jazz and blues, with narrative form and language.[9] For example, the poet Langston Hughes (1902–1967) incorporated jazz and blues rhythms as the basis for many of his poems including "Dream Boogie: Variation" (1951). By incorporating the rhythms of African American music and black vernacular expression into literature, Hughes attempted to link written and oral traditions of African American artistic expression.[10]

The relationship between African American musical and literary artistry can be found in the works of writers such as W. E. B. Du Bois (1868–1963). "Of the Sorrow Songs," a chapter of his *The Souls of Black Folk* (1903), examines the artistry of spirituals as having significance in American music and the human experience.[11] Sterling Brown (1901–1989) wrote a blues-like poem titled "Memphis Blues" (1931). Ralph Ellison's (1914–1994) award-winning novel *Invisible Man* (1952) also relies heavily on African American music, jazz in general and in particular the recordings of Louis Armstrong playing and singing "What Did I Do to Be So Black and Blue." Perhaps one of the prime examples of African American music manifested in words is the improvisational and free-flowing textual symmetry of *Jazz* (1992), a novel by Nobel Laureate Toni Morrison that depicts African American life in 1920s Harlem.

In addition to literature, some African American composers have integrated literary themes and forms with African American music. William Grant Still (1895–1978), often regarded as the dean of African American music, was highly influenced by jazz, blues, and spirituals and attempted to incorporate these traditions, along with his interest in African American literature, into his work. One of his most significant compositions is the *Afro-American Symphony* (1930), an orchestral work in four movements with each movement prefaced by excerpts from poems written by Paul Laurence Dunbar (1872–1906).

Works such as *Afro-American Symphony* and many styles and forms of African American music can be described as *migrating narratives, talking books,* or *speakerly texts,*[12] expressions that convey stories of the black experience that have given African American musicians and communities, a distinct voice and visibility during different time periods—from slavery in the Deep South to progression and movement of musicians and other African Americans to the freer urban areas in northern cities to engage in social, cultural, economic, and musical opportunities and performances encoded as power, agency, and artistic relevance in American society.

African American music can also be described as a matrix of inventiveness and aesthetic impulses that stem from cultural memory and survival of African heritage that has been manifested in artistic expressions involving songs, drums, texts, and dance that has continued to influence the creativity and innovation of African Americans, musicians, and communities in various ways.[13] Quincy Jones further explicates this particular notion and emphasizes that in the African American experience, musical and artistic innovations are traditions that have enabled people of African descent to survive and reinvent themselves in American society. Jones once commented: "Black [African American] music has always had to invent its own society, a subculture to help the disenfranchised survive, psychologically, spiritually, and creatively. We come up with our own slang, body language, sensibility, ideology, and lifestyle to go with the music."[14]

African American music, musicians, and culture have not always been received with positive responses from mainstream American society. Thus, being aware of careers and experiences of musicians such as Quincy Jones may greatly contribute to a better understanding of the struggles and challenges that some African American musicians have experienced in American society in attempting to pursue their careers and passions.

Historically there has also been in American society what can be described as a type of musical Jim Crowism and stereotype associated with African American popular music production that can be equated with racism. For example, in its origins early in the twentieth century, jazz—now considered to be America's classical music—was often regarded negatively in mainstream society. Jazz in essence was a "product of the Negro [African American]" and was often associated with promiscuity and a resulting moral decay in American society.

In the fifties the popularity of rock 'n' roll recordings was highly criticized and politicized in many parts of American mainstream society as encouraging juvenile delinquency and moral decay in young white teenagers, an argument similar to that earlier debated about the influence of jazz. One such criticism, published in the *New York Times* (1956), even featured comments by a noted psychiatrist on the effects popular music recordings had on young people: "Rock-and-roll music [records] is a communicable disease and another sign of adolescent rebellion. . . . Rock-and-roll [is] a cannibalistic and tribalistic form of music. . . . [It] is insecurity and rebellion [that] impels teenagers to affect 'ducktail' haircuts, wear zoot-suits and carry on boisterously at rock-and-roll affairs."[15]

In the public space of American society, African American music production often fell within the sentiments of segregationist ideology, pitting against one another older and younger generations. In March 1956 the *New York Times* published another riveting article, "Segregationist Wants Ban on Rock and Roll," in which a segregationist leader remarked:

> The National Association for the Advancement of Colored People [NAACP has] "infiltrated" Southern white teen-agers with "rock and roll music." [The executive secretary] of the North Alabama White Citizens Council . . . ask that juke box operators to throw out "immoral" records in the new rhythm. . . . [But] Coin music distributors said that this would mean eliminating most of their hits. [The executive secretary]

also said other records featuring Negro [African American] performers also should be "purged."[16]

Through musical expression Quincy Jones has often attempted to negate such sentiments by stimulating a positive sense of human dignity, civil rights, and a sense of positive African American/ethnic identity in individuals and communities. Jones recently remarked the following about the value and importance of styles such as jazz and blues: "For far too long, dating back to the emergence of Jazz and the Blues, our country has treated its only indigenous music as something unworthy of value because it was born on plantations and reared in jook joints. But the power that it possessed was mighty."[17]

Throughout his career Jones has constantly attempted to demonstrate the transformational effects and positive influences of popular styles from jazz to rap, their historical significance in American society, and how in many ways they transcend geographic and cultural boundaries. And in constantly stressing the value of these styles from a historical perspective while simultaneously being intimately involved in the creation of new music, Jones occupies a significant place in American popular music history.

Another goal of this book is to include a biographical discourse of an exceptional African American musician who I believe should be celebrated alongside what many intellectuals often regard as the canon of master musicians, a distinction most often associated with musicians in the Western classical music tradition (e.g., Bach, Beethoven, Mozart, Brahms, Chopin, Stravinsky, Copland, and Bernstein).

Some of the musicians that are distinguished as masters have been influenced by many styles of African American music that is evident in some of their works. For example, Antonín Dvořák (1841–1904) understood the value of African American music in American society; used elements thereof in his best-known symphony, no. 9 in E minor (*From the New World*) (1893); and also published an article titled *Music in America* (1895) in which he praised African American folksongs.[18] In the early twentieth century European composer Igor Stravinsky (1882–1971)—who was at the cutting edge of experimentation with melody, harmony, rhythm, texture, form, and instrumentation—incorporated elements of jazz in some of his works, such as *Petrushka* (1910–11), and others that were commissioned by Sergei Diaghilev for the Ballets Russes (Russian Ballet) dance company in Paris, France.[19] Swiss conductor Ernest Ansermet (1883–1969) publicly expressed that "Stravinsky knows the heart of all the good jazz dance music."[20]

Stravinsky was also influenced by African American music styles such as ragtime; this is evident in his works that include *L' histoire du soldat* (The Soldier's Tale, 1918) and *Ragtime for Eleven Instruments* (1917–18).[21] Other composers highly influenced by blues, jazz, and other styles of African American music include Aaron Copland, Maurice Ravel, George Gershwin, Leonard Bernstein, and others.

Many American music and historical reference sources provide only minimal focus on the contributions of a few talented African American musicians alongside a vast amount of research, writings, and discourses on many of the master musicians who are highly regarded in the Western classical music tradition. In many reference sources there often tends to be a focus on the influences of early African American musicians—Scott Joplin (ragtime), Bessie Smith (blues), Louis Armstrong, Duke Ellington, Charlie Parker, and Miles Davis—and how these musicians contributed and helped to shape the emergence and body of jazz in American society. Of this group of legendary African American musicians, Duke (Edward Kennedy) Ellington (1899–1974) was without a doubt the most prominent in his beliefs that styles such as jazz could serve not only as dance or entertainment music but also as a type of classical music, listened to for its own sake. Ellington composed complex pieces and multi-movement suites as *Black, Brown, and Beige* (1943), *Harlem* (1950), and *Suite Thursday* (1960). He also collaborated with composer and arranger Billy Strayhorn on jazz band arrangements of classical repertoire such as Peter Ilyich Tchaikovsky's *Nutcracker Suite* and Edvard Greig's *Peer Gynt Suite*.[22] In asserting the value of jazz as a type of classical music, Ellington declared that jazz was worthy of attentive listening and had a permanent place in American culture.[23]

In his career, Quincy Jones has achieved master musician status. He has collaborated with some of the best popular musicians. At the same time he has formal knowledge and training in the music of Western classical music composers such as Stravinsky and Ravel.

Jones's musical interest is a personification of a popular and classical music continuum that is steeped in the richness and value of all styles of music. Over the years he has continually influenced and produced a substantial body of work. Jones has also been noted for his ability to compose and arrange for string instruments and orchestral-type ensembles, and he has often attempted to blend popular and classical music in his works.

With the blending of jazz, ragtime, and classical music in works by composers as Ravel, Stravinsky, and Ellington, Quincy Jones is among this group of master musicians who have integrated innovative ideas in their work. Furthermore, Jones believes that European classical music and the music of Africa and African Americans have a close relationship because of what he describes as a sense of musical borrowing:

> It is interesting to note that European classical music has been greatly influenced by the music of Africa and Black America; and vice versa. [For example,] the blacks who came with the French to New Orleans were familiar with Western composers like [Wolfgang Amadeus] Mozart, and from them you began to see fusions like ragtime. . . . It has almost been like a relay team where one school of thought borrowed heavily from the other. Naturally both schools embellished on what they borrowed with their own sense of feeling.[24]

In many ways this statement demonstrates Jones's closeness, valuation, and embracement of different music traditions in his ideologies, integrative approaches, theoretical perceptions about music, and in his work with diverse groups of musicians and composers. As a master musician, Jones has greatly adhered to a sense of musical borrowing in his body of work in jazz, film, and popular music.

Can we in American society even imagine popular music without the contribution of Quincy Jones? Perhaps this question will garner many different responses. But his name has often been symbolic of professional success. Jones has continued to be highly regarded for his extensive expertise and longevity in the competitive entertainment industry. He is constantly sought out as an advisor and consultant on different types of music, humanitarian, and film projects.

Jones's many projects have ranged from serving as a composer and music consultant for the official music of the 23rd Olympiad in Los Angeles (1984)[25] to serving as a segment host for *Fantasia 2000—Rhapsody in Blue Segment* (Walt Disney Pictures), a sequel to the 1940 *Fantasia*. As with its predecessor, *Fantasia 2000* visualized classical music compositions with various forms of animation and live-action introductions.[26]

In public settings it is not unusual for Jones to be candid about his career and experiences. He has often appeared on talk shows such as Larry King, Tavis Smiley, and CNN, voicing his opinions about the arts, young musicians, social and cultural problems in the world, and also providing advice to fellow musicians. For example, after meeting some musicians in Johannesburg, South Africa, in 1985, Paul Simon set out to record there. Because of the apartheid problems, Simon was concerned with moral issues, and as a result one of the first musicians Simon consulted was Quincy Jones, along with Harry Belafonte and exiles Miriam Makeba and Hugh Masekela. They all gave Simon positive comments about his South African project. What resulted from this project was the album *Graceland* (1986), recorded with Joseph Shabalala and the South African group Ladysmith Black Mambazo.[27] Jones also served as one of the major commentators for *Under African Skies* (2012), a twenty-fifth-anniversary film documentary that focuses on Simon's return to South Africa to explore the journey and recording of *Graceland*.

Since the 1950s Jones has contributed numerous interviews in literary sources such as *Billboard, Down Beat, Ebony, Jet, Newsweek, Time, Variety, Stereo Review, High Fidelity/Musical America, Jazz Journal International*, and many others that feature profiles about his life, experiences, career, and his opinions about the influence of popular music in American society and throughout the world. There are also books, chapters, and other sources about Jones where he has contributed his ideas about music, the arts, the African American community, and humanitarian efforts.[28]

There are also some special film documentaries that feature performances and biographical profiles on Jones's life and career. These include *Quincy Jones in Concert* (1960), *Quincy Jones: A Celebration in Seattle* (1986), *Quincy Jones: A Celebration* (1990), *Listen Up: The Lives of Quincy Jones* (1990), *Quincy Jones: The First 50 Years* (1998), *Quincy Jones: In the Pocket* (2002), *Quincy Jones: The Story of an American Musician* (2005), *Quincy Jones: Live in '60/Reelin' in the Years* (2006[1960]), *Quincy Jones 50 Years in Music—Live at Montreux 1996* (2008), *Quincy Jones: The Many Lives of Q* (2008), and *Quincy Jones: The 75th Birthday Celebration Live at Montreux* (2009).

For those interested in pursuing further readings on Jones, this book can be a useful source in helping comprehend the significance of Jones's musical career and the reactions that have been given to his body of work. This book also includes discussions and background information about Jones and his work with many of the musicians he has collaborated with throughout his career. The topics that are included present not only a biographical profile of Jones but also discussions about his work as a composer, arranger, producer, recording artist, filmmaker, and so forth.

Chapter 1 presents an overview of the musical experiences, career, and artistic innovations of Jones and his contributions to popular music. Chapter 2 examines Jones's work as a bandleader and his experience assembling a group of the most talented musicians for his jazz bands. Chapter 3 includes a perspective about Jones's work as a composer and arranger.

Chapter 4 focuses on Jones's career in the recording industry and his collaborations with many jazz and popular musicians. Chapter 5 provides details about Jones's career in the Hollywood film industry and his challenges of being an African American composer and arranger attempting to succeed in a primarily white industry. The final section presents some insights on how Jones has continued to keep music making a vibrant aspect of his life. This vibrancy has influenced many musicians and humanitarians around the world. It is hoped that the contents of this book may inspire people in all areas of life to excel diligently in their own endeavors.

QUINCY JONES

1

A RETROSPECTIVE
OF QUINCY JONES
An American Music Icon

For more than six decades Quincy Jones has continually helped shape many styles of American music. To comprehend his global status, one needs only to refer to the popularity of works such as Michael Jackson's *Thriller* (1982), the "We Are the World" collaboration (1985), or "Soul Bossa Nova" (1962), a composition later incorporated as the theme song for the movie, *Austin Powers: International Man of Mystery* (1997). With such accomplishments, it seems that Jones's musical experiences and career warrants a study on many levels. This chapter presents a retrospective of the musical experiences, career, and artistic innovations of Jones and his contributions to American music.

Quincy Jones was born in Chicago, Illinois, on March 14, 1933. As a young child Jones experienced hard living on the South Side of Chicago, an area with a rich history of African American music and culture. For example, in 1893 Chicago hosted the World's Columbian Exposition (World's Fair) where ragtime as a popular music style and performances by Scott Joplin received broad public exposure. During the 1930s, Chicago was a major city of opportunity and part of a massive migratory movement of African Americans to northern areas of the United States from the Jim Crow South, seeking better economic opportunities. Also, similar to the New York City Harlem Renaissance in the 1930s and 1940s, Chicago was an important cultural center for African American expression in music and other artistic forms.

Chicago thrived with different sounds of popular music. The South Side was known as the "vice district" or as the "Levee." It became the home for many African Americans and black-owned social clubs. Many of these clubs supported African American entertainers and fostered a sense of racial pride on the South Side. Many of the social clubs (cabarets and saloons) were referred to as black and tans because they catered to a mix African American and white clientele.[1] In this setting some of the best musicians were major attractions. This include several New Orleans jazz musicians—Freddie Keppard, Kid (Edward) Ory, Joe King Oliver, Louis Armstrong, Jelly Roll Morton, Lillian Hardin, Earl Hines, and Jimmy Noone.

During the 1930s and 1940s Chicago's South Side was also one of the major urban centers for the further development of the blues, particularly with a style that became referred to Chicago blues. Early blues artists such as Big Bill Broonzy, Tampa Red, Memphis Minnie, John Lee "Sonny Boy" Williamson, Big Joe Williams, Bukka White, Washboard Sam, and Arthur "Big Boy" Crudup greatly contributed to the Chicago blues tradition. But although many of these musicians had dominated the blues scene in Chicago, when Muddy Waters (McKinley Morganfield) (1915–1983) arrived from the Mississippi Delta area in early 1940s, the sound of Chicago blues was truly born. Waters who became known as "Father of Chicago Blues" and the "Godfather of the Blues," first worked as a musician and became recognized on Chicago's South Side especially with his innovative use of a sturdy electric guitar with an amplifier that could be played very loudly. This made an impression among many blues musicians in Chicago and in other areas.

In the mid-1940s, the South Side also became a significant haven for the development of urban gospel music, a tradition that was greatly influenced by the innovations of Thomas Andrew Dorsey (1899–1993), who became known as the "Father of African American gospel music." Dorsey incorporated jazz, blues, and religious music into a rich urban gospel music texture that was nurtured in Chicago by musicians such as Mahalia Jackson, Sallie Martin, Roberta Martin, and many others.

Jones acquired an early indoctrination into jazz, blues, and gospel because of the constant and tangible musical presence on the South Side, where he was constantly exposed to the rich musical culture that he experienced in the city, at home (especially from his mother.

who often sang religious songs), and in his local neighborhood as one of his female neighbors on a daily basis performed stride piano.[2] Even at a young age Jones exhibited skills in musicianship. He was often drawn by his inner aesthetic emotions that were energized with the sounds of music in his neighborhood as being positive experiences that would affect his entire life. But it was in another city during the 1940s where his personal engagement with music would be fully realized.

Jones and his family were part of a second wave of migratory movement of African Americans to western regions of the United States, especially during the 1940s, when some African Americans relocated to the area to seek better economic and performing opportunities. Jones and his family relocated to the Seattle, Washington, area to pursue a better life. During this time he began to have a personal experience with music.

In Seattle Jones would be exposed to musical and cultural diversity similar to New Orleans, New York, Chicago, or Los Angeles. By the mid- to late 1940s Seattle had an established African American community as well as social clubs (jook joints) where territorial bands (traveling and touring bands from different cities) often performed.[3] In the city there were several important neighborhoods such as Jackson Street from 1st to 14th Streets and Madison Street between 21st and 33rd. In these neighborhoods the soundscapes were comprised of an array bebop, blues, rhythm & blues, Dixieland, and classical. Also, located in several of these neighborhoods were popular social clubs such as Trianon Ballroom, Palomar Theater, and the Washington Social and Education Club. Musicians of the highest caliber were readily available in Seattle—Clark Terry, Billy Eckstine, Bobby Tucker, Sarah Vaughan, Duke Ellington, and Count Basie.

Jones's personal experience with music began in 1945, when he was approximately eleven years old, in Sinclair Heights, an African American neighborhood in the Navy town of Bremerton close to Seattle. At a recreation center called the Armory, he and some neighborhood friends broke into the soda fountain area and found a freezer where lemon meringue pie and ice cream were stored. But for Jones, there was a much greater experience in that in the Armory he discovered a tiny stage in the room and on it was an old upright piano. As he tinkled on the keys he began to find a sense of peace.[4] This experience changed the direction of his entire life—in essence the beginning of his personal engagement with music.

As time progressed, music became for Jones a form of expression, a way of knowing, and a skill in problem-solving and high-order comprehension. Since that time, music has always been something in his inner being that he could control but that also offered a type of freedom. Music became a type of communicative language where Jones could openly express himself artistically and creatively. When he played music his nightmares ended, his family problems disappeared, and he did not have to search for answers. This positive experience with music made Jones feel a sense of fullness and self-reliance.

In a pedagogical sense, Jones's early experiences with music involved an integrative process of an eclectic curriculum. This involved a creative and continual use of community resources, social venues, mentor/teacher relationships, and observations and interactions with performing musicians. Jones's early experiences also involved an active exploration of music in the city of Seattle, where over time he was able to musically develop a deep sense of inner hearing and memory. This also involved his constant in-depth focus of acquiring knowledge about the concepts and functions of music (e.g., harmony, structure, form, and style).

One early musical experience involved a local barber. As Jones wandered past the house of the barber in Sinclair Heights, a man named Eddie Lewis stepped out onto the front steps of his house holding a trumpet, blasted a few notes, and then stepped back inside. Jones was amazed that Lewis could play many notes on the trumpet only using three valves. After this, Jones had an opportunity to ask Lewis several questions about the intricacies of playing the trumpet.

Jones began to nurture his musical ability in a more formal setting at the racially integrated Robert A. Coontz Junior High School, where he sang in the choir and performed in the band. He became obsessed with the inner workings of the school band ensemble, musical instruments, and arrangements. He also studied many different musical instruments—drums, tuba, B-flat baritone horn, French horn, E-flat alto horn, Sousaphone, piano, violin, and clarinet—but these were not suited for him.

As a member of the band, Jones possessed an inquisitive mind about the fundamentals of music, style, and form. In this experience with his school band Jones described that, "I was curious about orchestration [writing music]. I [often wondered] how could people [in the band] play together and not be playing the same notes? But I got totally obsessed with playing. I would stay in the band room all day and play [every musical instrument]."[5] But ultimately, Jones began to concentrate on the trumpet as his principal instrument. His father was supportive and provided Jones with his first trumpet.

In addition to his interest in musical instruments, Jones also performed as a singer in a gospel quartet called the Challengers under the direction of a local music teacher named Joseph Powe. In his home library Powe collected books on arranging and film scoring. Jones took the opportunity to study many of these scores and arrangements. This initial inquiry allowed Jones to concentrate more on the technical aspects of arranging music and learn the ranges and notation of certain instruments (e.g., B-flat trumpet) on a music score.

In his early experience Jones once described that, "I used to babysit for Powe. I'd look at his Glenn Miller arranging books and it was just like walking into fantasyland, just to be able to look at those things with the trombones and how they worked. How you put the [saxophones] and trombones and stuff together. I was just hooked on it. I must have been about thirteen. It took over my life."[6]

Jazz trumpeter Clark Terry served as one of Jones's early important mentor/teachers. Terry performed with many bands over the course of his long career, including those of Charlie Barnet, Count Basie (both big bands and small ensembles), and Duke Ellington.[7] He greatly influenced modern jazz and invented a unique style of trumpet playing that bridged the gap between the swing era of the 1930s and approaches to the bebop style of 1940s by musicians such as Dizzy Gillespie. Clark Terry constantly displayed an effortless command on the trumpet. He had an ability to play fast and intricate passages and elaborate melodic lines.

In 1947 when Jones was thirteen years old, he constantly sought music lessons from Clark Terry, who would often travel to Seattle to perform gigs. On one occasion when Terry was performing at the Palomar Theater in Seattle, Jones approached Terry and introduced himself and mentioned that he was in the process of learning how to play the trumpet and write music. When Terry was in town, Jones would often arrive at Terry's place of residence early in the morning for lessons. Jones and Terry would work for hours and when the sessions ended Jones would attend school. The lessons were beneficial to Jones's future as a musician. Jones noted that, "[Clark Terry] taught me and talked to me and gave me the confidence to get out there and see what I could do on my own."[8] This experience with Clark Terry greatly influenced Jones's continued growth and development in music.

In addition to his work with Clark Terry, Jones attended James A. Garfield High School, where he had opportunities to interact with students of different ethnic and socio-cultural backgrounds and musical interests. By this time it was undeniable that Jones possessed an artistic gift and a distinct ability to hear, perform, and respond to harmony.

Jones and his friend Charles Taylor performed in the Garfield High School concert band under the direction of Parker Cook, a teacher and musician who was very supportive of Jones's interests in composing and arranging. Jones and Taylor both also studied with a musician named Frank Waldron.

In 1948 Jones was a member of the Garfield High School military band. Many African American and white musicians of the band shared a deep friendship and camaraderie that influenced Jones's ideologies of cultural diversity. Among the band members for this particular ensemble was Jones's white friend Norm Calvo, who stated that "we were at least 10 years ahead of the curve of camaraderie when it came to race, everybody just sort of blended."[9] No one found it unusual when Jones and other African American members of the band walked to Calvo's house after school to jam in Calvo's parents' music room.

As early as 1947 Jones had already established his talent as a vibrant trumpet player outside of high school by performing in a semi-professional band organized by his school friend, Charles Taylor. Some of the band members included: Oscar Holden Jr. (tenor saxophone), Grace Holden (piano), Billy Johnson (bass), Major Pigford (trombone), Waymond Jones (temporary drummer), Harold Redmond (drummer), and Buddy Catlett (alto saxophone). This band was later reorganized and incorporated as the Bumps Blackwell Junior Band. "Bumps," whose real name was Robert Blackwell, played the vibraphone and served as the bandleader for the group.[10]

The Bumps Blackwell Junior Band consisted of Billy Johnson (bass), Harold Redmond (drums), Charles Taylor (tenor saxophone), Buddy Catlett (alto saxophone, but he later became known for playing bass), Quincy Jones (trumpet), Bumps Blackwell (vibraphone), Major Pigford (trombone), and Tommy Adams (vocalist and sometimes drums). Blackwell also added to the group two female performers: August Mae, a tap dancer, and vocalist Ernestine Anderson, who later became a famous jazz singer with talents often regarded similar to that of Ella Fitzgerald and Sarah Vaughan.

Performing with these early bands was important in Jones's musical development, helping shape his aspirations of pursuing music as a career and exposing him to different types of collaborative projects with talented jazz musicians in Seattle and other parts of the United States. For example, the Bumps Blackwell Junior Band performed as a backup for Billie Holiday and Billy Eckstine when they performed in the Seattle area.

The Bumps Blackwell Junior Band in many ways prepared Jones to be competitive with more professional ensembles. When he became a member of the Lionel Hampton Orchestra a few years later, he understood firsthand the inner workings of the performance stage, big band ensemble format, instrumentation, audience and performer response, and jazz and rhythm & blues repertoire.

Jazz bassist Buddy Catlett, one of the original members of the Bumps Blackwell Junior Band who himself became a legendary musician, has pointed out that he personally witnessed that Quincy Jones possessed an ability to compose and arrange at a very young age. Catlett witnessed firsthand that even before Jones became a member of the Lionel Hampton Orchestra, he had progressed to mastering his composing and arranging skills. Catlett pointed out that as a teenager, "during this period with Bumps [Jones] wrote most of the book [arrangements]. He was only 15. . . . He was serious about everything. He really took his time to figure out what he was doing."[11]

In addition to performing popular music, Jones and other members of the Bumps Blackwell Junior Band were also proficient in performing military marches, a skill they learned as members of a military regiment located at Camp Murray in the Seattle area. They were officially sworn in the African American Washington National Guard 41st Infantry Division Band. The young men were provided with uniforms and new musical instruments and they were required to participate in drills at the Armory in Seattle. For a time, Jones was an official bugler for the regiment. During several months each summer the members of this regiment were also assigned active duty with the army at Camp Murray.

As a young musician Jones developed a strong-willed personality and tenacity for meeting, performing, and dialoging with established musicians, a skill that contributed to his success in the popular music industry. In his mid-teenage years he had already become personally acquainted with Count Basie, Duke Ellington, Woody Herman, and Milt Hinton, always seeking music lessons. One of his most poignant experiences in Seattle was observing an open rehearsal of a professional symphonic orchestra under conductor Arturo Toscanini (1867–1957) and Harry Lookofsky (violinist and concertmaster). This experience contributed another dimension of music by opening his insights into the Western classical music tradition. He observed not only the intricacies of melodies, rhythms, and textures but also how the orchestrated music scores were invigorated through the performances of an ensemble of professional musicians. This experience also greatly influenced Jones's musical ideas, interests, and future development in the music profession.

Lionel Hampton (1908–2002) and Dizzy Gillespie (1917–1993) were two of the prominent bandleaders that greatly influenced Quincy Jones's early musical career. Hampton and Jones first became acquainted in Seattle during the late 1940s. Hampton was a well-known performer, and his musical excellence sparked Jones's interest. Hampton not only provided many performing opportunities but, for Jones and many other aspiring young musicians, was a symbol of success as a professional African American musician in the competitive white popular music industry during a time in American society (1930s and 1940s) when many African Americans experienced racial discrimination.

Although there was a rich heritage of artistic ingenuity among many African Americans, social, cultural, and political segregation in American society often led to inequality and fewer opportunities for African Americans to freely pursue artistic passions. African American musicians often were challenged by racism that involved discrimination in employment, recording and commercial markets, booking contracts, performance venues and tours, hotel accommodations, management, and media coverage.

Hampton was at the center of change and racial integration in jazz and popular music. He was well known in both white and African American communities because he and pianist Teddy Wilson had been the first African Americans to play regularly in a white band, with Benny Goodman's small ensembles. Because of this achievement, Hampton was often regarded as something of a hero in Seattle and other areas.

Hampton had the ability to attract large audiences with his music. He was a musician who could think outside the box and innovate compositions that excited both musicians and audiences. In his autobiography Hampton notes that the first out-of-town booking that Joe Glaser of the Associated Booking Corporation arranged for his group was at the Trianon Ballroom, a popular social club in Seattle that mainly catered to white clientele.

In the 1940s, the Trianon did not admit African Americans. However, things became racially heated in 1940 when Lionel Hampton's new orchestra was booked; both African Americans and whites wanted to see the Hampton orchestra. As a result, the African American community approached the Trianon establishment and persuaded the management to open the ballroom to African Americans. After Hampton's performance the Trianon instituted a regular policy of hosting what was called Colored Folks Monday night dances while continuing to bar African Americans the rest of the week.

In 1948 Hampton again performed a concert in Seattle, this time at the Palomar Theater. At the age of fifteen, Jones made his way backstage and showed Hampton his first composition *The Four Winds Suite*, an intricate instrumental work. This suite showed Jones's promise in learning how to master a craft of writing and arranging compositions—transposing instrumental parts, exploring timbres, textures, harmonies, and various underlying rhythmic structures in orchestral works. After playing it, Hampton was very impressed and invited Jones to join his orchestra. But Hampton's wife Gladys objected and encouraged Jones to remain in Seattle and finish his education.

Hampton stated the following about Jones and his promise in music:

> The same year I hired Betty Carter, I tried to hire a young cat named Quincy Jones. We were in Seattle, and this fifteen-year-old kid came backstage at the theater and showed me a suite he had written called "The Four Winds Suite." I played it, and it was really good. In the meantime, I found out that he'd been born in Chicago and he also played the trumpet. I offered him a job, and he accepted, and he played third trumpet for a little while. It must have been the summertime, when he wasn't in school. . . . I wanted him to stay with the band, and he wanted to stay with me, but [my wife] Gladys overruled us both. She was not going to take a kid out of school. So I left him with an open invitation to join me after he graduated.[12]

Jones later express how upset he had been that he was unable to perform with Hampton:

> I wanted to go with that band so badly. I never wanted to play with a band so much. Hamp had all these guys! Jimmy Cleveland, and Benny Bailey, Betty Carter, . . . and Jerome Richardson. Incredible band! It was like, "God!" you know, "Please!" I wanted to leave home. I was dying to leave home. I just wanted to go. I didn't want to finish school or anything. So when Hamp said, 'You're with the band,' I didn't want to take a chance!" I just got on the bus. . . . Then Gladys got on the bus and she said, 'No. Get that kid back to school. Get him off of the bus.' I was so hurt.[13]

Jones did complete his high school education. But before his graduation he performed with a jazz workshop band under the direction of Gus Mankertz of Seattle University. This band performed innovative bebop arrangements by musicians such as Dizzy Gillespie, Woody Herman, and Stan Kenton. The band also performed Jones's first composition, *The Four Winds Suite*. Because of his significant talent and compositional skills, Jones later received several music scholarships from Seattle University, followed by advanced study in contemporary music at Schillinger House in Boston (now known as Berklee College of Music). At Schillinger House, Jones studied a core curriculum of arranging, big-band ensembles, the Schillinger system of music theory, and jazz solo analysis.

Outside of his formal training at Schillinger House, Boston offered performing opportunities and allowed Jones to interact with popular musicians of the highest caliber. While in Boston he found a local club called Izzy Ort's located close to the Paramount Theater, one of Boston's major entertainment venues. Some of the musicians that performed in these venues included bandleader and alto sax player Bunny Campbell and pianist Preston "Sandy" Sandiford.

On many occasions Jones brought his arrangements to Sandiford, who would review them and encourage Jones to arrange and work out the technical aspects of the composition. Sandiford suggested that Jones first notate (write out) the chords and rhythm parts, then add in the top lines for the lead horn parts. This is one method of compositional writing; Jones would later master his individual style of composing and arranging in jazz and popular music.[14]

Jones also became a more professional working musician and performed at local clubs with on occasions that famous jazz bassist Oscar Pettiford came to town with his band. Pettiford soon sent for Jones to come to New York and do several arrangements. Through Pettiford, word of Jones's talent got back to Lionel Hampton, who again attempted to recruit Jones for his orchestra.

In 1951 Jones was again invited to join the Lionel Hampton Orchestra as a trumpet player and arranger. Hampton's road manager, George "Kingfish" Hart, contacted Jones with the invitation. Janet Thurlow—a white vocalist from Seattle who sang in Hampton's orchestra, and one of the first white singers ever to sing with an African American band—also persuaded Hampton to hire Jones. Both Thurlow and Jones became major performers in Hampton's orchestra.

In 1951 they shared a marquee with Hampton for another Seattle concert at the Trianon, the social club that had previously discriminated against African Americans.

Jones toured with Hampton for approximately two years, from 1951 to 1953. As a bandleader Hampton had his own way of doing things. One of the things that made his orchestra a unique and major attraction was their attire. Jones described some of his early experiences performing and working with Lionel Hampton, especially in New York City and wearing the special attire:

> Clifford Brown, Art Farmer and I were in the trumpet section. We had to wear Bermuda shorts with purple jackets and Tyrolian hats, man, when we played *Flying Home*, Hamp marched the band outside. You have to imagine this—I was 19 years old, so hip it was pitiful and didn't want to know about anything that was close to being commercial. So Hamp would be in front of the sax section, and most of the band behind him. But Brownie (Clifford Brown) and I would stop to tie our shoes or do something so we wouldn't have to go outside, because next door was [the club] Birdland and there was [Thelonious] Monk, Dizzy [Gillespie], and Bud Powell, all the Bebop idols standing in front at intermission. . . . You'd do anything to get away.[15]

Although as a hip nineteen-year old, Jones desired to do anything to get away from wearing the Bermuda shorts, purple jackets, and Tyrolian hats, he knew that being a member of the Lionel Hampton Orchestra offered possibility and a future in the American popular music industry. Hampton became a friend and mentor. Hampton was aware of talent when he saw it and did his best in nurturing Jones's many abilities as a trumpet player, arranger, and composer.

Jones's talent as trumpeter was showcased in Hampton's orchestra. One improvisational trumpet solo was featured in film footage of a "Slide Hamp Slide" (1951). This black and white film short was recorded at *Showtime at the Apollo*, a series of musical segments filmed and performed at the Apollo Theater in New York City. The musical segment was also known as the "Harlem Variety Review," and was hosted by Willie Bryant.[16]

As Jones describes, "bandleaders such as Hampton helped to give young people an identity."[17] In essence, bandleaders such as Hampton provided a model of talent and success for aspiring young musicians to emulate. Jones also leaned from Hampton the importance of entertaining and enlightening audiences at the same time through musical performance. One of the most important things Jones learned was what it meant to be a perfectionist, by observing Hampton's work and performance ethic and his having one of the best bands in jazz/popular music history.

One of the highlights of Jones's time with Hampton was touring with Lionel Hampton and the All Stars in 1953. While in Europe the group recorded several albums that include *Lionel Hampton—European Concert* (1953), *Lionel Hampton—European Tour* (1953), and *Lionel Hampton and his Orchestra Live in Sweden* (1953). Members of the All Stars included Clifford Brown, Art Farmer, Walter Williams (trumpets), Jimmy Cleveland, George Cooper, Al Hayse (trombones), Gigi Gryce, Anthony Ortega (alto saxophones), Clifford Solomon, Clifford Scott (tenor saxophones), Oscar Estelle (baritone saxophone), George Wallington (piano), Billy Mackel (guitar), Monk Montgomery[18] (bass), Alan Dawson, Curley Hamner (drums), Sonny Parker, and Annie Ross (vocals).

Hampton stated the following about Jones and his involvement with the band and travel to Europe:

> I also took Quincy Jones along on that trip. He was the kid who I'd met in Seattle back in 1948 when he was fifteen years old. Well, in the intervening years, Quincy had gone to [Schillinger House] Berklee College of Music in Boston and then arrived in New York to become a record producer and arranger. We kept in touch, and whenever I was on the West Coast, he'd try to sit in with me. He played trumpet when we recorded in Los Angeles in 1951. I took him to Europe with me in 1953 as a trumpet player and arranger. He stayed over there for a while to study music some more.[19]

After performing with Hampton's band, Jones formed his own big bands and small ensembles. The following chapter includes discussion of jazz bands organized by Jones after his work with Hampton. But it should be noted that the musicians that Jones collaborated with after working with Hampton were not all jazz musicians. He became more and more proficient in working with various musicians, writing music outside of the jazz idiom, and keeping up with contemporary trends in popular music.

Some of Jones's collaborations and recordings after working with Hampton were with rhythm & blues musicians but in many of these collaborations there is an integration of jazz; Jones often included jazz musicians as improvisational soloists and background perform- ers. For example, Jones recorded an arrangement of "Whole Lot of Shakin' Goin' On" (1955),[20] a gutsy vocal performance by Big Maybelle (Mabel Louise Smith) (1924–1972), a prominent rhythm & blues singer in the 1950s. Jazz musicians on this recording include Jerome Richardson, Budd Johnson, and Billy Byers. However, although Jones was writing and recording various popular styles, he did not divorce himself from jazz. In fact, he played a crucial role in international exposure of jazz in his affiliation with Dizzy Gillespie's big band.

Like Lionel Hampton, Dizzy (John Birks) Gillespie created a rich history in jazz and American popular music, as one of the major innovators of trumpet improvisation during the bebop era of jazz. One of Gillespie's major accomplishments was assembling a talented group of musicians for the first official U.S. jazz goodwill tour. The tour was initiated by New York Congressman Adam Clayton Pow- ell Jr., with the idea of forming international/goodwill relationships with foreign countries through the performance of African American popular music.[21] Part of the rationalization for the tour stemmed from the 1950s Cold War, the Soviet Union, and a global struggle of world communism versus democracy.

The U.S. government presented performances of jazz abroad as a powerful symbol of American freedom, creativity, and optimism. Through the government-sponsored radio program *Voice of America*, jazz was heard in Eastern Europe, the Middle East, and other Soviet- controlled areas of the world.[22] In addition, the U.S. government began to commission jazz musicians to make goodwill State Depart- ment tours to other countries. These tours provided opportunities for many African American jazz musicians to represent the United States as cultural and musical ambassadors.

Gillespie was impressed enough with the musicianship and compositional skills of Jones that he sought out Jones to assist in organizing the tour. Gillespie stated that "since I was already set to go on tour in Europe . . . , I got in touch with Quincy Jones, who'd helped me to organize the big bands I recorded and played with occasionally in 1954 and 1955, and told him to get the band together for me."[23]

In 1956 Gillespie appointed Jones as music director, frontline trumpeter, and arranger for the Dizzy Gillespie band official tour of the Middle East, Far East, and South America.[24] This valuable opportunity not only solidified Jones's remarkable talents and ability but gave him the opportunity to perfect his compositional skills and interact with many talented musicians in Gillespie's tour band, similar to his musical experience with the Lionel Hampton Orchestra.

Gillespie's goodwill tour band included Idress Suliemkan, Ermet Perry (trumpets), Jimmy Cleveland, Melba Liston, Frank Rehak (trombones), Sahib Shihab, Jerome Richardson, Lucky Thompson, Marty Flax, Ernie Wilkins (saxophones), Charlie Persip (drums), Nelson Boyd (bass), Walter Davis (piano), Candido (bongos and conga drums), and Herb Lance and Dottie Saulters (vocals). Other musicians later added to the tour band included Lee Morgan, Al Stewart, Carl Warwick, Joe Cariani, (trumpets), Rod Levitt (trombone), Phil Woods, Billy Mitchell, Jimmy Powell, Benny Golson (saxophones), Al Haig (piano), Paul West (bass), and Austin Cromes (vocals). Marshall Stearns, a white jazz scholar and founder of the Institute of Jazz Studies at Rutgers University in Newark, New Jersey, also accompanied the band tour as a public relations liaison.

One major significance of the tour was that it brought together African American and white musicians during a time when America continued to be a segregated society. The musicians considered it a high honor to have been selected to participate in the State Department tour and having an opportunity to represent the United States in cultural affairs. Gillespie remarked that, "I've sort of liked the idea of representing America, but I wasn't going over to apologize for the racist policies in America."[25]

Gillespie was the leader of an interracial band. To many audiences this was unusual to experience whites and African Americans performing in the same band. Gillespie remarked, "that was strange to them because they'd heard about [African Americans] being lynched and burned, and here I come with half whites and [African Americans] and a girl [Melba Liston] playing in the [same band]."[26]

In many areas included on the goodwill tour itinerary (e.g., Greece, Turkey, Syria, Iran, Pakistan, Argentina) it was quite unusual for the locals to experience African Americans and interact with jazz musicians. Many of these performances are recorded on the albums *Dizzy Gillespie World Statesman* (1956) and *Dizzy in Greece* (1956), and *Dizzy in South America Official U.S. State Department Tour, Vols. 1 & 2* (1956). These compilations feature Jones as trumpeter and include many of his arrangements and compositions. Also, an additional compilation titled *Dizzy in South America: Tangos, Sambas, Interviews, and More Big Band Bebop, Vol. 3* (1956) includes several interviews with Jones and other members of the band. The tour was successful in garnering cultural exchanges between audiences and the musicians and was a landmark in the dissemination of jazz on a global level.

The musical experiences that Jones gained from performing in the bands of both Hampton and Gillespie were invaluable to his life and career. After these experiences he soon found many other opportunities and many jazz musicians and commentators also acknowledged his musical ability. In 1957 Billy Taylor published comments on several creative jazz musicians by stating: "[M]ost of the popular jazzmen of today are serious minded, creative artists who are trying to contribute something worthwhile to the society in which they live. Men like John Lewis, Dave Brubeck, Quincy Jones, and Shorty Rogers are typical of this kind of musician."[27] At the time that of these comments Jones was only twenty-four years old; the other musicians mentioned were almost ten years Jones's senior and had begun to establish their careers in jazz.

But perhaps one of Jones's greatest contributions to society and jazz at a young age during the 1950s was his strong work ethic, focus, and efforts to encourage audiences to experience jazz as a true art form. Moreover, he did so during the 1950s, when the jazz profession was often stereotyped in the media as a style of popular music that was associated with illicit activities (e.g., drugs and alcohol). The career path and choices that Jones carved out at a young age also had significant implications for his future endeavors as a jazz bandleader and in pursuing new opportunities in Europe.

Paris was one of the European areas where African American artists and musicians often settled. During the years between the world wars, while the Harlem Renaissance was active in American society, groups of African American artists and jazz musicians, centered in Montmartre, contributed to a thriving jazz culture in Paris. Jazz in Paris became a cultural movement in which African American artists and musicians such as Josephine Baker, Sidney Bechet, James Reese Europe, and others could escape the harsh realities of racism in American society and pursue unlimited performing opportunities.

Paris in many ways offered Jones more opportunities, as an African American musician, than he had experienced in American society. In 1957 he assumed a position in Paris as a musical director, arranger, and conductor for Barclay Records, a company that was owned by Nicole and Eddie Barclay. One of the reasons Jones accepted the position at Barclay was to concentrate more on composing and writing for string instruments. Thus, when Nicole Barclay (at the recommendation of Billy Eckstine) telephoned Jones to offer him the position, one of his first inquiries was whether he would be able to compose and arrange for strings. Jones was initially going to remain in Paris for only a few months, but his career blossomed and he was allowed to write whatever he desired. His stay in Paris lasted longer than he had expected. At Barclay, Jones wrote arrangements for the label's artists and also for Eddie Barclay's 55-piece orchestra.

In Paris, Western classical artists such as Igor Stravinsky, Maurice Ravel, and Olivier Messiaen also influenced Jones. But a woman soon crossed his path who challenged him to expand his musical skills in new and innovative ways in composition, theory, harmony, and orchestration. With this experience Jones acquired the tools to transform himself into a serious composer and arranger. The woman was Nadia Boulanger (1887–1979), one of the first staff members of the Ecole Normale du Musique, where she taught harmony, counterpoint, music history, analysis, organ, composition, and keyboard harmony. She was also a founding member of the American Conservatory in Fontainebleau in 1921 and became its director in 1948.

Although Boulanger and Jones were from different backgrounds—classical (Boulanger) and popular music (Jones)—they seemed to complement each other in their musical experiences, careers, and in opening many social barriers. Similar to Jones, Boulanger possessed a strong professional work ethic that greatly contributed to her accomplishments. Boulanger made her debut in 1912 conducting her own music. She was also the first woman to conduct orchestras in Paris, Washington, D.C., and New York. In her lifetime she received many accolades, honorary degrees, and certificates, and greatly contributed to the success of many of the students she mentored.

Boulanger was selective in the students she chose.[28] Her requirements were stringent in that students were first required to audition, demonstrate analytical and compositional skills, and discuss what they wanted to accomplish as a student in her studio. In Boulanger's studio Jones was required to analyze complex classical works such as Ravel's *Daphnis et Chloé* and Stravinsky's *The Firebird*.[29]

In studying with Boulanger, Jones gained deeper insight into the fundamentals of Western classical music harmony, orchestration, structure, and form, expanding his ideas and concepts about various styles of music outside of jazz. He stated that, "in music [the Western classical tradition], I'm basically an impressionist and a romantic. I think my favorite composer is Ravel. I didn't know too much about him until I went to study under Nadia Boulanger in Paris and was introduced to people who knew him well."[30] Working with Boulanger gave Jones the artistic validation of a being serious composer and arranger.

Although Boulanger was not a total connoisseur of jazz, this did not affect her ability to assist Jones in developing his musical skills that would also contribute to his successful music career. He desired to write complex symphonies; but Boulanger, who encouraged her students to explore their distinctive styles, encouraged Jones to find his own path in music. Her suggestion was, "learn your skills but forget about American symphonies. You already have something unique and important. Music can never be more or less than the creators. . . . The more specific and peripheral boundaries you choose for your work the more freedom you have."[31]

In essence, Boulanger helped Jones develop his individuality and his own unique skills in music composition. Jones's musical experiences with Boulanger became an integral part of his training and experience working, composing, and arranging in the popular music and film industries as he pursued new opportunities in the decade of the 1960s and throughout his career.[32]

Over a period of thirty years, Jones made several successful career transitions and excelled as a bandleader, recording executive, Hollywood film composer, and business entrepreneur. Musically, he made a transition from jazz to concentrating on other popular styles and artists.

In 1961 Jones was promoted to the position of executive vice president of Mercury Records, the first African American to hold such an executive position for a white-owned record company.

In addition to his work in the recording industry, in the 1960s Jones became one of the few African American composers and arrangers to make a transition to the Hollywood studios while continuing to be active in the recording industry. Jones scored numerous films and television series, working with such notable directors as Sidney Lumet, Sydney Pollack, and Steven Spielberg.

In the 1970s Jones's work in music and film was highly influenced by his interest in the African/African American historical experience. One of his personal quests was not only to comprehend the complexities of the African American experience but also to understand how music related to the historical experience of displaced Africans. This type of inquiry was important to his understanding of the evolution of African American music within the context of historical and musical roots linked with the African continent. This involved extensive study and an analysis of numerous books and sound recordings.[33]

From his research Jones arrived at a theoretical notion of a correlation between music and culture embodying the African American experience. That is, in American society the African American experience was very much grounded in black musical production. Jones was involved in other projects in the 1970s that centered on the African American experience. He assisting in organizing both the Chicago Black Expo (that was similar in function to Operation PUSH with Rev. Jesse Jackson) and the Institute for Research in Black American Music.[34]

Jones's incorporation of his knowledge of the African American experience into his compositional writing is reflected in extended works such as *The Black Requiem*, first performed in 1971 by Ray

Charles with the Houston Symphony and an 80-voice choir.[35] One of Jones's most significant accomplishments after this was his work on the television score of Alex Haley's *Roots* (1977), one of the most-watched mini-series in television history.

By the mid-1970s with so much success it seemed as though Jones was invincible. He constantly worked on various stressful projects. But he faced one of the most challenging experiences of his life by suffering a brain aneurysm that some believed could result in his death. Because of extensive brain surgery, Jones could no longer play the trumpet. The recovery period may have been a slight setback. But Jones regarded this experience as a wakeup call and a period of recovery that allowed him to reconsider the more important aspects of his life, religion, family, and career.[36]

The 1980s was also a period of re-transitioning. After recovering from a near-death experience, Jones grew to value life, health, and family in more positive ways. He also continued his interest in African American cultural history by working on several film projects such as his work as a producer and composer for the film *The Color Purple* (1985).

In the popular music recording industry Jones achieved a high level of success by producing Michael Jackson's *Thriller* (1982) album. This was followed by the success of the "We Are the World" (1985) single in collaboration with Lionel Richie, Michael Jackson, and many other popular musicians.

In the mid-1980s to 1990s Jones ventured into the business aspects of the recording industry, in addition to generating albums such as *Back on the Block* (1989) and *Q's Jook Joint* (1995). He formed several corporate enterprises including Qwest Records and Quincy Jones Music Publishing. He also formed Quincy Jones Entertainment (QJE), a joint enterprise with Time Warner, Qwest Broadcasting Company, and the Tribune television stations in Atlanta and New Orleans.

Jones also partnered and invested in a new cable TV network known as New Urban Entertainment (NUE) Television. He also founded *Vibe*, a hip hop magazine series jointly owned with Time Ventures. Having founded *Vibe* and in his role as the CEO of Qwest Records, Jones constantly served as a role model for excellence in music and attempted to offer advice to the contemporary rap community.

Having worked with contemporary rappers, Jones constantly serves as a mentor for many aspiring musicians and continues to be concerned with how they value African American history and musical traditions. Jones suggested that many rappers should take a trip to Africa, as did comedian Richard Pryor—because it will make them think twice about using the N-word, a derogatory term.[37] Jones is also critical of modern rappers in what he describes as "turning their backs on jazz and blues." He believes most rappers and young people do not have substantial knowledge of past great musicians such as Duke Ellington or Charlie Parker.[38] This is one reason he became more and more involved in humanitarian work and especially interested in organizing music education programs for young people.

In his leadership role as a humanitarian, Jones has used his success in the popular music and film industries to contribute to the betterment of the world by advocating for human, civil, and children's rights. He has also taken his advocacy for the rights of others to Capitol Hill in Washington, D.C., and to many other countries, including South Africa with Nelson Mandela.

Throughout most of his career Jones has continued to envision a philosophy of empowering children as the future leaders of the world. He has sponsored many projects in areas such as South Africa, Italy, and on various social and civic music collaborations—USA for Africa and Save the Children. Similar to the mentorship roles of Clark Terry, Jones has continued this tradition and has often served as role a model for young and aspiring musicians.[39] He is very much a proponent of education and intellectualism.

One of his most recent projects is working with the Global Youth Parliament, an organization that brings together hundreds of young people from industrialized and Third World countries to come up with solutions to their nation's biggest challenges. Jones also currently serves as an active member of the board of directors of the famous Apollo Theater, in Harlem, New York City.

With recent the election of Barack Obama as the nation's first African American president, one of Jones's campaigns is advocating the creation of a cabinet-level position for Secretary of the Arts. Jones believes strongly that this is an important position. Furthermore, the United States is one of the few Western democracies that do not have a high cabinet minister or secretary in charge of the arts or cultural affairs. He hopes that President Obama will create such as position in the United States and believes that such an appointment would help ensure that music and other arts remain a vital part of America's school curriculum.

Jones has also advocated for jazz education in the nation's capital. At a 2004 jazz festival sponsored by the National Museum of History in Washington, Jones was selected as one of the Smithsonian Ambassadors for Jazz. He stated, "I can only hope that one day America will recognize that our indigenous music—jazz—is the heart and soul of all popular music and that we cannot afford to let its legacy slip into obscurity. The creating of Jazz Appreciation month is a step toward that legacy."[40]

Jones is also an author. He has contributed forewords and introductions in books covering many different subjects,[41] and has also written several interesting articles on subjects as wide-ranging as African American music history, starting up a professional band and the problems that bandleaders often experience with repertoire and personnel, techniques in composing, and providing advice to the younger generation of aspiring music.

Jones wrote an article surveying rap music and violence in which he focused on the murders of Tupac Shakur and Christopher Wallace (also known as Notorious B.I.G.), examining the effect the gangster ethos has had on rap (hip hop) music. He argued for rap and hip hop to be seen in a historical context and attempted to link the style to bebop jazz and other forms of African American musical expression.[42]

Jones has contributed several articles to *Music Alive!*, a journal series geared for children published by Cherry Hill Music Company. He recently offered this advice to people who want to break into the music business: find approximately ten musicians that he or she admires the most and sing or play with their records in order to find his or her own style.[43] Jones has written on the subject of the music industry and Napster and how to save the album in the popular music industry. He suggests that single tracks are the cutting edge into album sales, which are more profitable. As a solution to the problem, songwriters and A&R representatives should attempt to make their albums so good that fans (consumers) will want to buy the entire album. Special packaging for the physical product will also encourage fans to buy more albums.[44]

Jones continues to be a man of learning. He encourages the integration of advancement in technology in learning for people of all ages. He often interacts with scholars, intellectuals, students, and communities as a public speaker, presenting lectures and seminars at some of the most prestigious institutions of higher learning.

Jones has been the recipient of many awards and accolades, including the National Medal of the Arts (2010). The year 2003 was officially designated as the "Year of the Blues." In so doing, members of the United States Congress paid tribute to Jones for his international achievements, work, and contributions to the music industry and music education.[45] Jones was also inducted as a prestigious Kennedy Center Honoree (2001). In addition to all of this, Jones has received numerous awards in the recording industry and has been the recipient of an Academy Award, an Emmy, and several other honors for his work in film and television.

Jones has received honorary doctoral degrees, awards, and distinctions from some of the most prestigious academic institutions. This includes the establishment of the Quincy Jones Professorship of African American Music, an endowed professorship (currently held by Ingrid Monson) at Harvard University. Jones and the Harvard School of Public Health recently joined together to advance the health and well-being of children worldwide.

In 2007 Jones was selected as the first-ever "Mentor of the Year" with the Q Prize, named in his honor. The Q Prize is an international award, presented by the Harvard School of Public Health, intended to challenge leaders and citizens of the world to provide essential resources to enable young people to achieve their potential.[46]

In 2008, James A. Garfield High School in Seattle dedicated its Quincy Jones Performing Arts Center. In 2010 the Los Angeles Unified School District (LAUSD) honored Jones by naming an elementary school after him. The Quincy Jones Elementary School is located in Los Angeles' Central Avenue Historic Jazz Corridor. This school offers students an education with an emphasis on learning jazz music and arts education. The school also partnered with organizations such as Los Angeles County Music Center, the Los Angeles Philharmonic, the Thelonious Monk Institute of Jazz (University of Southern California), the Harmony Project, Little Kids Rock, California State University, Northridge, and the University of California, Los Angeles.[47]

Quincy Jones is a musician who has constantly employed innovative techniques and ideas in popular music. This is part of his musical DNA/biological makeup. Even as a youth he was constantly in contact with future cutting-edge musicians. For example, in Seattle, Jones was a close friend with guitarist Jimi Hendrix, both attended Garfield High School. Jones commented that, "[Jimi] was dying to play jazz. He used to come over to the house and sit under the grapefruit tree and stuff. He was a reflexive person. I knew his daddy."[48] Collaborating with many different musicians provided Jones with opportunities to explore various types of music. This diverse interest in music may be one of Jones's greatest assets in his career.

Musicians generally specialize in mastering a limited amount of styles and genres. For example, a classical musician may seldom venture out into playing popular music. A jazz or popular musician may choose to play only one style. But throughout his career Jones has challenged musicians and has demonstrated how all types of music are valuable. For Jones, musical choices in essence equal musical freedom. Jones is what can be described as a crossover artist in that he has made successful transitions in embracing new popular music and contemporary artists. But in some instances he has been criticized for embracing popular music outside of jazz. He once stated:

> I've been accused of selling out, but what I play is my choice; what I
> write is my own choice. How can you place restrictions on art? I can't
> imagine any of my colleagues telling me to my face that I'm selling out.
> Besides the really good musicians understand what I'm doing. It just
> so happens a lot of things turn me on—from rhythm & blues [popular
> music] to Penderecki [classical music].[49]

Working with a diverse group of artists on many levels, Jones throughout his career has continued to be aware of the principle of not placing restrictions on his musical creativity. He has seen jazz as the popular music of the day having to share space with emerging newer styles such as rhythm & blues, rock 'n' roll, and soul. But rather than feeling restrictions, Jones possessed an ability and interest to make the transition and delve into more contemporary styles.

Even as a young musician Jones felt no restrictions in his musical preferences. He learned early on how to interact with professional musicians. For example, since the beginning of his career performing as teenage musician in the Bumps Blackwell Junior Band, in many photos and album covers Jones seems to be gazing straight into the eyes of the audiences with a look of optimism. As Jones developed into a mature musician his contributions and optimism in the entertainment world have had an impact on generations of aspiring musicians.

In preparing this retrospective a major concern was determining what topics to include in a discussion that would adequately describe a man that has achieved success at the highest levels in his life. Similar to his musical experiences, career, and artistic innovations, a retrospective on Jones is a work in progress.

2

THE QUINCY JONES
BANDS

Quincy Jones has organized several recording and touring bands in his career, with some of the most talented musicians in jazz history. One of the major challenges in his career was working with the 1959 Free and Easy tour, based on a remake of *St. Louis Woman*, a Broadway musical with a story centered on African American characters. Jones has often noted that taking on such a project was one of the major mistakes in his career. This chapter examines Quincy Jones's musical experiences and work as a bandleader with many talented jazz musicians and how Jones transformed the challenging experience of the Free and Easy tour into a type of positive energy that has enhanced his ability, body of work, competitiveness, and longevity in the popular music and film industries.

In the swing/big band era of the 1930s and 1940s, well-known bandleaders such as Count Basie, Duke Ellington, Paul Whiteman, Benny Goodman, and others performed a vast amount of dance arrangements that often attracted large audiences. Many of these bands were built on the leaders and their musical instruments— Benny Goodman and Artie Shaw (clarinets), Duke Ellington and Count Basie (pianos), Lionel Hampton (vibraphone), Dizzy Gillespie (trumpet), and so forth. Each of these bands had a distinctive identity that was associated with musical repertoire, dress, performance etiquette, and ensemble of performers that, in addition to instrumentalists, may have included vocalists and sometimes dancers.

But in the late 1940s and 1950s bebop and cool jazz ushered in new trends of different and more intimate types of jazz with improvisational arrangements often performed by smaller, more intimate ensembles.

In forming his early bands Jones employed influences from both big band and small ensemble traditions. In addition, Jones's personal experience performing in the bands of Lionel Hampton and Dizzy Gillespie greatly influenced the establishment of his own jazz bands in that he understood early in his career that the success of a professional jazz band most often depended not only on appropriate repertoire but also on talented and versatile musicians.

What distinguished Jones from many other jazz bandleaders who employed or contracted staff arrangers is that he had the experience and ability to prepare his own compositions and arrangements for his bands. Some of these compositions and arrangements will be discussed in chapter three of this book.

For Jones, name designations such as All Stars, Big Bands, and Orchestra were an important type of identity and status for many of his ensembles. In the early 1950s, at the age of twenty, Jones organized one of his first instrumental ensembles in Europe known as Clifford Brown & Art Farmer with the Swedish All Stars. This particular ensemble was one of collegiality and musicianship. In addition to American jazz trumpeters Clifford Brown and Art Farmer, other members of the ensemble included Swedes Arne Domnérus (alto saxophone), Bengt Hallberg (piano), Lars Gullin (baritone sax), Åke Persson (trombone), Gunnar Johnson (bass), and Jack Norén (drums).

Clifford Brown (1930–1956) and Art Farmer (1928–1999), who both had been members of Lionel Hampton's Orchestra, were dynamic trumpeters who made substantial contributions to jazz history.[1] Brown's playing reflected a combination of influences from trumpeters such as Dizzy Gillespie, Miles Davis, and Fats Navarro. He developed an extraordinary technical facility on the trumpet at a very early age. In the 1950s he also performed briefly with Charlie Parker. Brown made his first recordings with Chris Powell's Blue Flames, a rhythm & blues group. After this he performed and recorded with the Tadd Dameron band.[2]

In the mid-1940s Farmer performed with Benny Carter, Jay McShann, Gerald Wilson, and others. In the early 1950s, in addition to performing with the Hampton orchestra, Farmer also formed several small ensembles such as The Jazztet with Benny Golson. He also formed a septet with Jimmy Cleveland (trombone), Oscar Estelle (alto and baritone saxophones), Clifford Solomon (tenor sax), Monk Montgomery (bass), and Sonny Johnson (drums).[3]

The Swedes—Arne Domnérus, Bengt Hallberg, Lars Gullin, Åke Persson, Gunnar Johnson, and Jack Norén—were also very accomplished musicians. They were pioneers of big bands and in the dissemination of jazz in Europe. Several of these musicians played with noted American bands, including those of Duke Ellington, Count Basie, Dizzy Gillespie, and Benny Bailey.

The All Star ensemble proved that Jones possessed a certain skill to organize a distinguished group of musicians to perform his works. He selected an international cast of musicians to convey his ideas. By doing this he engaged in a type of international jazz music dialogue.[4]

In the 1950s after his collaboration with the All Stars, Jones assembled some of the best jazz musicians in his formation and organization of several big bands and orchestras. He organized groups for his recording sessions and later formed some groups as traveling ensembles. The size of his bands ranged from approximately seventeen to forty members. In some of his early ensembles he recruited musicians that had performed with him in the Hampton and Gillespie bands because he was familiar with the personalities, skills, and abilities of those musicians and vice versa. He also recruited musicians that possessed skills in playing certain types of musical instruments for his particular compositions and arrangements; for example, some of his arrangements required instrumentalists such as xylophone or flute players for special parts. Musicians were often drawn to Jones's ensembles because he already had achieved a status and reputation in jazz.

In the mid-1950s, one of the first big bands that Jones organized was named Quincy Jones and His All Stars. The members of this group included Ernie Royal, Bernie Glow, Al Porcino, Jimmy Nottingham (trumpets), J. J. Johnson, Kai Winding, Urbie Green, Jimmy Cleveland (trombones), Herbie Mann (flute), Dave Schildkraut, Sonny Stitt,[5] Al Cohn, Jack Nimitz (saxophones), Horace Silver (piano), Oscar Pettiford (bass), and Osie Johnson and Art Blakey (drums). Many of the members of this group were prominent figures in jazz and came from different musical backgrounds—swing (Cleveland), bebop (Pettiford), cool (Winding), funky (Silver), and hard bop (Blakey).

Jones also formed several groups known as Quincy Jones and His Orchestra, as studio and background musicians to support particular performers for his work on recordings with Dinah Washington and Sarah Vaughan, especially when his arrangements required string accompaniment and a full symphonic sound. He also formed orchestras to record many of his own albums and compilations.

In selecting his ensemble members, Jones experienced many challenges. Some of these stemmed from the fact that the heyday of the big band era in jazz had greatly declined and musicians had moved on to smaller ensembles. Also, Jones preferred musicians who had experience performing diverse repertoire. In an early interview Jones made some interesting comments about jazz musicians. He noted that many young jazz musicians seemed to be confused and only desired to perform specific repertoire (jazz standards such as those by Charlie Parker and Dizzy Gillespie). He suggested that jazz musicians become versatile and learn all aspects of jazz performance. Jones also believed that, as much as possible, jazz musicians should possess the ability to integrate themselves with many different types of bands, not just specific bands that they preferred to perform with. He emphasized that many jazz musicians in contemporary times have the ability to do progressive (and innovative) things.[6]

But, in addition, Jones was very selective in his choices of musicians because he believed that talent was not the only major requirement for his bands. Thus, whether it was with the All Stars, big bands, or orchestras, Jones continued to express a philosophy of cohesiveness when working with and maintaining his instrumental ensembles. He continued to be concerned with the longevity and musical and artistic growth of his ensembles. Furthermore, he believed that musicians working together for a sufficient amount of time in his ensembles could achieve band mastery.

In 1959 Jones continued to be highly committed in forming what he believed would be an exceptional traveling big band. This traveling big band in essence was to be a type of territorial band where Jones and his instrumental ensemble would perform in different venues in America and abroad. When Jones was twenty-six years old, an article titled "Jones Forming Band" was published in *Down Beat* magazine (April 1959) stating that Jones was expected to add his name to the growing list of traveling big bands. He had recently returned to New York after a lengthy amount of time writing and studying in Paris and had recently signed a record contract with Mercury Records. While in Chicago during a conversation with a Mercury executive, Jones revealed that the organization of his band was well beyond the planning stage. Some personnel had been chosen. Jones commented that, "I'm getting my chops [trumpet skills] in shape. The [traveling] band [that I am attempting to organize] will have a complement of 17 men."[7]

Jones detailed what he believed were the major facets of organizing a traveling band. But he soon realized that the amount of preparation for organizing his band required a great amount of effort. He noted that in Europe there was usually a large demand for first-rate big bands.[8] But, after his European experience, he often found himself discouraged and frustrated in finding recording opportunities and financial backing for his bands.[9]

Jones was also often frustrated in attempting to assemble a superior group of serious musicians for his bands. He was blunt about his requirements for band membership. In addition to finding talented musicians, Jones was specific in attempting to avoid musicians who possessed what he described as "dissonant personalities" that he believed would affect band behavior, attitude, and work output:

When I came back last November [of 1958] after 19 months in Europe, I decided to try to form a [traveling] band. I'd seen signs that indicated—to me, anyway—that this is the time. I soon discovered that the amount of planning required was more than most writers on the subject—and most people asking what's happened to the bands—realize.

A key reason for wanting a band—and I know this feeling is shared by many musicians—was the constant discouragement and frustration of assembling a superior group of musicians for recording, of having them right there, and knowing what could happen if they could stay together for a month. . . . Finding musicians who'll travel at all was one problem. Finding musicians who had big band experience—in a period when there was practically nowhere for them to get it—was another.

I also had to have musicians who were men as well as creative. Oddly enough, the two elements don't often seem to go together. My men had to have good conception—not a studio approach—but they also had to be straight guys. One man with a dissonant personality can ruin a section, no matter how skilled a musician he is. . . . And no junkies [drug addicts]. . . . Their attitude runs through everything they do on and off the stand. They're late to gigs, careless in appearance, and they goof musically. It's hard enough to get a big band going without them on hand. . . .

You can't fully plan the personality of a band. It's created by what happens when the men get to know each other, feel the rhythm section, react to the book [of arrangements]. . . .[10]

Jones later extended his requirements to include musicians that possessed a dependable work ethic:

Jazz brings out the truth in a guy. To get a real band sound you must have the right guys. And to find guys who have the same musical outlook is so difficult. . . . To get a fine band sound those guys have got to fight and love each other. It's blood I want. The men I want must be amiable and dependable, though they mustn't be so dependable that they can't play. There are so many like that. I don't care what their idiosyncrasies are as long as they are discrete.[11]

In Jones's experiences, perhaps the events that occurred in the year of 1959 can be described as a type of antithesis—the best and yet the worst of times. This was one of the most challenging time periods in Jones's entire professional career. But, on the other hand, during that year he also produced Ray Charles's successful album *The Genius of Ray Charles* (1959), and had written numerous arrangements for other musicians.

Jones also recorded one of his most significant jazz albums, *The Birth of a Band*. With such success, why not take on a Broadway show? In 1959 Jones assumed a position as the music director of a Broadway show called *Free and Easy* that was a remake of *St. Louis Woman*, a musical that was based on the novel *God Sends Sunday* (1931) by Harlem Renaissance writer Arna Bontemps (1902–1973) about a jockey name Little Augie. This musical was written by Harold Arlen (1905–1986), a composer who contributed greatly to American popular music repertoire.[12]

St. Louis Woman originally premiered at the Martin Beck Theatre in New York City on March 30, 1946, and ran for approximately 113 performances.[13] However, even before the show premiered, it received much criticism from the NAACP, critics, and the African American community alleging that it portrayed roles that distracted from the dignity of the African American race.[14]

Thirteen years later, *Free and Easy* was to be a reinvention of this musical. But this time it was conceived as a new American jazz musical, and Jones would play a significant role in the musical production. This musical is set in a Mississippi betting saloon at the turn of the century; the main character Augie is down on his luck, but later makes money from gambling. Some of the actors in the musical included Martha Flowers, Irene Williams, Irving Barnes, and Moses Barr. Many of these performers were classically trained.

The producer of the musical was Stanley Chase, who had by the age of thirty-two already produced Broadway musicals and original plays such as *Threepenny Opera* (1952), *The Potting Shed* (1957), *A Moon for the Misbegotten* (1957), and *The Cave Dwellers* (1958). The program director was Robert Breen, the arts executive and theatrical producer who had received international success with the 1952 critically acclaimed revival of the musical *Porgy & Bess* that toured twenty-nine countries in four years.[15]

With a cast of over seventy-five members, the producers decided to premier *Free and Easy* in Europe for a period of over nine months instead of having a typical New York City debut. This was a strategic way of starting fresh in a new geographic location and with different audiences that were often more welcoming to African American musicians than those in the United States. After all, *Porgy & Bess* had made a lasting impression on European audiences; it was expected that *Free and Easy* would succeed in similar ways.

Part of the reasoning for beginning the show in Europe may have been the fact that many African American performers had relocated to Europe to pursue their careers. Some of the producers believed that by premiering the show first in Europe, *Free and Easy* would establish legitimacy as a theatrical musical and would possibly receive a different response when it premiered in the United States.

In the remake of the show after its European premiere, Sammy Davis Jr. would assume the role of Augie. Also expected to be featured in the show was young Patti Austin, and Robert Guillaume, who later became an Emmy Award–winning actor for his role in the television series *Benson*. The premiere of the show was scheduled in Europe in mid-December 1959. The remake of *Free and Easy* was intended to be re-worked as a musical featuring jazz, stylized pantomime, costumes, and a full jazz band performing onstage in acting roles.

In October 1959 *Down Beat* published an article about *Free and Easy* stating:

> the show is dripping with firsts. Since Quincy Jones is writing the score for the show it will be the first Broadway musical ever scored by a jazz composer and arranger, possibly the first that ever used a jazz orchestra [onstage] in place of a pit band. It will also be the first Broadway show that ever went through its tryout performances in Europe instead of the customary Boston, Hartford, Bridgeport, and Philadelphia.[16]

In many ways *Free and Easy* was also envisioned as a type of goodwill tour with the musicians involved acting as cultural ambassadors, similar to the Gillespie tour of 1956 that showcased jazz in many geographic areas. The excitement of *Free and Easy* as a type of goodwill venture was also evident in a *Down Beat* article that stated: "[T]he show is all Negro, excepting the white musicians in the mixed band. . . . It will play Amsterdam; Lauzanne, Switzerland; Munich; Essen; Brussels; Utrecht; Stockholm; London; and possibly some cities in Iron Curtain countries. Then it will come back to America and play a month in San Francisco and a month in Los Angeles before New Yorkers even get a peek at it."[17]

Jones was excited about his work on *Free and Easy*. He stated that "It's a fabulous thing man. . . . We expect it's going to run a long time on Broadway. . . . When a show has nine months under its belt, as this one will have, it can survive. Besides, we should have absolutely all the kinks worked out by then."[18]

Jones's work on *Free and Easy* was acknowledged in the *New York Times*:

If you are a lover of jazz you are supposed to quake at the mention of Quincy Jones. If that portion of this congregation will stop quaking it will be possible to elaborate for the non-quakers that Mr. Jones happens to be one of the foremost jazz artists in the U. S. A., a man no less hailed across the Atlantic, a man who at the age of 26 already can be mentioned in the same breath with Count Basie and Duke Ellington. Hence, big news this morning: Mr. Jones has decided to turn his talents to the theatre, specifically to Stanley Chase's production of Harold Arlen's blues opera.

Indeed, Mr. Jones is going deep into "Free and Easy." Not only has he agreed to conduct it, but he also will play his trumpet, appear on the stage when occasion requires and with Billy Byers be responsible for the orchestration. What has lured Mr. Jones from the more lucrative fee to which he is accustomed is his belief that jazz, in order to grow, must eventually fuse with the lyric theatre and the symphony.

He sees "Free and Easy" a chance to contribute to that growth—the first show for the lyric theatre orchestrated completely in the new jazz idiom and cast with singers of operatic training who also can act. Mr. Jones says with the fervor of a novitiate, "We're either going to rock the boat or sink it."[19]

Jones succeeded in organizing an impressive group of musicians for the *Free and Easy* tour. He stated, "I always wanted to try a Broadway show and I agreed. In New York I immediately called every person (musician) I dreamed about working with."[20] Jones described this group of musicians as a type of United Nations ensemble.

With an active agenda and a cadre of band members, Jones was very excited about the possibilities of a successful show and tour. The tour seemed to be a major step forward in Jones's ambitions about starting a band and having an active band schedule. Rehearsals began on November 16 in Brussels, Belgium. The production was to open at the Théatre Carré in Amsterdam on December 14, 1959.[21]

In addition to the male musicians, Jones also had two female musicians during a time when the inclusion of females as instrumentalists in jazz band ensembles was rare. Members of the band included Floyd Standifer (trumpet), Sahib Shihab (baritone saxophone, flute),

Porter Kilbert (alto saxophone), Joe Harris (drums), Phil Woods (alto saxophone), Budd Johnson (clarinet, tenor saxophone), Patti Bown (piano), Benny Bailey (trumpet), Julius Watkins (French horn), Jerome Richardson (piccolo, flute, tenor saxophone), Les Spann (guitar, flute), Åke Persson (trombone), Buddy Catlett (bass), Clark Terry (trumpet, flügelhorn), Quentin Jackson (trombone), Jimmy Cleveland (trombone), Leonard Johnson (trumpet), and Melba Liston (trombone).

The musicians formed a great working relationship with Jones as their bandleader. Many of these musicians were well established in their professional careers. For example, Clark Terry, who was one of Jones's early mentors, played in several big bands.[22] Åke Persson was a well-known musician in Europe. In the 1940s Porter Kilbert performed in the Coleman Hawkins Orchestra. Jimmy Cleveland and Jerome Richardson had performed with Jones in the Lionel Hampton Orchestra. In the mid-1950s Cleveland formed an octet and also performed on many of Jones's recordings—"Swingin' Till the Girls Come Home" (from *Basically Duke*), "The Song is You" (from *Julian "Cannonball" Adderley*), "Let Me Off Uptown" (from *Drummer Man*), and others. Cleveland produced a sensitive and refined sound on trombone that was influenced by cool jazz. He performed on studio recordings with Miles Davis on the albums *Miles Ahead* (1957) and *Porgy & Bess* (1958).[23]

Jerome Richardson was one of the pioneer musicians in popularizing the flute in jazz. Richardson also played alto, tenor, and soprano saxophones. In the 1950s he played with the Earl Hines band (1954–55). After settling in New York he played with Ernie Wilkins and Quincy Jones. Quentin Jackson (1909–1976) had performed in the 1930s in the McKinney's Cotton Pickers and in the bands of Duke Ellington and Cab Calloway. Joe Harris and Leonard Johnson were quite well-known in the drum and tenor saxophone jazz communities. Les Spann had performed with Dizzy Gillespie on several recordings.

Floyd Standifer and Buddy Catlett were both Seattle natives and early on began to carve out extensive careers and long-lasting friendships with Jones. Sahib Shihab (1925–1989) played baritone, alto, and soprano saxophones and flute. In the mid-1940s he performed with Fletcher Henderson and Roy Eldridge and recorded in New York with Art Blakey. In the 1950s, before joining the *Free and Easy* tour

Shihab, performed in the bands of Dizzy Gillespie, Illinois Jacquet, Oscar Pettiford, and Dakota Staton. He also formed his own band in 1956.

Phil Woods toured with several big bands in the 1950s including those of Jimmy Raney (1955) and George Wallington (1956–57). He also played with the Dizzy Gillespie goodwill tour in 1956, and was one of the musicians that published comments about his experience performing jazz overseas. In addition, Woods performed with the Quincy Jones bands for several years and was featured as an alto saxophonist soloist on several of Jones's recordings.[24] Budd Johnson (1910–1984) had an extensive career in jazz. He played tenor, alto, and soprano saxophones and clarinet and was also an arranger. In the early 1930s he performed with Louis Armstrong and later in the bands of Earl Hines (1935–42), Dizzy Gillespie (1944 and 1948), Billy Eckstine (1944–45), Sy Oliver (1947), Machito (1949), Benny Goodman (1956–57), Gil Evans (1959), Quincy Jones (1959–61), and Count Basie (1964–69). In the 1950s Johnson arranged and produced many early rock 'n' roll records.

Before performing with the *Free and Easy* tour band, pianist Patti Bown, a Seattle native, had performed in New York recording sessions with Billy Eckstine and Jimmy Rushing. She also recorded with the Ed Shaughnessy trio. Bown released an album, *Patti Bown Plays Big Piano*, in 1958.[25] Melba Liston (1926–1999) was a jazz composer, arranger, and performer. She performed with several bands including those of Gerald Wilson, Dexter Gordon, Count Basie, and Randy Weston. In 1956 Liston was also a member and an arranger for the Dizzy Gillespie goodwill tour band.[26] While performing with Jones in Europe, Liston was also featured as a trombone soloist on several recordings and performances.[27]

Benny Bailey performed in several big bands including Dizzy Gillespie (1947–48) and Lionel Hampton (1949–53). Julius Watkins (1921–1977) was one of the first musicians to showcase the performing capabilities of the French horn in jazz.[28] Early on he played trumpet with Ernie Fields's band from 1943–46. In 1949 he recorded on French horn for Kenny Clarke, Babs Gonzales, and the Milt Buckner band. In the 1950s Watkins made recordings with Thelonious Monk. He also led a combo known as Les Jazz Modes with Charlie Rouse (1956–59).

On the tour Jones described Watkins by stating: "Julius Watkins, the French horn player we called 'Phantom' because he was so quiet and performed backstage during the Free 'n' Greasy show as Clark Terry dubbed it, left his mouthpiece at the top of the Eiffel Tower in Paris before we played a concert there. Our road manager had to climb up there and find it."[29] Some of the band members also later contributed interviews about their experiences working with Jones.[30]

Robert Breen, the director of the show, referred to the *Free and Easy* band members as "free spirits." When the show opened in Amsterdam it received a negative review:

> This city probably offers the warmest audience in Europe for an American musical featuring blues, jazz bands, and Negroes. But Harold Arlen's "Free and Easy" which has all three in a package labeled "blues drama" could hardly have got off to a shakier start than it did here last week. Monday's performance was being billed as the world premiere and Robert Breen of "Porgy & Bess" fame was on the program as director. But before the curtain went up Breen was arguing that the premiere should wait until the Paris opening next month. . . . This was the first time, Breen said, that there had ever been a complete jazz orchestration for an entire musical. It was the first time that a jazz band had appeared on stage not only as musicians doing their work in their own way, but also as characters in a play. And they had to memorize their scores. . . . [T]hese free spirits . . . represented the cream of jazz musicianship.[31]

When *Free and Easy* premiered in Europe, many theatergoers compared it to the European premiere of *Porgy & Bess* a few years previously. Here it should be re-emphasized that *Porgy & Bess* was conceived as an opera with orchestration, scenes, and dramatic roles, a classical form to which many European audiences could relate. Take note that in the above comments, the author described *Free and Easy* as a blues drama.

Also, several members of the *Free and Easy* cast had previously performed with the international tour of *Porgy & Bess*. For example, Martha Flowers and Irene Williams had played the character of Bess on the international tour. Some of the European audience members may have evaluated the performances in *Free and Easy* on the same artistic level. One Dutch critic commented, "We all have seen 'Porgy & Bess,' and that is our only standard."[32]

The showed opened in Paris on January 15, 1960, at the Alhambra Theatre, where it also turned out to be unsuccessful and not so free and easy. Instead of running for several months the show closed in Paris only after a few weeks. Part of the reason was that during this time the Algerian war crisis (a war of independence and decolonization from France) erupted, and France soon focused much of its attention on politics.[33] The crisis was complex and characterized by guerilla warfare, terrorism against civilians, use of torture on both sides, and counter-terrorism operations by the French army.

The particular events of the Algerian war crisis greatly affected the presence of people of color but also, in a broader scope, influenced other nations and intellectuals to systemically examine the psychological effects of racism and colonization in the world. This sentiment is reflected in the emergence of Afro-centric studies such as by Frantz Fanon (1925–1961), who wrote the book *The Wretched of the Earth* (*Damnés de la terre*) (1961) examining the Algerian war crisis and the psychological effects of colonization on the psyche (mind set) of nations/states, cultures, and people of color.[34] The political crisis extended into the arts, and even performing venues began to suffer in terms of patronization. As a result, after only a few months *Free and Easy* closed for good in March 1960 without making it to the United States or the Broadway stage.

Several days into the Algerian crisis, Jones experienced a cash flow problem with meeting payroll and expenses. He called a meeting of the band and announced that anyone who wanted to return to the United States had a ticket waiting for him or her. Jones felt an obligation to the many musicians that had sacrificed so much of their time to undertake such a challenging engagement and travel abroad to perform with the show.

Because of his deep sense of obligation, Jones attempted to continue the band and generate a payroll of thousands of dollars to the musicians on a weekly basis as he sought to find other performing opportunities for the band in Europe. If they desired to stay, he would attempt to book the band for a series of European concert tours. Desperate to keep the band working, Jones was able to organize a series of bookings from one week to the next in Yugoslavia, Sweden, Denmark, Portugal, Spain, Holland, France, and Austria.

Jones found a few performances including a three-week tour with Nat King Cole that was sponsored by jazz impresario Norman Granz. He described the experience as follows:

> Well the Algerian war was going on and we didn't draw enough people, so one Thursday we were told the show was closing and we're going home in two days. Idealist, I said we have a gig to play at the Olympia in Paris. I called our booking agent, Willard Alexander in New York and said, "We're in trouble." We missed our plane and now there are 30 people including the 18-piece band stranded. We didn't have a manager or agent, so you use your instincts. I called friends to get us booked. We stayed in Europe ten months. This took me to the edge. Guys were asking me for loans and draws in different countries. It was a nightmare. I was $60,000 in debt. . . . It was one of the lowest points in my career. We couldn't make it because it was just too much of a load, and by this time big bands were dying.[35]

Although there were hardships, most of the band members were supportive of Jones's efforts to find other performing opportunities in Europe. For example, Quentin Jackson remarked:

> When I left Duke [Ellington] in 1959, it was to go with Quincy Jones in the show Free and Easy. . . . I thought it would mean I would not have to go on the road anymore and do one-nighters anymore, and that I could stay in New York and get recording dates, because I knew a lot of contractors. But the show fell through. Quincy wanted to keep the band, and because he's such a wonderful guy we all agreed to stay with him. We toured Europe, and I like that. We did a couple of months in Sweden and toured all the folk parks. We settled in Paris for a few weeks and then traveled around.[36]

The failure of *Free and Easy* left Jones over $100,000 in debt, at that time a large amount that took him several years to clear. He even contemplated committing suicide. But the adversity of the tour seems to have made Jones a more determined individual and musician. He later remarked about this challenging experience: "you learn from your mistakes. It took me seven years to get out of the debt from *Free and Easy*. It's always a question of survival—you learn because you have to."[37]

We will never know whether or not *Free and Easy* would have succeeded in Europe or on Broadway. But this experience was another opportunity for Jones to reinvent himself in the popular music industry. In the 1960s he formed the Quincy Jones Big Band, which basically was comprised of the members of the *Free and Easy* band. The group performed in Paris at the Alhambra Theater. The band also recorded the album *Q Live in Paris Circa 1960*.[38] Members of this band also recorded on several of Jones's other 1960s jazz albums.

On his return to the United States after the *Free and Easy* tour experience, Jones became the first African American musician to be featured on the National Guard Show. The show had been in existence for twelve years and was a recruiting promotion show used on 3,800 radio shows throughout the United States. In collaboration with popular music vocalist Andy Williams, Jones and his eighteen-piece band recorded several tunes released as a public-service radio show in January 1961.[39]

Jones also remarked of his experience with *Free and Easy*: "with the big band I had an impossible situation on my hands. I kept saying 'I'll never do it again'—well, I tried, and I lied. I did do it again and again."[40] Upon his return to the United States, Jones also formed other larger bands that included some of the musicians from his earlier ensembles. Other prominent jazz musicians joined Jones's ensembles, such as Kenny Burrell (guitar), Milt Hinton (bass), Snooky Young, Nat Adderley, Dizzy Gillespie, Freddie Hubbard (trumpets), Gloria Agostini and Margaretha Ross (harps), Milt Jackson and Gary Burton (vibraphones), and many others. During this time Jones on occasion added African and Latin American percussionists to his ensembles, including Babatunde Olatunji, Tito Puente, and Carlos "Patato" Valdes.

Quincy Jones: Live in '60/Reelin' in the Years (2006) is a video that features performances by Jones as a bandleader in the 1960s.[41] This video is comprised of two European concerts filmed in Belgium and Switzerland. The repertoire for the Belgium concert consists of several of Jones's compositions and arrangements: "Birth of a Band," "Moanin'," "Lester Leaps In," "The Gypsy," "Tickle Toe," "Everybody's Blues," and "Big Red." In Switzerland the repertoire consists of "Birth of a Band," "I Remember Clifford," "Walkin'," "Parisian Thoroughfare," "The Midnight Sun Will Never Set," "Everybody's Blues," "Stockholm Sweetnin'," "My Reverie," "Ghana," and "Big Red."

Since the 1970s Jones has worked on many different projects involving large and small ensembles. As Jones delved more into writing and performing contemporary styles of music in that decade, he tapped into a new generation of bands and ensembles made up of talented instrumentalists such as N'dugu Chancler (drums), Dann Huff (guitar), Paulinho DaCosta (percussion), and Greg Phillinganes (keyboards and synthesizers). This is another way that Jones has reinvented himself philosophically and as bandleader.

Over the years Jones has continued to work with many talented musicians on the stage and in recording studios. His grace, manners, and poise as a bandleader is also a manifestation of his musical expertise. In overcoming the negative events of 1959, Jones proved that he could continue to thrive and survive through difficult times and experiences. He is a prime example of how a musician must often find solutions and other opportunities; though adversity, resilience is achieved. Whether on a Broadway stage, recording studio, big band, or other venues, Jones has made a significant contribution as a bandleader.

3

COMPOSER
+
ARRANGER
=
"Q"

Quincy Jones has described the art of composing and arranging as hearing "a tapestry of different colors and textures, and densities." But he cautions: "arranging is also sweatshop work, a blend of experience, architecture, soul, and science. When one is arranging, that musician is in many ways tearing fears, observations, harmonies, and rhythms down to their essence and building them back up to support and re-create the songs."[1]

This chapter focuses on his body of work as a composer and arranger and discusses some of his compositions and arrangements in jazz and popular music, as well as some of the musicians, styles, and trends that have influenced his compositional writing. Jones has over five hundred compositions and arrangements cataloged and registered with the American Society of Composers, Authors, and Publishers (ASCAP).[2] Over the years, jazz bands, small instrumental ensembles, individual artists, and popular music groups have performed many of these works.

As a composer and arranger Jones's creative agency is energized by his ability to generate works that reflect the influences of many different styles. For example, his arrangement of "I'm Gone" (1954) for King Pleasure (Clarence Beeks) (1922–1981) incorporated a technique known as *vocalese*, a jazz vocal technique where a musician adds lyrics to existing instrumental solos and replaces instruments with vocal parts. This arrangement was a version of a chart titled "NJR" that Jones had written for saxophonist James Moody.[3]

Jones has written arrangements of many popular tunes, often for specific performers and bands. For example, his collaboration with alto saxophonist Julian "Cannonball" Adderley (1928–1975) on the album *Julian "Cannonball" Adderley* (1955)[4] includes an arrangement of "The Song Is You," composed by Jerome Kern and Oscar Hammerstein. This arrangement is structured to showcase the lightness of the instrumental texture of Adderley's delicate, complex solo improvisation combined with several horn parts—alto, tenor, baritone saxophones, trombone, and cornet.

In some arrangements Jones conveys a sense of whimsy and savvy, as in the arrangement of "Makin' Whoopee" (1956) he wrote for Dinah Washington (1924–1963).[5] Jones also prepared a jazz, gospel, and soul arrangement of Leonard Bernstein's "Somewhere" (from the musical *West Side Story*) for Aretha Franklin on her album *Hey Now Hey (The Other Side of the Sky)* (1973).

Jones has written instrumental compositions that feature lyrical-type melodies, such as "The Quintessence," "The Witching Hour," "The Twitch," "Jessica's Day," and "The Midnight Sun Will Never Set." Other arrangements are centered on a swing dance and rhythmic feel, such as in "Hard Sock Dance" and "Trumpet Mambos." Cultural roots, current events, and suggestive titles such as "Gula Matari," "Walking in Space," and *Roots* have also inspired Jones in the creative output of his compositions and arrangements.

In his compositional writing Jones has often explored various shades of timbres, textures, and nuances. His music may even incorporate techniques such as finger snaps, whistles, field hollers, handclaps, clanking bottles, sounds of locomotives, and background vocals. His music may also incorporate an assortment of musical instruments—banjo, trumpet, mandolin, koto,[6] harmonica, congas, African djembe drums, cowbell, violin, chimes, cello, tube shaker, synthesizer, Hammond B-3 organ, and many others.

"Faith" (1966) is a trumpet and vocal arrangement set in a New Orleans Dixieland jazz band style that Jones prepared for Louis Armstrong (1901–1971). This arrangement incorporates intricate and interweaving melodies of trumpet, clarinet, trombone, banjo, and drums. The arrangement employs a type of collective improvisation technique where the musical instruments ornament and embellish on melodies at the same time.[7] There is also a strumming banjo that supports and accompanies the other instruments with recurring melodic and rhythmic motives.

Many of Jones's compositions and arrangements are written with a technique of manipulating the sound and tonal ranges of musical instruments. For example, his arrangement of "Let Me Off Uptown" (1956) showcases the virtuosic improvisational skills of trumpeter soloist Roy Eldridge (1911–1989) in a performance with the Gene Krupa Big Band and jazz vocalist Anita O'Day.[8] Eldridge had a distinct technical ability to play in high-register, scale-like passages, and long sweeping vibratos on the trumpet; Jones incorporated these techniques in the arrangement.[9]

Jones may prepare an arrangement of horns that sound similar to strings and vice versa. At the same time, he may combine interweaving brisk and flowing passages of a harp with the sensuous sounds of an alto saxophone. He can create a whimsical melodic line of high-pitched flutes that seem to be dancing on top of the brassy sounds of trumpets and trombones. An example of Jones's ability to manipulate the sound of flutes, trumpets, and trombones can be found his original composition "Soul Bossa Nova" (1962): flutes provide a light instrumental texture while trumpet and trombone parts are arranged to play sounds like slides and growls.

These are only a few examples of Jones's art, creative touch, and ability in compositional writing. Over the years, his writing has adhered to an open and welcoming philosophy steeped the value of musical diversity. Part of this philosophy stems from his early years of creative thinking and development.

One musician who greatly influenced Jones's compositional writing, early creative thinking, development, and ideas about musical diversity was Ray Charles (1930–2004). Jones met Charles in Seattle when he was fourteen years old and Charles was sixteen.[10] Charles read music in Braille, a skill he passed on to Jones. Charles was also an independent musician who pursued many activities and had an ability to perform styles ranging from jazz to classical music. In their close friendship, Charles emphasized to Jones the idea of inclusiveness and being open to performing all styles of music. Jones performed in Charles's band at engagements held at places like the Seattle Tennis Club, Washington Social Club, bar mitzvahs, and frat dances. The band was required to play all kinds of music, which greatly benefitted Jones's development as a musician, composer, and arranger.

Jones stated that "when Ray Charles showed up and that's when it really got going. . . . I remember we couldn't wait for Ray to get through with his jobs at night—we all had three jobs. We'd meet at the Elks Club and get into Bebop."[11] This was in 1947, '48. . . . Ray was so good then he used to frighten me; he could play anything. And he had such a democratic attitude towards music."[12] Charles inspired Jones's interests in musical diversity but he also taught Jones some notational and score-writing skills that would be beneficial to Jones's compositions and arrangements throughout his career. Jones applied many of these skills in his early writings for jazz big band and ensembles.

Jones's compositions "Kingfish" and "Stockholm Sweetnin'" are important early works in several ways. First, they show wide contrast in terms of style, instrumentation, textures, and rhythms. Second, they were composed for different types of ensembles—big band and small ensemble. Third, they are prima facie evidence of early influence of different musical styles on Jones's composing (e.g., swing, bebop, and cool jazz).

"Kingfish" (1951) was Jones's first professional composition, written at the age of eighteen when he was a member of the Lionel Hampton Orchestra. The significance of this work is that, even as a teenager, Jones showed great promise as a composer and arranger. The writing of "Kingfish" also served several purposes. Hampton wanted his arrangements to be exciting and full of notes; this is exactly what Jones learned to accomplish. He wrote arrangements for Hampton that flutist Jerome Richardson described as "thunder-and-lightning" arrangements.[13] The composition integrates different rhythms and textures showing different stylistic influences—swing, bebop, cool jazz, rhythm & blues—with introductory melodic material arranged for a vibraphone (played by Hampton); an improvisational trumpet solo (played by Jones); passages played in unison by horns and flute; walking bass[14] patterns; virtuosic improvisation on several instruments;

harmonic chords and rhythmic accompaniment on piano that supports the soloists; and call-and-response, short repeated patterns
(riffs) played between instrumental sections. "Kingfish" is also one of
the earliest examples of an arranger incorporating flute as a major part
of the instrumental texture in a jazz composition.

The Hampton orchestra performed other compositions and
arrangements by Jones, including "Brand New Baby," "Comme
ci Comme ca," "Love for Sale," "Evening in Paris (An Evening in
Paris)," and "On the Sunny Side of the Street."[15]

"Stockholm Sweetnin'" (1953), an original composition that was
first recorded by the Clifford Brown, Art Farmer, and Swedish All
Stars, is a masterful jazz work comprised of complex harmony and
tonal colors. This composition features a rich textural arrangement of
instrumentation geared for a small ensemble format, with influences
from of Miles Davis's *Birth of the Cool* sound and lyrical melodies
played by a combination four horn parts—trumpet, alto and baritone
saxophones, and trombone[16]—and is also an example of the influence
of Ray Charles on Jones's expertise in writing horn arrangements. He
has stated: "I was actually into that four-horn sound all of my life.
Ray Charles also knew how to write all that stuff, and he taught me
what some of the advance notations were, what some of the voicings
were. And we used them to do arrangements . . . that we'd hear from
the East Coast."[17]

Jones gained a vast amount of writing experience working with
Dizzy Gillespie and the U.S. State Department jazz goodwill tour
(1956), during which he had to prepare many different types of
arrangements. Part of his task was to rework some of Gillespie's old
arrangements, but he also wrote new compositions. As the musical
director of the tour, Jones enlisted band members Melba Liston and
Ernie Wilkins to compose a few original charts. Together, they also
wrote arrangements for the national anthems of each country they
visited. In addition, many of the arrangements were intended to be a
symbolic representation of African American historical roots, music,
and culture. Jones along with his writing crew composed a work, titled
"The History of Jazz," to showcase the evolution of jazz and different
musical styles. This work also included a demonstration of African
drum rhythms.[18]

During the late 1950s and 1960s, Jones completed many compositions for his own big bands. Some of these were influenced by Western
classical music, such as "My Reverie," based on the French Impressionist composer Claude Debussy's piano composition *Rêverie* (1890).
Jones also wrote many jazz arrangements. For example "Moanin',"
written by Bobby Timmons in 1958 and performed by Art Blakey
and the Jazz Messengers, is often categorized as hard bop, a style that
developed in the late 1950s out of the bebop movement by musicians
who desired to incorporate more African American music (e.g., blues,
gospel) in jazz. Timmons's arrangement is arranged in a call-and-
response style with passages played by a piano followed by harmonic
passages played by other instruments. Timmons cleverly incorporates
an Amen harmonic church cadence or "Yes Lord" musical response
that is influenced from traditional gospel music and congregational
singing of sacred hymns. In Jones's arrangement of "Moanin'" (1960),
this Amen church cadence consists of flügelhorn, French horn, four
trumpets, four trombones, and five saxophones. Other instruments
include flute, guitar, drums, piano, and bass. In this arrangement Jones
took familiar musical material and transformed the hard bop style to
integrate his own distinct big band sound and feel. He also included a
flügelhorn improvisation performed by Clark Terry.[19]

On several occasions Jones has noted the difficulty in pursuing
a career as a composer and arranger in jazz, recalling many experiences as a young musician in New York City and how composers
and arrangers like him constantly sought out job assignments. He
described hanging out with other composers and arrangers at the
famous jazz club Birdland, the Brill Building, and other popular music
industry locations:[20] "songwriters and arrangers hung out in front of
the Brill Building doorway like Mafia hit men, hands in pockets, col-
lars up . . . broke, hungry, always looking for the next job. Broadway
shows, television and film scores, records, nightclub acts, commercials,
industrial shows—we did it all."[21]

But, Jones's talents did not go unnoticed. The respect he had
gained among his peers was considerable. Music critics were very
much interested in his opinions about innovations in jazz and arranging. In an early interview Jones discussed many of the challenges for
jazz composers and arrangers; he also discussed compositions such

as "Flying Home" (Lionel Hampton), "Moody's Mood for Love" (James Moody), and what he believed were examples of new, innovative, and experimental compositions that made them unique to the jazz repertoire.[22]

In a biographical profile, Raymond Horricks described Jones as a brilliant young arranger-composer belonging to a contemporary school of African American musicians in New York. The profile describes Jones as an ideal arranger and composer with an ability to write instinctively for the art of jazz improvisation and a remarkable versatility in remolding compositions to suit all manner of instruments and voices. His style did not evoke the formal dignity of John Lewis, the pre-eminent jazz composer of the New York school.[23] Rather, Jones was considered to be a composer and arranger with a deep sense of precision and emotion in his body of work that had impact in the jazz world.[24] In essence, Jones exhibited a commitment to his craft by continually expanding his body of work and possessing a desire to pursue more advanced compositional writing opportunities in the jazz world.

Possessing a deep desire to develop his skills in string arranging, Jones became a composer and arranger who would not settle for limited opportunities in compositional writing, even if this meant accepting musical projects abroad. As musical director, composer, and arranger for Barclay Records in Paris, Jones was provided with many opportunities to expand his compositional skills and incorporate symphonic/orchestral instruments such as violins, cellos, violas, and harps in many of his works. This includes his arrangements and collaborations with vocalist Sarah Vaughan, tenor saxophonist Zoot Sims, and the Eddie Barclay orchestra on the album *Vaughan and Violins* (1958).[25] Jones also produced this album, which includes his arrangement of "Misty," originally composed by Erroll Garner (music) and Johnny Burke (lyrics).

Sarah "Sassy" Vaughan (1924–1990) was often known as the Queen of Bebop. Without a doubt one of the most innovative and versatile singers in jazz history,[26] Vaughan was also an accomplished pianist who performed with many musicians and bandleaders, including Earl Hines and Billy Eckstine. But it was her rich vocal technical ability that cemented her legendary status. Vaughan was highly influenced by bebop musicians Dizzy Gillespie and Charlie Parker. She recorded as a vocalist on many labels, including Columbia (1949–53).

The arrangement of "Misty" was very much suited to Vaughan's versatility and vocal range. She had a distinct ability to interpret many styles of music in performances and recordings with a variety of musicians and instrumental ensembles. Jones had high regard for Vaughan and it was not a difficult task to write a string and vocal arrangement to accompany her elegant interpretation of the melody and lyrics.[27] Jones's arrangement of "Misty" has become a popular music standard.

Jones also collaborated with Peggy Lee on several arrangements. Often described as having a sultry voice, Lee (1920–2002) was one of the most versatile vocalists in jazz and American popular music history.[28] In many recordings and performances she expressed a deep sense of drama through textual and melodic lyricism. Such expressions in music were ideal for her collaborations with Jones.

Lee began her career in jazz/popular music in the 1940s when she became a featured vocalist with the Benny Goodman band. She later had major hits with "Why Don't You Do Right?" and "The Way You Look Tonight." During the 1950s Lee extended her career to acting in television shows and films including *Mr. Music* (1950), *The Jazz Singer* (1953), and a noteworthy acting performance in *Pete Kelly's Blues* (1955), for which she received an Academy Award nomination. She is probably best known for her recording of the popular song "Fever" (1958).

Lee very much wanted to work with Jones. She had heard and admired the arrangements that Jones had previously prepared for Ray Charles. When her office telephoned Jones in Europe and asked if he would be interested in arranging for Lee, he accepted the invitation and returned to the United States. Lee and Jones seemed to complement each other musically, in that they both had an ability to delve into many popular music styles in order to produce memorable recordings and performances. In his arrangement for Lee of "As Time Goes By" (1961) (originally composed by Herman Hupfield), Jones created sensuous sonorities using twelve violins, four violas, four cellos, harp, piano, guitar, vibraphone, bass, drums, congas, and bongos that weave over the flowing passages of Lee's voice and Benny Carter's improvisational alto saxophone solo. Many of the other arrangements that Jones completed for Lee are recorded on her Capitol albums *If You Go* (1961) and *Blues Cross Country* (1961).

In addition to working with Sarah Vaughan and Peggy Lee, Jones also wrote string and vocal arrangements for bands and other noted musicians. For example, he wrote jazz compositions and arrangements for the bandleader William "Count" Basie (1904–1984), one of the legendary swing bandleaders. Basie was primarily centered in Kansas City, Missouri, where in the 1920s and 1930s there was a thriving jazz scene. He helped popularize a Kansas City dance style of swing jazz arrangements. Many of these arrangements were based on a fast-paced, danceable style of blues and boogie-woogie[29] that Basie himself often performed on piano in the background with short musical phrases (riffs) that were repeated continuously by different instrumental sections (trumpets, saxophones) of the band. These musical phrases were arranged to serve as background to complement improvised solo passages. Many band members performed instrumental improvisations called head arrangements.

Jones's arrangements gave the Count Basie band a new voice without losing the essence and integrity of the original Basie style. He often wrote arrangements to showcase the individual talents of band members: the light and syncopated piano playing by Basie, the melodic tenor saxophone playing by Ben Webster, and the balanced strumming/acoustic playing by guitarist Freddie Green.

Jones composed and arranged in a melodic instrumental jazz style several selections on the album *String Along with Basie* (1959). Although Basie was known for his "all rhythm section,"[30] on this album Jones concentrated more on the flow and continuity of melody, even in the integration of Basie's slow improvisational piano parts. For example, "Blues Bittersweet" is arranged with flowing string passages. The arrangement begins with a slow, repeating syncopated (offbeat) boogie-woogie-like rhythmic pattern played on bassoon; as the bassoon continues, the strings enter and play a sweeping blues melody that is answered by the trumpet/horn section. The piano (played by Basie) also integrates an improvisational melodic section with slow-moving chords. The arrangement is highlighted with a bluesy improvisational sax solo by Ben Webster.

Jones has often remarked that arranging and recording with Ella Fitzgerald (1917–1996) is an important aspect of his career. Fitzgerald was known as the First Lady of Jazz and the Queen of Scat.[31] For over fifty years she led the jazz industry as a remarkable vocalist who touched audiences with her performances and recordings.

Jones recorded the album *Ella and Basie* (1963) that showcased an arrangement of "I'm Beginning to See the Light," a song Fitzgerald had previously recorded in 1944. Jones's arrangement incorporates a balance between Fitzgerald's refined style of scatting and instruments—especially the soft, smooth guitar part performed by Freddie Green. The perfection of the Fitzgerald/Jones collaboration was acknowledged with the following commentary by Geoffrey Mark Fidelman (1994), the author of Fitzgerald's biography:

> What can you say about an album that was nearly perfect—one that had so many gems that more than half of them ended up in Ella's permanent repertoire? One that shuffled the greatest singer of the era (Ella), the finest musicians of the era (the Basie band), and one of the most imaginative young arrangers of the era (Quincy Jones who himself ended up being one of the biggest arranger/producer/writers of any era)?[32]

Jones, Count Basie, and Frank Sinatra make up an important triumvirate who together contributed some of the most memorable arrangements in popular music and recording history. Sinatra's vocal career spanned several decades with bandleaders such as Harry James (1939), Tommy Dorsey (1940–42), Axel Stordahl (1942), Count Basie (1964), and many others. Sinatra was familiar to many as a dynamic crooner, and was also highly regarded for his acting roles in Hollywood films. Sinatra's many film appearances include *Anchors Aweigh* (1945), *On the Town* (1947), *From Here to Eternity* (1954) (for which he received an Academy Award for Best Supporting Actor for his acting performance), and *The Man with the Golden Arm* (1955), a film about the problems of dealing with drug addition. But his vocal performances continue to be Sinatra's lasting legacy.

Jones has often reflected on his personal experience of arranging and recording with Frank Sinatra.[33] Sinatra was familiar with Jones's arrangements for Basie. In 1964 Sinatra, in the process of performing with the Basie band, telephoned Jones and invited him to arrange, conduct some works, and add a string section for arrangements to be compiled in an upcoming album (*It Might As Well Be Spring*). Arranging and conducting for Sinatra was a significant opportunity in Jones's musical career. Furthermore, Sinatra and Jones shared a common bond in that they both excelled in popular music and film. Their music and talent in performances and on recordings have continued to appeal to generations of audiences.

Jones's arrangements with Sinatra and Basie also contributed to Sinatra's musical legacy. His arrangement of the song "Fly Me to the Moon" (1964) (composed by Bart Howard) is one of the most familiar songs in the Frank Sinatra/Count Basie Band repertoire.[34] This arrangement became even more popular in 1969 as the theme song for the historical event of the American astronauts' walk on the moon. When Apollo 11 landed on the moon astronaut Buzz Aldrin chose the Quincy Jones–Frank Sinatra rendition of "Fly Me to the Moon" as the first song to be played on lunar soil. With several album compilations (e.g., *L.A. Is My Lady*, 1984), Sinatra and Jones created a dynamic collaboration between two extraordinary musicians. Mediating this experience was Count Basie and his famous band.

Outside of jazz some of Jones's compositional writing was influenced by rhythm & blues (R&B) and jump band styles. In its earliest manifestations, R&B was dance music that developed in the 1940s. Rooted in the boogie-woogie, blues, and jump/dance rhythms of swing bands of the late 1930s, the style was generally characterized by small instrumental combos consisting of a rhythm section (piano, guitar, bass, and drums) and the sound of honking horns. It combined a boogie-woogie bass pattern, an underlying swing feel, jazz and urban blues electric guitar styles, and gospel-influenced singing characterized by an improvised, half-spoken, half-sung quality of shouts, moans, and high-pitched falsettos. The blues often served as the basis of the style. The lyrics were often based on themes reflecting the background, lifestyles, and street language of urban African Americans. Similar to jazz big bands, jump bands retained a rhythm section but were smaller in format and incorporated fewer horns.

In his arrangement of "Whole Lot of Shakin' Goin' On" (1955) for Big Maybelle, Jones used stylistic elements of rhythm & blues, jump band, and gospel music and a combination of instruments consisting of three saxophones, trombone, drums, guitar, piano, and bass. Jones also structured this arrangement with accented percussive rhythms in the drum part and a danceable tempo.

The arrangement is given much vitality with the gospel-influenced singing of Big Maybelle as she continually sings and improvises on words such as "Come on baby" and "Shakin' it" (followed by a series of horns riffs). The boogie-woogie pattern and blues feel is arranged in the piano part. This particular arrangement also includes an improvisational tenor saxophone solo (performed by jazz musician Budd Johnson).

Jones collaborated on several arrangements with Louis Jordan (1908–1975), a musician and vocalist who is often considered the father of rhythm & blues. Jordan was highly regarded for his technical virtuosity and included extensive alto saxophone improvisations in many of his popular hits. Jordan had previously worked on what was known as the Theatre Owners' Booking Association (T.O.B.A.) and chitlin' circuits with such groups as the Rabbit Foot Minstrels.[35] He recorded his first vocal number with the Clarence Williams band and later joined the Chick Webb Orchestra. From the early 1940s to the 1950s Jordan, with his own group the Tympany Five, had several popular music hits such as "Caldonia" and "Choo-Choo-Ch'-Boogie."[36] Jones produced and composed several arrangements for Jordan's album *Somebody Up There Digs Me (Greatest Hits)* (1956).

In the mid-1950s an article was published citing Jones as being one of the top new composers and arranging talents in rhythm & blues. He was recognized as having a substantial body of arrangements to his credit and having successfully arranged for both jazz and popular musicians. In the article Jones made several comments about the importance of jazz and rhythm & blues and shared his views about the integration of these two styles in the categorization of African American popular music. He also emphasized that it was up to arrangers to raise the quality of rhythm & blues by adding new types of orchestration to arrangements, and that he was hopeful that there would be many more talented arrangers and musicians in the popular music industry.[37]

Some of Jones's works reflect a geospatial connection and influence in that he often incorporated elements of foreign styles in his compositions and arrangements. One major influence was bossa nova, an altered type of samba that emerged in Rio de Janeiro in the late 1950s and 1960s. In Brazil, bossa nova was a popular style that appealed to the middle- and upper-class sectors of society. Part of the innovation of bossa nova was that it expanded the stylistic and musical vocabulary of traditional samba with more subdued tempi and poetic symmetry. Bossa nova added the textures of strumming guitars and vocals. It integrated melodies, harmony, rhythm, syncopation, and other stylistic influences from American cool jazz of the 1950s, played by musicians such as Miles Davies, Chet Baker, and Gerry Mulligan.

Brazilian innovators of bossa nova included Luiz Bonfá, who wrote influential music for the film *Black Orpheus* (1959), guitarist João Gilberto, who recorded the album *Chega de Saudade* (1959), and Antonio Carlos Jobim (1927–1994), one of the most frequently recorded bossa nova composers, who achieved recognition on an international level with compositions such as "The Girl from Ipanema (Garota de Ipanema)" (1962). Bossa nova was also important in the American jazz and popular music communities because it contributed a number of songs that readily became standards in the popular music repertoire: "The Girl from Ipanema," "Desafinado," "Samba de Una Nota Só (One Note Samba)," "Chega de Saudade (No More Blues)," and others.

In the 1960s bossa nova enjoyed enormous success in Brazil and abroad. Besides receiving recording contracts, Brazilian musicians such as Antonio Carlos Jobim were given opportunities to perform concert engagements in the United States, where the increasingly popular style was also promoted as a dance craze. American jazz musicians such as Charlie Byrd, John Coltrane, and Stan Getz recorded numerous bossa nova albums. American musicians experimented with incorporating bossa nova influences into other styles of African American popular music, such as with funk and soul.

One of the international composers and arrangers that inspired Jones in bringing the bossa nova style to the forefront in popular music was Lalo Schifrin. Schifrin was born in Buenos Aires, Argentina, of

Jewish heritage and initially studied classical music. Some of his early training included piano lessons with Enrique Barenboim, the father of pianist and conductor Daniel Barenboim. Schifrin became interested in jazz in his early teens. He received a scholarship to study at the Paris Conservatory with Olivier Messiaen. But at night he would perform jazz in Paris local clubs. While studying in Paris, Schifrin also had an opportunity to perform with bandoneón player Astor Piazzolla,[38] who at that time was also in Paris studying with Nadia Boulanger. After Schifrin's return to Argentina he formed a sixteen-piece jazz orchestra.

Schifrin met Jones in 1956, during the Dizzy Gillespie South American goodwill tour.[39] Jones described that while on tour he and Gillespie were in a club and observed a young "dude" (Schifrin) playing some fine jazz piano. Schifrin later introduced Jones and Gillespie to Astor Piazzolla. It was Schifrin that informed them about the bossa nova movement in Brazil, which was their next stop after Buenos Aires. Also, it was Schifrin who informed Jones of the possibility of studying with Nadia Boulanger in France.[40]

Both rhythmically and harmonically, bossa nova was a new trend in Jones's compositional writing. Brazilian bossa nova seemed to him a good combination because in the style, it was possible for jazz musicians to play fast tempi but in a more subdued and refined style. Thus, arrangers such as Jones could write arrangements in the style and manipulate the basic bossa nova rhythmic structures in different ways. Jones also felt that the bossa nova offered new directions for jazz musicians:

> You have to keep [bossa nova] from sounding too weighty, because it's a floating rhythm. One of the things that makes bossa nova so rich is that it is strong rhythmically and harmonically. I think its influence on jazz will be lasting rather than temporary. It will produce in jazz musicians a greater respect for polyrhythms. It has opened an escape hatch from the 2/4 and 4/4 [two- and four-beat time signatures] trap jazz has been in. Jazz musicians have been experimenting with other time figures for the last few years of course, but bossa nova really provides a fresh new direction.[41]

In the early 1960s Jones collaborated with Schifrin on the album *Big Band Bossa Nova* (1962).[42] Jones was one of the first musicians in American popular music to arrange complex pieces in the bossa nova style for a big band ensemble. In essence, he took the style that originally was intended for small intimate ensembles and incorporated a brass sound for a big band made of musicians such as Clark Terry (trumpet), Jerome Richardson (flute), Phil Woods (alto saxophone), Lalo Schifrin (piano), Jim Hall (electric guitar), and many others. But his arrangements preserved the sound of Brazilian traditional instruments—Rio de Janeiro samba drum and percussion ensembles (*baterias*) of low-sounding *surdos*, *cuícas*, *pandeiros*, bells, and other percussion—all enmeshed with the complex rhythms of full/brilliant brass, flutes, and electric guitar melodies.[43]

The album includes "Boogie Bossa Nova," a bossa nova arrangement of "Boogie Stop Shuffle" (an original hard bop composition by bassist Charles Mingus) as well as bossa nova standards "Desafinado" and "Chega de Saudade." He also masterfully included a samba/Carnival-style arrangement of Lerner and Lowe's "On the Street Where You Live" (from the musical *My Fair Lady*) with the techniques and sounds of a traditional samba drum and percussion ensemble enmeshed with the brilliant sounds of brass instruments. There is also a beautiful arrangement of "Lalo Bossa Nova," a composition by Schifrin.

Other early compositions and arrangements display international influences. The album *Around the World: Quincy Jones and His Orchestra* (1961) includes musical sketches and arrangements that have a multicultural flavor and identity: "Hot Sake" (Japan), "Strike Up the band" (USA), "Africana" (Africa), "Meadowlands" (Russia), "Under Paris Skies" (France), "Mack the Knife" (Germany), "Manolete de España" (Spain), "Baia" (Brazil), "Come Back to Sorrento" (Italy), and "Dear Old Stockholm" (Sweden).

Also with an international flavor, "Invitation," from his album *The Quintessence* (1961), is an arrangement of a song by Bronislaw Kaper written in style similar to that of "On Green Dolphin Street," with a Latin rhythmic and melodic feel. Jones incorporated a slow rhythmic tempo at the beginning of the arrangement; a transitional section of a faster swing jazz rhythmic tempo; an exotic modal flavor juxtaposed with a simple melody performed by flute; a countermelodic response arranged for wind and brass instruments; improvisational parts with sweet-sounding textures of alto and tenor saxophones; and French horn with parts written for harps.

In the late 1960s Jones was highly involved in popularizing fusion styles and promoting the use of electronic keyboards and synthesizers in popular music and in his compositional writing. The fusion styles developed during the late 1960s and involved musicians incorporating rock, soul, and funk elements into jazz. Fusion styles often integrated the incorporation of rock or funk rhythms into jazz compositions and the use of simple harmonies and chord progressions. Some musicians began using electric musical instruments, often replacing acoustic bass with electric bass guitar and acoustic pianos with electric keyboards and synthesizers. One of the major influences was the use of intensive amplification for electronic effects, especially with electric guitars.

Miles Davis was a pivotal figure in innovating jazz-fusion works with his album *Filles de Kilimanjaro* (1968), where he included electronic keyboards, repetitive funk bass lines, and rock influenced drumming techniques. Davis also developed a distinct fusion sound with his recordings *In a Silent Way* (1969) and *Bitches Brew* (1969–70). Herbie Hancock, also greatly influenced jazz-fusion styles with many of his compositions, arrangements, and recordings. Other innovative musicians include Jimi Hendrix, Blood, Sweat & Tears, and Larry Coryell.

Jones is recognized as having been the first musician to record an electric bass as early as 1953 and a synthesizer in 1964. He once commented:

> [The synthesizer] expanded the [popular music] vocabulary. People always talk about it replacing acoustic instruments. I think that's ridiculous. If you've got that kind of an ear, maybe it can, but I think the effective usage is to have the synths do what they can do specifically. They expand the alphabet from twenty-six to forty letters. They have a personality, millions of sonic designs that can't come from other instruments.[44]

Many of the arrangements Jones wrote for the album *Walking in Space* (1969) display his jazz-funk fusion writing, combining a jazz big band sound and the contemporary world of electronic musical instruments.[45] These are good examples of Jones's ability to be progressive innovative in his compositions and arrangements. For example, Jones incorporated the styles of funk, soul music, jazz, and gospel in his arrangement of the song "Oh Happy Day."[46]

Some of the arrangements were influenced by the musical *Hair*, at the time a thriving Broadway musical. The title song is arranged as a collage of sounds and styles comprised of funk and swing jazz, with vocal parts consisting of melodic and lyrical material from *Hair*— suggesting a collage of moods and scenery that involve locked doors, pulled blinds in a room encircled with low lights, and the heat of high flames, all influencing the singer's musical interpretation, which is performed and sung by Valerie Simpson and accompanying vocalists. Throughout the arrangement Jones juxtaposed a series of sonorities, rhythms, and instrumental textures that in some ways convey images of someone walking in space. This is also done with manipulations of acoustic and dynamics levels, as the music gradually rises (crescendos) and falls (decrescendos).

This work begins with a slow introduction played on a few instruments, but progresses into a swing jazz feel with a walking bass, steady drumming, and improvisational solos performed by Hubert Laws (flute) and Freddie Hubbard (Harmon mute trumpet). This is followed by a swing jazz improvisational section of the melodic material performed by the horns. Also included in the arrangement is a funk/ jazz solo for guitar (performed by Eric Gale). Throughout the work Jones uses transitions in which the different styles continually elide into each other, seeming to form a cohesive unit or entity of contemporary music sounds.

Many of Jones's arrangements in the 1970s demonstrate his ability to incorporate a symphonic sound combined with jazz, rock, and funk fusions. This can readily be seen in some of the arrangements and writings he prepared with particular musicians/performers in mind for the album *Gula Matari* (1970). Jones initially included an arrangement of Nat Adderley's composition "Hummin'," with the intention that Jimi Hendrix perform the solo part on the recording. He commented that this arrangement "was originally written for Jimi Hendrix. Hendrix wanted to solo over that and I wrote it for him. He was supposed to be featured on that tune, but he got hung up or got too high."[47] As a result, the solo part was given to Toots Thielemans, the harmonica virtuoso who had appeared on several of Jones's albums.

Some of Jones's contemporary works combine classical and popular music influences with a symphonic/funk sound that he arranged for strings. An example of this type of arrangement is "Tell Me a Bedtime Story" (1978), an original piano solo composition by Herbie Hancock. Jones transcribed this work to incorporate a violin improvisation performed by concertmaster Harry Lookofsky, a musician that Jones initially met as a youth residing in the Seattle area. This arrangement is another example of Jones's ability to write dynamic parts for strings.

Jones also recorded a jazz/soul/gospel arrangement of the Doobie Brothers song "Takin' It to the Streets" (1978)[48] that integrates a contrast of instrumental riffs, funk bass passages, call-and-response sections performed by the soloists, background singers, and an elaborate solo improvisation written for tenor saxophone. The arrangement also includes a soulful gospel music section with an increase in tempo, interjections of vocal shouts performed by the soloists and background singers, all combined with the playing of tambourines and interspersed handclaps.

As early as the 1960s, Jones had already experimented with various types of rapping techniques and spoken lyrics inspired by performers such as the Last Poets and Gil-Scott Heron (1949–2011). Evidence can be found on the album titled *Mellow Madness* (1975), which featured a lover's rap called "Beautiful Black Girl," performed by a toasting group known as the Watts Prophets (Richard Dedeaux, Anthony Hamilton, and Otis O' Solomon).[49] In the song, Jones experimented with poetic rap verses/lyrics arranged as call-and-response chants, which he formulated with funk rhythms and African percussion instruments. Although Jones had experimented with rapping in years before, the music industry did not take note of rap until the release of "Rappers' Delight" (1979) by the Sugar Hill Gang, a trio from Englewood, New Jersey. After that breakthrough hit, rap music began its rise as one of the most vital popular music forms in the 1980s.[50]

Stylistically, rap or rapping refers to a vocal style in which the artist speaks in rhythm and verse, generally to an instrumental or

synthesized beat. The rhythm is most often in a four beat (4/4) pattern. The rhythm can be created by looping portions of other songs,
usually by a DJ (disc jockey) or sampled portions of other songs. Rappers often improvise their lyrics and perform their works a cappella
or to a beat.

Rap music emerged as an expression of hip-hop culture encoded
in speech, gesture, dress, posture, and other artistic expressions such
as graffiti painting and break dancing. It became a way of life for
many low-income youths. Beginning in the 1980s African American
rappers such as Ice-T and Kool Moe Dee used rap music to produce
social commentary by including lyrical content that reflected life in
low-income ghetto neighborhoods (e.g., crime, poverty).[51]

In the music industry skeptics debated whether rap music would
continue to be a popular style. But, in spite of this negativity, as the
style was developing Jones continued to be an advocate for the significance of rap music and its artistic longevity. By the late 1980s, he
integrated rap into an arrangement for contemporary rappers QDIII,
Ice-T, Melle Mel, Big Daddy Kane, and Kool Moe Dee in his album
Back on the Block (1989). Jones himself raps on the album.

Many of the arrangements on *Back on the Block* incorporate extensive use of electronic/digital drumming and synthesizer programming,
non-traditional musical instruments such as the African hindehoo,[52]
and various types of African percussion. He also incorporated as a
time/rhythmic element the pulsations of syncopated handclaps.

Back on the Block was intended to have a special message (a social
commentary) from Jones's memory of a "dude" (a low-income
African American male) located on the corner in every ghetto in
America. But Jones had previously used this imagery in an earlier
album, *The Dude* (1981). The dude in this album is described in the
music and lyrics as an educated African American male who did not
receive his doctoral degree from a formal university and academic
program, but instead received his education from a daily curriculum
that includes his lived experiences, family, friends, and by attend-
ing classes in the streets of his local neighborhood where he could
always be found. The dude is not concerned about inflation or a broken economy because he always has access to financial gratification.
He considers himself to be an expertise in the artistry of rap and

usage of words and is comfortable in his status and position in his local neighborhood.

Several years later *Back on the Block* was intended to be a reinvention of the imagery of *The Dude* written for both a cross-cultural and cross-generational inclusion of a diverse group of musicians. Thus, in addition to the rappers, the other musicians featured include Ella Fitzgerald, Miles Davis, Sarah Vaughan, Dizzy Gillespie, George Benson, Luther Vandross, Dionne Warwick, Barry White, Chaka Khan, Bobby McFerrin, Al Jarreau, James Ingram, Take Six, Herbie Hancock, Andrae and Sandra Crouch, Tevin Campbell, Ray Charles, and Josef Zawinul. Jesse Jackson presented a speech-like comment, "rap is here to stay."

In the arrangement of the title song, Jones included melodies sung in Zulu, jazz improvisation, and a gospel choir with rendition of poetic rap/lyrical content relating to the victimization of poverty, drugs, and violence that many young African Americans often experience in the inner cities. The major theme presented in the lyrics centers on an awareness of African spiritual ancestry as being part of a block of knowledge and appreciation of the African American experience. Part of the special message was also intended to convey that when one returns to his/her block (or becomes more aware of the African/African American experience), they have come full circle.

Jones uses the term *Block* as symbol of engagement and dialogue with a living, active community steeped in black pride where African Americans have knowledge and appreciation of their African ancestral heritage. But, the term is also used to represent a symbol of hope and faith in the future success of African Americans in American society. In the song the rappers reinvent Jones as the "Dude," an authority figure that has experienced the world in many facets and who continues to encourage the creative innovations of African American youths. The rap lyrics of the song also refer to Jones's use of diverse popular music styles such as soul, rhythm & blues, bebop, and hip-hop. Jones is also referred to as an experienced Dude familiar with the environs of African American local streets and neighborhoods, but he believes in empowerment, upward mobility, intellectual knowledge, and the commitment to one's artistic craft and creativity such as the art of rapping. Jones is a Dude who is constantly inspiring rappers such as Ice-T not to be concerned with the critics of rap; instead he admonishes rappers to be persistent in making meaningful rap music from the heart.

On *Q's Jook Joint* (1995) Jones creates an assortment of arrangements that integrate new sounds with electronic keyboards, synthesizer, drumming, and bass programming. With this album, Jones created images of the "jook joint" or social club as a musical/social space.[53] Many of the arrangements feature a montage of musicians with emphasis on music, rapping, rhythm, and special lyrical content with a cross-cultural and cross-generational group of musicians. Jones collaborated with James Moody (1925–2010) (a musician he highly regarded) on a contemporary version of the song "Moody's Mood for Love." The arrangement features improvisations by James Moody (alto saxophone), Brian McKnight, Rachelle Ferrell, and Take Six (vocals).[54] Jones was inspired to work on this arrangement because he had written several other arrangements for Moody in the past:

> In 1953, while I was working in New York as an arranger, I had the opportunity to work with James Moody, one of the most nurturing men I have ever met. Eleven of us had just left Lionel Hampton's band and decided to try out in New York.... Moody heard the arrangements I was writing for Dinah [Washington's] road band and gave me the chance to arrange for his eight-piece band, at $12 an arrangement. So after being personally involved in producing/arranging this arrangement [of the popular song "Moody's Mood for Love"] for Aretha Franklin in 1972 and George Benson in 1980 you can imagine the joy of having the good fortune to hear this dear friend and originator's solo open and close the [*Q's Jook Joint*] version.[55]

Other tracks on *Q's Jook Joint* include "Let the Good Times Roll" (featuring Stevie Wonder, Bono, and Ray Charles) and "Cool Joe, Mean Joe (Killer Joe)" (featuring Queen Latifah). In particular, the arrangement of "Cool Joe, Mean Joe (Killer Joe)" is a musical hybridization of old (jazz) and new (rap) styles. This arrangement stems from a popular jazz standard, "Killer Joe," that was composed by Benny Golson in the mid-1950s.[56] Jones made an arrangement of Golson's composition featuring flute and trumpet solos in his *Walking in Space*

(1969) album. But twenty-six years later, in *Q's Jook Joint*, Jones created a contemporary arrangement of "Killer Joe," this time featuring different rhythms, electronic instruments, and musicians. He also included an improvisational rap/lyrical solo performed by Queen Latifah.

Also, included in *Q's Jook Joint* is an arrangement of "At the End of the Day (Grace)," originally a theme song he composed for the 1984 Olympics in Los Angeles. The song was written in collaboration with Jeremy Lubbock as the official gymnastics theme "Grace." But Jones transformed the song into a magical number with an arrangement that included the sensual vocals of Barry White and the soulful harmonica playing of Toots Thielemans.

In this arrangement Jones used the texture of electronic instruments—synthesizers that play slow-moving chord progressions against the improvisational melody of a harmonica. But it is the textual symmetry of the vocal part against the chords that sets the mood for the composition as Barry White speaks slowly in a seductive voice words and phrases such as "yeah baby," "let me play all night," and "just for you." In between these softly spoken words and rhythmic phrases, Jones arranged a series of harmonized "doos" sung by a group of background vocalists. The textures, instrumentation, tempi, and mood of this composition are similar to other colorful arrangements by Jones such as "Septembro" ("Brazilian Wedding Song") and "The Secret Garden" ("Sweet Seduction Suite"), selections from the *Back on the Block* album.

Over the years Jones has excelled in compositional writing and the manipulation of rhythm, melody, instrumentation, and form in many different ways. One of his most aesthetically pleasing compositions is the title track of his album *The Quintessence.*[57] The title of this song seems to describe the essence of Jones's writings. The arrangement includes an alto saxophone solo performed by the skillful and artistic Phil Woods, who performed with Jones for many years.

With the arrangements compiled in this album, Jones's compositional writing ability was also recognized favorably. One review stated:

> Among the younger jazzmen, Quincy Jones is already indicating that he may be able to rise above the ebb and flow of jazz tastes. He is not like Mr. [Coleman] Hawkins and Mr. [Pee Wee] Russell, primarily a

performer, although he still plays trumpet on occasion. Rather, he is more comparable to Mr. [Benny] Carter, who has been active as arranger and conductor as he has as a performer. . . . Mr. Jones's strong musical personality as both composer and bandleader can be heard in [his album] *Quintessence*. . . . His writing has a warm, resilient quality.[58]

In his writings, Jones has often expressed high esteem for musicians who have influenced his career and has written some of his most memorable works as special tributes. For example, one of Jones's most popular instrumental jazz compositions, included in *The Quintessence*, is "For Lena and Lennie," a tribute to legendary musician, Lena Horne (1917–2010)[59] and her husband, composer, conductor, and arranger Lennie Hayton (1908–1971).

Another impressive arrangement by Jones is the work titled "A Tribute to Benny Carter" (1971). In terms of its richness of rhythm, harmony, textures, timbres, and nuances, this arrangement is an excellent example of his mature compositional writing. The original recording of this arrangement features Carmen McRae singing the lyrical content in an emotional blues style that greatly complements Jones's compositional writing.[60] This composition features horn parts that are extremely complex and instrumentation that sound similar to strings. In this arrangement Jones also included an bluesy tenor saxophone solo (performed by Flip Phillips).[61]

4

THE GREAT
WIDE WORLD OF
QUINCY JONES
IN THE POPULAR
MUSIC RECORDING
INDUSTRY

Quincy Jones's greatest accomplishments and legacy in popular music continue to be his contributions to the recording industry. This chapter focuses on some of the ways that Quincy Jones has created a world of musical innovations through his many albums and recordings. In the competitive recording industry, Jones has recorded as a composer, arranger, instrumentalist (trumpet, piano), vocalist, rapper, music director, conductor, and producer.

In his career Jones has generated records, albums, tape cassettes, compact discs, and music videos on many prestigious record labels that are constantly marketed around the world. For example, the album *Quincy Jones: Music Is My Life* (1983) was produced on the Pickwick label in the United Kingdom.[1] Other examples include the albums *The Q in Jazz* (2007), on Golden Stars label in Holland, and *Moanin': Quincy Jones Big Band Vol. 2* (1977), a Japanese Mercury release.[2] Many other albums could be presented to demonstrate Jones's productivity in the recording industry.

It should be noted that Quincy Jones began his recording career in the beginning of the 1950s, during a time in American history when the society was still racially segregated. In a historical prospective Jones began his recording career before the Supreme Court decision of *Brown v. Board of Education of Topeka* (1954) and the civil rights and black pride movements.[3]

Examining Jones's recording career within a historical perspective is important because in the 1950s there were limited recording opportunities for African American musicians at prestigious record labels. The record-buying public mainly purchased what was played on the radio. White businessmen, who owned most radio stations, mainly programmed white musicians. Music by African Americans was labeled as inferior and often received little airtime on white radio stations. As a result, such records were poor sellers in the white communities.[4]

African American musicians were often limited to what in the music industry was known as "race records." Representatives of record companies, the music industry, and the mass media often encouraged exclusion of African American popular music by creating such labels and categories to identify African American musicians, who they believed would appeal to only African American communities.

Quincy Jones contributed to breaking down racial barriers and opening doors of opportunities for musicians of different racial and musical backgrounds. In the 1950s Jones recorded with African American and white musicians on such labels as RCA-Victor, Bethlehem, Columbia, EmArcy, Blue Note, Prestige, and others. Some of the albums to his credit on these labels include *Lullaby of Birdland* (1955),[5] *The Giants of Jazz* (1955), *This Is How I Feel About Jazz* (1956), and *Go West Man!* (1957).

Jones also recorded several albums with jazz musicians, including Oscar Pettiford, *The New Oscar Pettiford Sextet* (1951); Gigi Gryce, *Jazz Time in Paris* (1953); Art Farmer, *A. Farmer Septet Plays Arrangements of Gigi Gryce and Quincy Jones* (1953); Paul Quinichette, *Moods* (1954); and Harry Lookofsky, *Miracle in Strings* (1954). These albums and others reflect Jones's ability to compile compositions, arrangements, and writing to showcase the talents of various artists.

In the 1950s Quincy Jones recorded as a trumpeter and arranger for a recording project with several jazz musicians with the same last name: Thad Jones, Jimmy Jones, Eddie Jones, Jo Jones, Renauld Jones, and Elvin Jones. For recording purposes this group of musicians was referred to as the Jones Boys. These musicians assembled on the basis of a recording session and album known as *The Jones Boys* (1956).[6] Though none of them were related, Leonard Feather conceived the recording session to feature a number of musicians named Jones.[7]

The Jones Boys ensemble came from various backgrounds. Thad Jones (trumpet) (1923–1986) performed with Count Basie (1954–63). He also co-founded the Thad Jones–Mel Lewis Orchestra (1965–78). During the 1940s and 1950s Jimmy Jones (piano) (1918–1982) served as accompanist for Sarah Vaughan and Ella Fitzgerald. Eddie Jones (1929–1997) (bass) performed with Sarah Vaughan and Lester Young in the early 1950s. He also performed with the Count Basie Band and small ensembles. Jo Jones (1911–1985) (drums) was often regarded as one of the most proficient drummers of the Swing Era. Jo Jones also performed as vital member of the Count Basie Band for many years.

Renauld Jones (1910–1989) (trumpet) performed with big bands led by Chick Webb, Don Redman, Duke Ellington, Count Basie, and others. Finally, Elvin Jones (1927–2004) (drums) was one of the most prominent drummers of the post-bebop era. He was especially known for his work with John Coltrane and Miles Davis. Between 1956 and 1957 the Jones Boys recorded several albums that include *The Jones Boys*; *Jump for Jones*; *The Jones Boys: Quincy, Thad, Jimmy, Jo, Eddie, Elvin*; *The Jones Bash: Thad Jones, Renauld Jones, Quincy Jones, Jimmy Jones, Jo Jones, Eddie Jones*.

Quincy Jones also recorded with several jazz and popular musicians on the Okeh and Atlantic record labels in the 1950s. Historically, Okeh was one of the race record labels and a pioneer in recording African American musicians; but most importantly, it provided a major path for the American recording industry into African American music that became part of the periphery of popular culture during the first decades of the twentieth century.[8] The company continued to play an important part in recording African American music in the 1950s, especially rhythm & blues.

On the Okeh label Jones collaborated with several popular music-recording artists. This includes his work with the Wild Bill Davis Trio on the arrangements of "Belle of the Ball," "Syncopated Clock," and "Serenade to Benny." Davis was the stage name of William Strethen Davis (1918–1995), a pianist and an arranger and one of the pioneers of the electronic organ in jazz.

Jones also recorded with Brook Benton (1931–1988), one of the prominent African Americans singers in popular music. He also recorded with the Sandmen, one of the most popular African American male harmony groups of the 1950s;[9] Chuck Willis (1928–1958), a rhythm & blues and rock 'n' roll vocalist and songwriter; and with several doo wop groups such as the Treniers ("Say Hey—The Willie Mays Song"), a popular music group led by brothers Clifford and Claude Trenier.[10]

On the Atlantic label, Jones recorded arrangements with LaVern Baker (1929–1997), one of the major female rhythm & blues singers of the 1950s.[11] He also recorded with the Clovers, a successful rhythm & blues harmony group of the 1950s, and the Cardinals, one of the founding members of what was known as the "bird" groups of the 1940s, 1950s, and 1960s.[12] In addition, he recorded several albums with Ray Charles and Milt Jackson. This includes the albums *The Great Ray Charles* (1956), *The Genius of Ray Charles* (1959), and *Genius + Soul = Jazz* (1960).[13] With jazz vibraphonist Milt Jackson, Jones recorded the album *Plenty, Plenty Soul* (1957).[14]

In the early 1950s, in addition to recording several albums as a member of the Lionel Hampton and Dizzy Gillespie bands, Jones also achieved a significant amount of international experience with several albums he recorded in Paris, France. Jones recorded several jam session albums with trumpeter Clifford Brown, including *The Clifford Brown Big Band in Paris* (1953).[15] While he was music director at Barclay Records, Jones recorded the albums *Et Voilà* (1957), *Twilight Time* (1959), *Americans in Paris* (1959), *Eddie Barclay présente Swing & Sweet* (1958), *Eddie Barclay présente Swing & Sweet Vol. 2* (1958), *Eddie Barclay* (1959), *Confetti* (1959), *Surprise Party Caniche Vol. 1* (1959), and *Surprise Party Caniche Vol. 2* (1960[1959]).

Also for Barclay, Jones arranged and recorded with French jazz guitarist Jean-Pierre Sasson on the album *Jean-Pierre Sasson & The Muskrats-Dixie Downbeat* (1958). He also recorded several arrangements with Henri Renaud[16] ("Meet Quincy Jones," "Dillon," and "Wallington Special") and an album with Billy Eckstine, *Mr. B. in Paris with the Bobby Tucker Orchestra* (1957).[17]

Jones recorded the album *The Double Six Meet Quincy Jones* (1960) for Columbia with the Double Six of Paris, a French vocal sextet group that performed a special repertory of jazz themes with added lyrics.[18] This particular style of *vocalese* was influenced by American musicians such as King Pleasure (Clarence Beeks) and the vocal trio of Lambert, Hendricks, and Ross. Also, on the Phillips record label, Jones performed and recorded as a trumpeter on the album *Jazz et Jazz* (1963) with André Hodeir, a composer, critic, and novelist best known for his scholarship, which influenced the area of jazz criticism.[19]

In the recording industry, Mercury Records was one of the "Big Five" record companies along with RCA-Victor, Columbia, Capitol, and Decca.[20] In the early 1960s Jones assumed an executive position at Mercury Records, where he recorded a number of albums and compilations. Many of his albums received highly favorable reviews. The album *I Dig Dancers* (1960) included the compositions "Pleasingly Plump" and "The Midnight Sun Will Never Set." Critic Dorothy Kilgallen commented on this compilation:"[m]y favorite band on this album is Quincy's composition, The Midnight Sun Will Never Set [that features Phil Woods on the alto saxophone]. It reveals him as a flagrant romantic in the space of the jazz age; Puccini would have appreciated him, Ravel would have embraced him, so—some day—will the kid around the corner."[21]

Producing numerous albums with some of the leading popular musicians and singers was a significant aspect of Jones's tenure at Mercury records:

> The thing I like about producing is that it pulls out every thing you're trained in. You're dealing with singers, rhythm sections, finding tempos getting the right keys. . . . If everything is okay, you let it keep going, but if it's not, you have to be able to tell why. I don't [normally] write the string charts on the albums I produce, because as a producer, if you don't take care of the master shots and deal with too many closeups, you forget what you're making. I have a great relationship with arrangers. Usually we talk and decide where we're going ahead of time.[22]

Jones once commented, "I only work with artists [musicians] I respect and love what they do. . . . So once the musician learns to trust me, learns that he[/she] can go without the net, that I won't let him[/her] fall, we have a great time."[23] Jones produced several albums in collaboration with artists such as Sarah Vaughan and Dinah Washington. Vaughan's albums include *Vaughan and Violins* (1958), *Sassy Swings the Tivoli* (1963), *Vaughan with Voices* (1963) *Viva! Vaughan* (1964), and *Sarah Vaughan Sings the Mancini Songbook* (1965). Washington's albums include *For Those in Love* (1955), *The Swingin' Miss D* (1956), *The Queen and Quincy* (1956), *I Wanna Be Loved* (1961), *Tears & Laughter* (1961), and *This is My Story (Vols. 1 & 2)* (1962). Jones also produced an album of Duke Ellington compositions and arrangements, *Impressions of Duke Ellington* (1961), that featured Billy Byers (conductor and arranger) and the Quincy Jones Orchestra.[24]

As an executive at Mercury, Jones often attempted to explore recording opportunities in collaboration with an array of musicians from different racial and artistic backgrounds. For example, Jones produced recordings by artists such as Terry Gibbs, *Terry Gibbs Plays Jewish Melodies in Jazztime* (1963). Making this album was one of the high points in Gibbs's career:

> [In 1963] we recorded an album for Mercury Records. Quincy Jones was now a vice president of Mercury, so I went to him with an idea. I always wanted to do an album playing Jewish music, and play it almost like you'd play Latin Jazz. . . . Quincy loved the idea and he produced the album. I got to know Quincy fairly well when he was a young trumpet player with the Lionel Hampton band. . . . The music turned out great. I played a bunch of [Jewish] songs that had never been written on paper. All the Jewish musicians on the recording were real *klezmers*. . . .[25] I wanted to call the album *Jewish Jazz* but Mercury wouldn't let me. The world wasn't too hip those days and the album was eventually called *Terry Gibbs Plays Jewish Melodies in Jazztime*.[26]

Jones also brought a sense of African American music history into the Mercury recording studio by producing the album *At Town Hall* (1961) by Josh (Joshua Daniel) White (1914–1969), a legendary vocalist, songwriter, actor, and civil rights activist who was known for his powerful voice and stage presence and for singing African American folk, blues, and gospel music.[27]

Part of Jones's responsibility was scouting out and overseeing artistic projects and assisting in developing new recording artists. He was also greatly involved in being a liaison between the new artists and Mercury. Jones commented about doing A&R (artists & repertoire) work that provided him with many opportunities:

> There's a lot of sacrifices you have to make when you become an A and R man—if you're a musician, anyway—insomuch as it gives you a certain freedom to do the type of projects the way you want to do them. It's selfish, in a way.
>
> I don't know whether it's the ego or what—but it gives you a chance to use your imagination completely. If you use your imagination only in the music and don't think of overall packaging it still isn't complete. This way we have complete control. It's a dictatorship.
>
> Also your concern is to find talent every way possible. They're brought to you, you go out and look—everything that's new on the scene, you're aware of it. And in many ways being in that position does stimulate your awareness because, naturally, you have to look for all the new things that are happening. You have to be right on top of everything that's talked about, or that holds a possibility of becoming the "new thing." You have to feel the pulse of the whole music world.[28]

In scouting out new artists, Jones persuaded Nana Mouskouri, a vocalist from Chania, Crete, Greece, to travel to New York City to record an album, *The Girl from Greece Sings* (1962).[29] Jones also produced an album with Timi Yuro (Rosemary Timotea) (1940–2004), *The Amazing Timi Yuro* (1964). Yuro is often considered to be one of the first white soul music singers of the 1960s.

Jones also recorded Mercury's teen pop idol Lesley Gore. During the 1960s Gore was one of the most successful young white singers of her generation. She was only seventeen years old in 1963 when Jones produced her hit, "You Don't Own Me," which reached Number 2 on the pop charts. Gore was partly successful because of her image as a teenager who experienced the adolescent anxieties of many young girls her age. Jones promoted this image in many of Gore's successful top hit singles with such songs "It's My Party," "Hey Now," and "Look of Love." The albums that Jones produced with Gore include *I'll Cry If I Want To* (1963), *Boys, Boys, Boys* (1964), *Girl Talk* (1964), *California Nights* (1967), and *Love Me By Name* (1976).

Verve is an American label founded by Norman Granz in the mid-1950s primarily to record jazz.[30] In the 1960s Jones collaborated on several Verve albums that include *Li'l Ol' Groovemaker. . . . . Basie!* (1963) with Count Basie. Also, in conjunction with the Basie band, Jones recorded with Sammy Davis Jr. (1925–1990), a multi-talented singer, dancer, and actor who achieved iconic status in the entertainment industry. Like Frank Sinatra, Davis often performed with some of the best bands and arrangers. On the album *Our Shining Hour* (1964), Davis recorded and performed an array of songs with the Count Basie band, conducted and arranged by Jones.[31]

Herb Alpert and Jerry Moss established the A&M record label in 1962.[32] Jones's affiliation with A&M, beginning in 1969, greatly complemented his work as a crossover and fusion recording artist and with his recordings with many musicians outside of the jazz idiom. Jones's A&M albums include *Walking in Space* (1969), *Gula Matari* (1970), *Smackwater Jack* (1971), *You've Got It Bad, Girl* (1972), *Body Heat* (1974), *Mellow Madness* (1975), *Ironside* (1975), *I Heard That!* (1976), *Sounds . . . And Stuff Like That!!* (1978), *The Dude* (1981), and *Live at the Budokan* (1981).

On the A&M label, Jones produced, conducted, and arranged several works ("If You Hadn't Left Me [Crying]" and "One") for Marvin Hamlisch (1976). Two other A&M acts Jones recorded with were the Brothers Johnson and Billy Preston. The Brothers Johnson is a band consisting of brothers George ("Lightnin' Licks") and Louis ("Thunder Thumbs") Johnson.[33] Jones recorded four Johnson compositions on his 1975 album *Mellow Madness*. He recorded with the Brothers Johnson as a composer, arranger, and producer on four albums: *Look Out for #1* (1976), *Right on Time* (1977), *Blam* (1978), and *Light Up the Night* (1980). These albums received high positions on the pop and rhythm & blues charts. These albums include such popular hits as "Get the Funk Out Ma Face," "Strawberry Letter #23," and "Stomp!"[34]

Billy Preston recorded with Jones on the A&M album *I Wrote a Simple Song* (1971). Preston (1946–2006) was a prominent songwriter, keyboardist, and bandleader. He played the Hammond B-3 organ, piano, and Fender Rhodes electric piano. He was influenced by popular styles such as rhythm & blues, rock, funk, and soul music.[35] In the 1970s Preston established a solo career and recorded hits songs such as "Outa-Space" (1972), "Will It Go Round in Circles" (1973), and "Nothing from Nothing" (1974).

In the 1980s Jones became the proprietor of Qwest, a boutique label distributed by Warner Bros. Records, and continued to produce a variety of gospel, jazz, rap, and pop music albums. George Benson's album *Give Me the Night* (1980) was one of the first albums released by Qwest. One of the first popular musicians to sign with Qwest was Patti Austin, a singer who Jones has considered a daughter. In the 1980s Austin recorded the award-winning albums *Every Home Should Have One* (1981) and *Patti Austin* (1984), both produced by Jones. Austin is noted for her sensitive and romantic vocal style and duet with James Ingram of the song "Baby Come to Me" (1981). Also, on Qwest, Jones produced Frank Sinatra's album *L.A. Is My Lady* (1984).

The late 1970s through the 1980s was a historical record-making period in Jones's career, primarily due to his work with Michael Jackson. Jackson (1958–2009) was a unique individual. Who can forget the sequined glove and socks, the moonwalk, the brisk snaps and pops of his arm movements, the twirls and complex movements of his feet as they engaged in delicate, ballet-like movements, and even the sensuous pelvic motions as his hands embraced his lower extremities? Jackson's dance talents have been compared to that of dancers Fred Astaire, Sammy Davis Jr., and Gene Kelly.

Jackson played the role of the scarecrow in *The Wiz*, and working with Jones on this film greatly influenced Jackson's solo recording career. But Jackson had previously met Jones at another engagement: "I first met Michael Jackson when he was twelve at an afternoon party at Sammy Davis' house in LA in 1972 as we all watched the Ed Sullivan Show with the Jackson Five, which Sammy had pre-taped on a precursor to home video."[36]

During the filming of *The Wiz*, Jackson approached Jones for help on a solo recording:

The first time [Michael Jackson] came to my home he said to me, "I'm getting ready to do my first solo record for Epic Records. Do you think you can help me find a producer?" I said, "I've got my plate pretty full right now trying to get [*The Wiz*] preproduction going, but I'll think about it." As we rehearsed the musical scenes for *The Wiz*, I became more and more impressed. He was always super-prepared. He showed up at 5 A.M. for his scarecrow makeup call and had every detail of what he needed to do memorized and ready for shooting. He also knew every dance step, every word of dialogue, and all the lyrics of every song by every one in the entire production.[37]

Jones did later agree to record with Jackson and the result was the album *Off The Wall* (1979). Jones has noted that some of the arrangements for this album were quite innovative and initially involved a type of improvised percussion—for example, the arrangement of "Don't Stop 'Til You Get Enough" which has a strong disco influence. Jones remarked that it "began as an improvised percussion track with a few of us sitting around the studio banging on Perrier bottles. The arrangement was built around that groove."[38] By the time the album was finished it was a complete unit, the artistry "locked and airtight."

Off The Wall sold multi-platinum and yielded four Top Ten singles. It was the largest-selling African American record at that time and propelled Jackson to stardom. The album was also important because it revealed Jackson's versatility to perform both fast-paced dance songs and sentimental ballads.

Jackson achieved a lasting legacy in his recording with Jones on the album *Thriller* (1982).[39] Rod Temperton, an English songwriter and record producer, composed the title song.[40] The *Thriller* project was twofold. In the album, there is a visual and theatrical dimension in the music in that each song creates a distinctive atmosphere that seems to demand a visual depiction. The video was also a trendsetting piece of work and was an ideal medium for Jones, as he was able to incorporate his expertise and ideas from working in the film industry. The *Thriller* video was a mini-film directed by John Landis, who also directed the film *An American Werewolf in London* (1981).[41]

Before *Thriller*, music videos essentially had been promotional tools. But Jackson's were mini-movies that told the story of the song visually as well aurally. It was Jackson who broke MTV's color barrier, because the demand for his videos was so strong.[42] The *Thriller* video featured elaborate staging, visual effects, state-of-the art theatrical makeup, a mini-plot, and Jackson-style dancing. This video set the standards for future music videos. The most obvious is the opening, with sounds of werewolf-like howling in the background, squeaky door, and footsteps. But the song succeeds in sustaining the suspense with a constant funk bass riff, busy percussion, and the slowly rising melody that finally spills over on the chorus. The orchestration is given a special quality by Jones's production team.

The music and lyrical content of *Thriller* comprise a type of program music where music and use of descriptive lyrics serve as effective tools that inform the choreography, costumes, makeup, and scenery that as an entity tell a story and present a sense of horror, gloom, and doom. Famed actor Vincent Price added horror-spoken lyrics that describe in various ways the setting of the scene and event as darkness falling across the land, crawling blood-searching creatures, a putrid stench of death in air, shivering bodies, and grizzly ghouls. These lyrics are interspersed with werewolf howls that all contribute to the dramatization of the song.[43] There is also a sense of youthful hipness in Price's performance with his use of vernacular phrases such as "terrorizing y'all's neighborhood" and "the funk of forty thousand years."[44] Price's spoken part is heightened with sound effects and the rising dynamics of music played in a style reminiscent of a "Phantom of the Opera"-like organ performance. This is followed by Price's horrifying and maniacal laugh and the shutting of a door, which signifies the conclusion of the composition and performance. The other songs in the album also capture the tonal colors of the lyrics in different musical settings.

The *Thriller* video gave the album a special appeal because consumers could visually experience how the music, dance, and drama together informed Jackson's performance. The album was number one for thirty-seven weeks in 1983 and generated an unprecedented seven Top Ten singles. *The Making of Michael Jackson's Thriller*, an hourlong videocassette, sold hundreds of thousands of copies in the first few months of the album's release. The album also accounted for a record of twelve Grammy Awards in 1983, shared by Jackson and Jones. Thriller was a marketing achievement of the highest order, but also was an example of musical genius between Jones and Jackson. Its songs and arrangements were highly structured, its production was precise in its artistry, and its dance choreography and vocals were representative of the Jackson style.

The album offered a variety of popular music. Its first hit was "The Girl Is Mine," an upbeat pop duet with Paul McCartney. "Billie Jean," a song that had dance floor appeal that achieved a number one ranking for several weeks, followed it. After this the song "Beat It" (an overture to hard rockers that featured Eddie Van Halen on guitar) also achieved a high chart position.

By 1984 *Thriller* was well on its way toward earning a place in the *Guinness Book of World Records* as the best-selling album of all time. This album has sold over 100 million copies worldwide. It continues to be the best-selling album of all time.

In the 1980s Jackson and Jones also collaborated on the soundtrack of Steven Spielberg's film *E.T. The Extra-Terrestrial* (1982). This soundtrack was also a box-office hit.

Jackson's last collaboration with Jones was on the album *Bad* (1987). This album produced seven hit singles including five number one hits, the most drawn from a single album. The album compilation brought together some of the most talented keyboardists, instrumentalists, and vocalists such as Greg Phillinganes (synthesizer solo), Larry Williams (saxophones), Gary Grant and Jerry Hey (trumpets), Paulinho DaCosta (percussion), and others. The album is stylistically diverse: "Liberian Girl" includes a Swahili chant by Caiphus Semenya; "Man in the Mirror" incorporates gospel music vocals, featuring Siedah Garrett, the Winans, the Andrae Crouch Choir, Ollie E. Brown, and others.

Bad also incorporates a variety of recording techniques, textures, rhythms, instrumentation, and ideas into one album. Symbolically this album may be one of the most important inferences to world peace and how we as people may often judge others, or cultural differences, in a negative way. For example, since Jackson's passing the song "Man in the Mirror" has attained symbolic significance in cultural diversity and acceptance in the world.

The lyrics have many types of implications, such as improving personal negative qualities and then making changes in the world for the betterment of mankind. Jackson's message is that in order to make the world a better place one must strive for personal improvement in his or her life and then assist others in changing the world.[45] The song's message of an individual taking responsibility for spreading peace and hope is similar to that in the popular song "Let There Be Peace on Earth (and Let It Begin with Me)" (1955) by Sy Miller and Jill Jackson.

Jones and Jackson also made a substantial contribution to humanitarian efforts with the recording of the song "We Are the World" (1985), which was co-written with Lionel Richie. This socially conscious mass performance brought together a dynamic cast of popular music artists collectively known as USA for Africa. The ensemble included Dan Aykroyd, Harry Belafonte, Lindsey Buckingham, Kim Carnes, Ray Charles, Bob Dylan, Shelia E., Bob Geldof, Hall & Oates, James Ingram, Jackie Jackson, LaToya Jackson, Marlon Jackson, Michael Jackson, Randy Jackson, Tito Jackson, Al Jarreau, Waylon Jennings, Billy Joel, Cyndi Lauper, Huey Newton & the News, Kenny Loggins, Bette Midler, Willie Nelson, Jeffrey Osborne, Steve Perry, the Pointer Sisters, Lionel Richie, Smokey Robinson, Kenny Rogers, Diana Ross, Paul Simon, Bruce Springsteen, Tina Turner, Dionne Warwick, and Stevie Wonder.

USA for Africa was historic in that it brought many talented artists from different backgrounds together to make a special humanitarian relief recording.[46] Jones's work as a producer, conductor, and arranger of the USA for Africa ensemble continues to be a prototype for humanitarian efforts.

Jones and Jackson both achieved a special place in history and the globalization of American popular music. These two great artistic minds complemented each other in many ways: both knew how to electrify audiences with music; both possessed a significant admiration for the world and people at large. Perhaps the most important bond shared by Jones and Jackson is that together they broke down racial barriers in popular music recording industry. Through their albums, Jones and Jackson demonstrated how musical production can have an important significance in the world.[47]

Part of Jones's legacy in the recording industry is his distinction with the National Academy of Recording Arts and Sciences. He has won a record of twenty-seven Grammy Awards and received over seventy nominations. Jones received his first Grammy nominations in 1960 in both popular music and jazz categories for the arrangement of "Let the Good Times Roll," and for the jazz album *The Great Wide*

World of Quincy Jones. In 1963 he received his first Grammy Award for "I Can't Stop Loving You," an instrumental arrangement that he prepared for the Count Basie band. Since that time Jones has received many Grammy Awards for his albums in the categories of jazz, R&B, and rap. In addition Jones had received Grammys in the categories of album of the year, producer of the year, and record of the year. He has also been the recipient of Grammy Living Legend and Trustee Awards.

Albums are often the heart and soul of a musician. They often serve as a complete entity of a musician's ideas and body of work. Jones's albums represent his ideology of creativity and they are his works of art. Not only has he been continually concerned with the musical content of his albums, he also envisions an album as a complete package that involves giving special attention to the design of album covers, program notes, and many other details. He once commented, "album[s] should represent what you want to do."[48]

Perusing the covers of Jones's albums offers a type of pictorial iconography of the Quincy Jones image. For example, on some of his early album covers Jones is photographed with his arms folded and wearing a dress suit and tie. During the 1970s one of the pictorial depictions that reflected Jones's interests in African/African American history and culture was on the album *Ndeda* (1972), with Jones dressed in African attire.

Jones has been involved in a continual process of generating albums and other compilations that represent a network of communication and unlimited boundaries in recorded sound.[49] In addition to the albums and artists that have been presented in this chapter, Jones has also collaborated with many other artists on recording labels such as RCA-Victor, MCA, Reprise, Roulette, CBS, Apple, Geffen, Columbia, and Cadence. Some of these artists and albums include Lurlean Hunter, *Lonesome Gal* (1955); Tony Bennett, *The Movie Song Album* (1966); Rufus & Chaka Khan, *Masterjam* (1979); Paul Simon, *There Goes Rhymin' Simon* (1973);[50] Ringo Starr, *Sentimental Journey* (1970); and Donna Summer, *Donna Summer* (1982).

One musician who greatly influenced Jones's recording experience was Miles Davis (1926–1991). Jones persuaded Davis to perform at the Montreux, Switzerland, jazz festival's 25th anniversary and to perform original arrangements from the albums *Sketches of Spain, Birth of the Cool*, *Miles Ahead*, and *Porgy & Bess*. In 1991 Jones recorded, produced, and conducted this legendary performance with Davis on the Grammy Award–winning album, *Miles Davis and Quincy Jones Live at Montreux*.[51]

Jones also played a significant role in recording the album, *Hubert Laws–Quincy Jones–Chick Corea: New Earth Sonata/Telemann Suite in A minor* (1985), based on a multi-movement suite by classical composer Georg Philipp Telemann.[52] The album involved musicians skilled in performing various styles of music. For example, Hubert Laws is a flautist with an extensive background in jazz, classical music, pop, rhythm & blues, and other genres.[53] Complementing this collaboration was Chick Corea (piano), who is very much linked with fusion styles.[54] With this collaboration, Jones, Laws, and Corea made an important contribution to fusing elements of popular music and classical music in a commercial recording.

The album *Handel's Messiah: A Soulful Celebration* (1992) is a prime example of an African American musical re-interpretation of a classical composition.[55] This special project involved a sacred/secular contemporary re-interpretation of George Frideric Handel's well-known 1754 work.[56] Similar to the USA for Africa collaboration, Jones helped bring together an impressive group of musicians from gospel, rhythm & blues, soul, and rock—Stevie Wonder, Take Six, the Richard Smallwood Singers, Sounds of Blackness, Al Jarreau, Patti Austin, Tramaine Hawkins, the Yellowjackets, Dianne Reeves, the Clark Sisters, Tevin Campbell, and others.

Jones used his experience in the recording industry to emphasize and demonstrate the historical significance of jazz and other styles of African American music with literary forms in his collaboration with several artists on the album *Rhapsodies in Black: Music and Words from the Harlem Renaissance* (2000). This historically themed project showcases the artistic innovations of many African American writers and musicians that were active in Harlem between 1918 and 1935. Jones is featured reading the poem "The Negro Speaks Rivers," by Langston Hughes. Included on the album are performances by Duke Ellington, Fats Waller, James P. Johnson, and others.

Jones's recording career continues to be active. In 2010 he completed *Q: Soul Bossa Nova Nostra* with a new generation of popular musicians: Ludacris, Usher, Q-Tip, Mary J. Blige, Jennifer Hudson, John Legend, and others. The album includes contemporary arrangements of songs such as "Strawberry Letter #23" featuring Akon and "It's My Party" featuring Amy Winehouse.

Jones also collaborated that year on the recording of "We Are the World 25 for Haiti," a charity single recorded by a number of artists to benefit earthquake victims in Haiti. It is a remake of the 1985 song, "We Are the World." It had been suggested in 2009 by Jones and Lionel Richie, producers of the original, that a re-cut version of the song be released under the title "Live 25."

Following the earthquake in Haiti, which devastated the area and killed thousands of people, it was agreed that the song would be re-recorded by new artists in the hope that it would reach a new generation and benefit the people of Haiti. The song was recorded with over eighty artists including Justin Bieber, Jennifer Hudson, Josh Groban, Janet Jackson, Barbra Streisand, Enrique Iglesias, Wyclef Jean, LL Cool J, Snoop Dogg, Kanye West, and many others. "We Are the World 25 for Haiti" was premiered in February 2010 during the opening ceremony of the Winter Olympics ceremony.

For Jones the recording studio has been a social space where he has continually been involved in generating albums and compilations with musicians of different age groups, backgrounds, interests, and artistic talents. With all of his accomplishments, Jones continues to be one of the foremost musicians propelling the recording industry into a competitive, commercial, and global dialogue.

5

ON "Q" IN HOLLYWOOD

Quincy Jones has often noted his challenges in being accepted as a serious composer and arranger in the film industry. Jones is one of the few African American composers to have succeeded in Hollywood.[1] He possessed talents and fortitude that could not be denied, and this is evident in his many film and television scores. This chapter focuses on Jones's work as a composer, arranger, music supervisor, and producer in Hollywood and how he paved the way for many contemporary and innovative film composers.

Quincy Jones was not the first African American film composer;[2] He has often noted this historical fact in interviews and biographical sketches. Between 1929 and the 1940s there were what were known as race films. The themes of these films were music and dance, westerns, sports biographies, and comedies. Many of these films were low-budget; most were aimed at African American audiences in segregated movie houses of the Jim Crow South and in areas of the North where there was also a large concentration of African American consumers. Race films provided opportunities to a number of African American actors/entertainers seeking employment in film industry, but the mainly light comedy, music, and dance roles were often exaggerated and pervaded with stereotypical images of African American life and culture.

In spite of some early films that featured African American performers, African American film composers were rare.[3] For white composers and arrangers, the customary routes to the Hollywood studios were through Broadway, radio networks, and dance bands, but these channels were not readily accessible to African American composers.

Although on occasion some music by African American composers was used in films, these writers (or arrangers) were seldom employed by the major studio to write or arrange directly for the screen. Even African American musicians were often excluded from working in studio orchestras.

One early film composer, Phil Moore, alleged that stereotyping was a major reason why African American musicians were excluded from studio orchestras. Moore contended that many white executives believed that African American musicians would not play soundtrack music as written and were lacking in other necessary disciplines such as promptness. Such attitudes resulted in a steady exclusion of African Americans from staff orchestras whose annual contracts were negotiated by white musicians' local unions.[4]

Will Vodery, William Grant Still, Clarence Muse, Donald Heywood, Phil Moore, Calvin Jackson, and Benny Carter are some of the early African American film composers.[5] Will Vodery was probably the first; in 1929 he had a one-year contract with Twentieth Century Fox. William Grant Still worked for Columbia Pictures in 1936 and for Twentieth Century Fox in 1943. Clarence Muse had a distinguished career as a stage and screen actor, and as a composer he became a member of the American Society of Composers, Authors, and Publishers (ASCAP) in 1940. Muse co-wrote the song, "When It's Sleepy Time Down South," which Louis Armstrong adopted as his theme song. Muse played African American character roles in many films by major studios. However, he did not write music for the studios; instead, he wrote songs and background scores for African American films by independent producers.

Donald Heywood was one of the few African American composers that made the transition from Broadway to film composing. He wrote the composition "I Want My Sweet Daddy Now," that was recorded in 1923 by vocalist Ethel Waters accompanied by Fletcher Henderson. In 1927 Heywood wrote a jazz standard, "I'm Comin' Virginia" (lyrics by Will Marion Cook). He also later wrote the book, lyrics, and music for several Broadway musicals with all–African American casts. In the 1930s and 1940s Heywood worked on many all–African American films produced by independent companies, contributing scenarios, lyrics, songs, and background scores. Heywood never worked for a major studio in Hollywood.

Phil Moore began working in Hollywood in 1937 at the age of nineteen. Unlike those who followed the usual route from the East Coast, he came directly from Seattle, where he had already become known as an arranger for singers and bands. In Hollywood he was hired as a rehearsal pianist, playing for such stars as Judy Garland and Gene Kelly. He worked his way into arranging, and assisting composer George Stoll. Under contract, he orchestrated for several films including *Broadway Rhythm* (1944), for which the prominent composer Johnny Green was director.

From 1943 to 1947 Calvin Jackson wrote over a dozen Hollywood films, on several of which he received screen credits. He had studied at the Juilliard School on a fellowship from 1937 to 1941. During this time he met several prominent New York bandleaders, including Benny Carter. Jackson later joined the Harry James band as an arranger. When the band was engaged to make a film for MGM (*Bathing Beauty*, 1944) Jackson was asked to arrange for it. Jackson arranged songs in a number of musicals, for which he also wrote background music as well. Dissatisfied with his low pay at MGM, Jackson returned to New York in 1948.

Benny Carter was without a doubt the most productive African American film composer of his generation. The legendary jazz bandleader and saxophonist had his first experience writing for Hollywood films between 1943 and 1944.[6] But he also worked in Hollywood as performer: in 1948 he performed on screen in the film *A Song is Born*, along with other jazz musicians including Louis Armstrong, Benny Goodman, Lionel Hampton, Tommy Dorsey, Vic Dickerson, and Charlie Barnet. Carter later arranged a portion of Claude Debussy's original composition, *Maid with the Flaxen Hair* as background music for the film *Portrait of Jennie* (1948).

Carter was among the earliest African Americans who both wrote for Hollywood films and participated in the use of jazz as background music. In the 1950s Carter arranged music for six films such as *Love Happy* (starring the Marx Brothers), *Panic in the Streets*, and *My Blue Heaven*. From 1951 through 1957 Carter wrote compositions and arrangements for eight more films. This includes the film *An American in Paris* (1951) and *The Snows of Kilimanjaro* (1952). He was again on screen, leading an orchestra, in *The View from Pompey's Head* (1955) and *The Sun Also Rises* (1957), a story by Ernest Hemingway and starring

Ava Gardner. In all, Carter arranged for fifteen films in 1947 through 1957, while playing on the soundtracks of many more.

When Carter wrote other styles of film music, he often felt a lack of formal training and consulted other composers with questions and matters that he believed would help him write appropriate film music. As he became more experienced working for film studios, he began to help younger composers break in—just as, in the 1940s, he encouraged many young musicians playing in emerging jazz styles. One such composer was J. J. Johnson, a trombonist in Carter's band in 1942–45 whom Carter helped over two decades when Johnson turned to film scoring.[7] Carter also mentored Oliver Nelson,[8] Lalo Schifrin, and Quincy Jones, who all achieved success in film scoring.

Quincy Jones is distinguished among early African American film composers because he became successful in both film and television. He was the first African American to be regularly employed by major studios. In Hollywood, Jones scored for several studios—Columbia, United Artists, Universal, MGM, Cinerama, Paramount Pictures, and Twentieth Century Fox. Another thing that distinguishes Jones from many other African American film composers is his extensive body of work.

Jones's résumé in Hollywood is impressive, but his success in the film industry was not overnight. Working and establishing himself in a competitive, overwhelmingly white industry offered many difficult experiences. To a great extent, the groundwork for Jones's longevity in Hollywood stems from his early career in the popular music industry, specifically his intensive work ethic and his determination always to follow his passions of artistic creativity. Similar to earlier African American composers, in the beginning many doors were closed to Jones as a prospective film composer. Being accepted as a serious composer in Hollywood came through years of struggle and breaking down racial and musical barriers, a struggle that for Jones began in the 1960s.

Pursuing a career in Hollywood is challenging for entertainers on any level. But Jones was determined to follow his passions and pursue film scoring. Jones arrived in Hollywood in the early 1960s, during a time when many young African Americans were becoming more vocal in their quest for equal rights and better opportunities to pursue their careers and aspirations. American society was experiencing young African Americans and white students participating in free-dom movements, boycotts, sit-ins, and organization of the Student Non-violent Coordinating Committee.

One of the major culminations of this time period was the March on Washington on June 11, 1963, when millions of people heard Rev. Martin Luther King Jr.'s famous "I Have a Dream" speech. What was so significant about this event is that it drew people from different ethnic and racial backgrounds, and some in attendance were part of the entertainment industry.

Jones's struggle to succeed in the Hollywood film industry was similar to what many young African Americans were experiencing in other professional fields in the 1960s. Also, Jones's association with popular styles such as jazz and blues often resulted in studios express-ing a reluctance to take a chance on his compositional ability to write for films.

Although Jones had spent an extended amount of time in France studying with Nadia Boulanger, in his initial attempts to pursue film-scoring work he was often not accepted as a potential candidate to score movies. For the Swedish film *The Boy in the Tree* (*Pojken i trädet*) (1961), Jones had already scored his first film with a storyline about a young rebellious teenage boy who is constantly at odds with his parents. Jones had no American film-scoring résumé; but by working on the Swedish film, he gained basic knowledge of techniques involved in composing music to accommodate drama, emotions, sound, and movement.

Hollywood studios were hesitant to hire an African American composer and arranger to score a film featuring white actors. Jones has stated:

> It was hard getting into [the Hollywood film] business. Some producer would hire you by name and then when you walked in he'd see you were [an African American] and say, "Now wait man, I don't want blues in this picture" or how can an [African American] man relate to a love scene between a white man and a white woman? You had to go through a lot of nonsense.[9]

In attempting to establish himself in Hollywood, Jones was often stereotyped not only because of his racial heritage but also as being a composer possessing skills limited to writing only jazz and blues. Jones commented that, "the first four [film scores] I did, I had to be furtive. Producers would go out of their way to warn me: 'no jazz!'"[10] In this way skin color and not talent often dictated what some Hollywood executives assumed about Jones's ability. Jones studied so diligently in Europe in order to negate such stereotypes about his musical ability and to avoid being pigeonholed into specializing in one style of music.

Jones worked diligently to master the ability to play and write for strings and to understand the technicalities of the orchestral score. About his early Hollywood experience Jones observed: "if you'd ever been associated with jazz, that used to be one strike against you. Negro [African American] musicians were automatically identified with jazz; strike two."[11]

One of Jones's arguments with many studios was: why not incorporate jazz and other popular styles in film scores? His major problem was finding ways to make studios realize his uniqueness in creating innovative music on many levels. In his experience Jones had previously observed that, "the few [African American film composers] who got any credits in the 1940s and 1950s were assigned to write [small] sequences in which jazz was related to the storyline." But some white composers incorporated jazz in Hollywood films.[12] Some of these composers were not jazz musicians per se. For example, in his jazz-influenced score to *Laura* (1944), David Raskin (1912–2004) introduced the method of composing a theme song that was woven throughout the film and personified a particular character.

In the 1950s jazz was used for several films as background music to represent social settings and problems.[13] In many of these films jazz was associated with activities such as those in nightclubs, bars, dance halls, and sleazy urban scenes of drinking, crime, and drugs. One of the earliest films cited for its use of jazz is *A Streetcar Named Desire* (1951) by Alex North (1910–1991), in which jazz was used to represent urban settings, sexual situations, and social problems from alcoholism and crime. Elmer Bernstein's (1922–2004) score for *The Man with the Golden Arm* (1955) is another film cited for its use of jazz themes. Johnny Mandel's score for *I Want to Live* (1958) has been recognized for its innovative jazz theme.[14]

One of the major innovators of the use of jazz in Hollywood film scores was Henry Mancini (1924–1994). In his long career, Mancini scored numerous films such as *The Glenn Miller Story* (1954), *The Benny Goodman Story* (1955), *Peter Gunn* (TV show, 1959–62), *Breakfast at Tiffany's* (1961), *The Days of Wine and Roses* (1962), *The Pink Panther* (1964), *Charade* (1964), *The Great Waldo Pepper* (1975), and many others. Mancini established a reputation in Hollywood that few composers of his time rivaled. Many of his songs of the 1960s ("Moon River," "The Pink Panther," "Days of Wine and Roses") have become standards in American popular music. What made Mancini unique was that he was not afraid to explore new territories in lyrical and orchestral music; he inspired a new generation of composers, and this includes Quincy Jones.

In addition to Benny Carter, other African American composers used jazz in films. For example, Duke Ellington worked in Hollywood as a composer on a few films, such as *Anatomy of a Murder* (1959), a murder mystery directed by Otto Preminger.[15] Ellington also scored the film *Paris Blues* (1961), a romantic drama characterizing Paris as a city of blues, jazz, romance, and love.[16]

The negative reaction that Jones received in Hollywood about jazz and blues was a result of the conservative attitude of studio executives, who hired composers steeped in conventional European tradition. Prime examples include Leonard Bernstein, Bernard Herrmann, and Aaron Copland. Bernstein (1910–1990) used a dissonant, contemporary classical style in his score of *On the Waterfront* (1954). Herrmann (1911–1975), whose dissonant techniques drew upon the influences of modern composers such as Ives, Berg, and Hindemith, was famous for his scores of *Citizen Kane* (1941) and Alfred Hitchcock's *Vertigo* (1958), *North by Northwest* (1959), and *Psycho* (1960). One of the most successful film composers from a classical music background was Aaron Copland (1900–1990), like Jones a Nadia Boulanger protégé. Copland scored several films, including *The City* (1939), *Of Mice and Men* (1939), *Our Town* (1940), *The Red Pony* (1948), and *The Heiress* (1949).[17]

Of all of the composers included in this discussion, Benny Carter and Henry Mancini became Jones's greatest influences and mentors in the Hollywood film industry. Jones also has credited Mancini with breaking through the Eurocentric film-scoring tradition with his film and television scores. Jones also believed that some of the best music continued to be generated from films. But he also was critical of one-track-minded composers steeped only in the European tradition. He believed that this was a disadvantage for many film composers:

> The classical people are still brainwashed by the European tradition. They're such snobbish bastards that they haven't tapped one-tenth of America's musical resources. There have been exceptions, of course, such as Leonard Bernstein on Broadway, and Aaron Copland. But there's so much that most of those people don't know about. I like Alban Berg and James Brown—Stravinsky and Duke Ellington. Only in films, the good ones anyway do you have a chance to express as much as you know musically. The level of the music here is very high, and it's getting better all the time. Everybody's writing the best he can. Where else can you write good music for a living these days? I'm writing closer to what I want than I ever have in my life. As a matter of fact, I believe the best music being written in this country today is coming out of films.[18]

Some Hollywood film scores did integrate more popular styles, even becoming a type of marketable commodity. What influenced the use of jazz and other popular styles in film scores, especially in the 1960s, may have also been the popularity and sales of soundtrack albums. These popular albums consolidated the film and recording industries as moneymaking entities— soundtrack albums were a type of advertisement for films and profited the recording industry as well. For example, in the mid-1960s one of the highest-selling soundtracks was from *The Sandpiper* (1965) with its theme song "The Shadow of Your Smile," featuring music composed by Johnny Mandel.

Jones produced the *Sandpiper* soundtrack album when he was still an executive at Mercury Records.[19] What is unique among film composers is that in 1965, while Jones was pursuing a career in Hollywood, he generated arrangements and albums for a record label.

As a film composer Jones envisioned succeeding as an opportunity to open doors for other perspective African American composers:

> I don't think that it's presumptuous—but I hope by my efforts to open things up for other cats to make it. . . . I can never take the attitude, even when I'm working on a film which I don't dig too much, that this one

isn't too important. They're all important. If I do a bad job, then Hollywood will say 'Later for that bebopper. No more soul brothers for us.' But when Negro [African American] kids see me nominated for an Academy Award, that shows it can be done.[20]

Plots, characters, movements, emotions, scenery, actors, producers, and directors dictate what type of music should be composed for films. In many instances the musical tasks and creative processes of film composers require special skills in problem solving. They often work on what seems to be impossible time constraints. In the recording studio, time constraints and composing often turn into long days and months of hard work. But the finished product, a beautiful film score, is a rewarding experience that may come to live even outside of the film in recordings and compilations.

Jones has an ability to write music at a rapid pace, which greatly contributed to his success in Hollywood. When beginning a project he would first view the film and then come up with ideas of what types of music should accompany a particular scene. This was basically an analytical process that sometimes involved working continually through the night. He has commented:

scoring is a multifaceted process, an abstraction of science and soul: the psychology of scoring is totally subjective, reactive, and highly personal. . . . Above all, the music has to sound organic to the subject or even sometimes in direct contrast to the subject matter while accommodating a sequence of scenes that may be interiors, exteriors, medium shots, close-ups, quick seven-second shots (e.g. Star Wars), etc. Different composers will invariably see or hear a scene in different ways.[21]

Working on film and television scoring gave Jones a sense of what can be described as artistic power, integrating his art and craft in music with other forms of artistic expression (drama, comedy, acting, dance). But film and television work also became an area where he experimented with different styles, rhythms, and electronic instruments. He was one of the first composers to initiate a trend by bringing together in film scores elements like big band, funk, jazz, fusion, classical, African, Latin, and techno.

In an article titled "The New Sound on the Soundtracks," Jones (along with Lalo Schifrin, and Johnny Mandel)—a composer with extensive training in classical composition—was regarded as being part of a "third stream" generation of film composers that often integrated jazz, classical music, and other styles to create a new style of film music, as some jazz musicians had attempted to do in the 1950s.[22] The article also emphasized that the new trend in film scoring had also opened doors for jazz performers:

> Not only have jazz-trained composers moved into the field [of film scoring]—jazz players have invaded it too. A few years ago, film composers who wanted to use jazzmen for their soundtracks encountered adamant skepticism from heads of music departments at the big studios, because of an unfounded belief that jazzmen, though superb players, couldn't read [notated music]. The best of them are of course, alarmingly good sight-readers, commonly referred to as "hawks" for the sharp-eyed precision with which they can play an unfamiliar score.... These men too are important to the evolution of the new style in motion picture music.[23]

One of Jones's major contributions to new and innovative scores was his collaboration with jazz performers who could bring his written scores to life, including Ray Brown, Freddie Hubbard, Clark Terry, Hubert Laws, J. J. Johnson, Dizzy Gillespie, Dave Grusin, Gerry Mulligan, Sarah Vaughan, Shirley Horn, and Toots Thielemans. Jones also brought in popular musicians such as Tony Bennett, Donny Hathaway, B. B. King, Astrud Gilberto, Little Richard, and Johnny Mathis.

Between 1965 and 1969 Jones scored numerous blockbuster films—dramas, suspense, love stories, animation, comedies, and westerns. Each of these scores shows his distinctiveness as a talented composer, but most of all how he was able to work tirelessly on assignment after assignment. The 1970s through the 1980s were no different; scored numerous films and served as the musical director/supervisor on several projects.

His first American film assignment was provided by director Sidney Lumet (1924–2011), who hired Jones to score *The Pawnbroker* (1965), for which Rod Steiger received an Academy Award nomination for his performance.[24] Jones wrote *The Pawnbroker* score in two months and recorded it in a few days. Jones asked Phil Ramone, who owned A&R Studios, to record the score. Henry Mancini and Armando Travioli gave Jones advice on the art and technical aspects of film scoring.

The main character in *The Pawnbroker*, played by Rod Steiger, was a survivor of a Nazi death camp who was haunted by memories of the experience. Jones incorporated string instruments at the beginning of the film to accompany a dream/flashback sequence in which Steiger's character reminisces on a happy event with his wife, children, and relatives. The scene begins with the children running through a field to meet him. As he approaches from a distance the sound, mood of the music, and instrumentation change to convey a sense love, hope, and family. The strings weave in an out with haunting melodic passages. The scene culminates with abrupt musical, textural, and percussive changes—a drum roll engages in a dialogue with the other instruments, symbolizing a sense of fear and tragedy. After this, the dream/ fantasy ends and reality of the main character's current life begins in his daily interaction as a pawnbroker in New York City.

Jones's score received recognition as an original jazz-influenced composition. He recruited some of the best jazz musicians such as Freddie Hubbard, Elvin Jones, Dizzy Gillespie, Oliver Nelson, Bobby Scott, a harpist, a woodwind and string section, even Don Elliott on mouth percussion.

After Jones completed work on *The Pawnbroker*, he waited several months to be hired for another film. His agent Peter Faith was determined to get Jones another scoring assignment. Eventually Universal Pictures telephoned Jones about scoring a movie, but they very skeptical about hiring an African American composer. The producer said he would get back with Jones, and telephoned Henry Mancini, who gave Jones a high recommendation. Jones did get other film assignments.

Jones did the score for *In Cold Blood* (1967), based on Truman Capote's Pulitzer Prize–winning book about a horrific murder of a family in a small city in Kansas. This is one of the earliest films in which Jones incorporated electronic musical instruments in the score. In preparing the score Jones listened to the interrogation tapes of the two murder suspects as played by actors Scott Wilson and Robert Blake. He wrote bass parts, played by jazz musicians Ray Brown and

Andy Simpkins, to represent the personalities of the two actual murderers. This score combined electronic percussion, cellos, and basses with jazz, blues, and contemporary Western classical music.

The *In Cold Blood* score has been described as "gutsy." On one hand Jones used contemporary orchestral techniques that play on the fringes of tonality and other streetwise sounds such as finger snaps, body slaps, and even the clanking of bottles. Jones also incorporated mouth pops and down home blues tunes.²⁵ A good example of his innovation is the song "Lonely Bottles," in which Jones incorporated the electric bass, clavinet, string bass, trombone with a wire-buzz mute, mouth percussion, and the clanking sound of bottles within a blues guitar melody. Jones received an Academy Award nomination for this score.

In some film scores Jones used elements of classical music and folk songs. For example, *Bob & Carol & Ted & Alice* (1969), starring Natalie Wood, Robert Culp, Elliott Gould, and Dyan Cannon, is about a trendy married couple that attempts to lure their best friends, another married couple, into an extramarital affair as a reflection of the liberated lifestyles of the 1960s. Jones used fragments from Handel's *Messiah* (Hallelujah Chorus) on the score, in combination with his original compositions and an arrangement of "What the World Needs Now Is Love" (by Burt Bacharach and Hal David).

Another example is the film *John and Mary* (1969), a love story that starred Dustin Hoffman and Mia Farrow. For this film Jones incorporated excerpts from Fugue no. 22 from *The Well-Tempered Clavier* (J. S. Bach), Rondo no. 1 (Mozart), Variations Serieúses (Mendelssohn), and Allegro (from *Royal Fireworks Suite*) (Handel).

The Italian Job (1969) is considered one of Britain's best films of all time. Michael Caine plays a mobster named Charlie Croker who, after release from prison, plans and attempts with several friends a daring robbery. In the film score, Jones created a sense of whimsy using elements of folk music as a type of recurring motive to represent a British character named Mr. Bridger, played by Noel Coward. To convey the British flavor, he included a special rendition of the song "Britannia."

One of Jones's most complex scores was written for the film *MacKenna's Gold* (1969). This western, about the lure of gold and the corruption of a diverse group of people as they attempt to search for a hidden gold treasure in the Canyon del Oro, starred Gregory Peck, Omar Sharif, Edward G. Robinson, Julie Newmar, Ted Cassidy, and Telly Savalas. Jones's score, incorporating rich instrumental timbres and textures, dissonant harmonies, vibrant string and horn passages, and extensive orchestrations, is greatly representative of Jones's musical training with Boulanger and influences from composers such as Stravinsky and Ravel. Also included are what can be described as "westernscape" sounds and musical imagery of the Old West. For example, the overture has the sound of galloping horses, a gunshot, and sound of the echoing and rustling winds of a dissolute canyon. Other pieces include Native American drumming and flute playing ("Apache Camp"), and Spanish strumming guitar playing ("Ole Turkey Buzzard"). In a contrast that seems to be a transition between the complex harmonies and intense instrumental sections, Jones also incorporated an elegant instrumental waltz-like French melody accompanied by strings and accordion ("Rêve Parisien").

The influence of jazz/funk fusion, big band sounds, and use of electronic instruments can be found in Jones's film scores of the 1970s. *They Call Me Mister Tibbs* (1970) (a sequel to *In the Heat of the Night*) is about an African American police detective named Virgil Tibbs played by Sidney Poitier. The music can be described as Quincy Jones's 1970s hip, groovy, and jazz-funky style: an intense Hammond B-3 organ improvisation (performed by Billy Preston), instrumental vamps, funk bass guitar improvisations, funk drumming, and a trumpet improvisation all integrated with repeating melodic and rhythmic momentum.

The Anderson Tapes (1971), a crime drama centered on a character named John "Duke" Anderson (played by Sean Connery) who is released after several years of imprisonment, focuses on the surveillance and tracking devices of numerous government and private agencies and the lack of coordination between those agencies. The score features jazz-funk fusion, Moog synthesizer, piano, vibraphone, trumpets, trombones, organ, guitar, percussion, flügelhorn, flute, and tenor saxophones, Fender bass, string bass, harmonica, and drums. Jones also included a vibraphone solo (performed by Milt Jackson) that is an example of a traditional jazz and popular music fusion.²⁶ Throughout the score, Jones incorporated call-and-response passages where the main melodic material is performed in unison by trumpets and horns followed by a response or ornamented elaboration by various instruments. One call-and-response section sounds similar to imitative counterpoint that is highly influenced by Western classical music.

The Hot Rock (1972) is a comic caper movie based on a novel by Donald E. Westlake. This film centers on a character named Dortmunder (played by Robert Redford) who after release from prison is persuaded by his brother-in-law along with to assist in an elaborate heist to retrieve a gem for Dr. Amusa (played by Moses Gunn). Located in the Brooklyn Museum, the gem is supposed to be of great significance to the African people, and over different periods of time was stolen by colonists and various African nations. The score, again with a strong jazz/funk influence, is quite deceptive both rhythmically and harmonically. It includes a simple baritone saxophone solo (performed by Gerry Mulligan), but also vocal ensemble parts of harmonized whistling combined with an instrumental combo playing melodies in a Dixieland jazz style.

The Getaway (1972) is a crime and action film based on a novel by Jim Thompson. The plot centers on Carter "Doc" McCoy (played by Steve McQueen), a criminal mastermind who, upon his release from prison, is coerced into helping forge a bank robbery. The "Love Theme" of this score is arranged as a simple melody played on harmonica (by Toots Thielemans) accompanied by electric bass, vibraphone, string bass, synthesizer, and drums. Jones's arrangement builds tension and motion through a series of slow harmonic progressions supported by the plucking of the string bass. Jones also incorporated contrasts of loud and soft passages at the end of the arrangement, when the melody seems to fade away into silence.²⁷

Examples of Jones's film scores incorporating vocal theme songs include his work on the films *Mirage, Walk, Don't Run, Banning, In the Heat of the Night, The Deadly Affair, For Love of Ivy, A Dandy in Aspic, Cactus Flower, $ [Dollars], The Wiz,* and *The Color Purple. Mirage* (1965), starring Gregory Peck and Walter Matthau, is about a man suffering from amnesia who soon realizes that he is in a life-and-death situation.

Jones employs interesting sound and musical techniques in this score with his incorporation of string instruments in the orchestration. The title song "Mirage" features a lyrical vocal by Johnny Mathis. A vibrato technique employed in the violins parts conveys a shimmering, dreaming effect as the vocal fills in with the melody and lyrics. At the end the vocal part imitates the vibrato on the words "My mirage."

Working on the film *Walk, Don't Run* (1966) included an experience Jones may never forget. The film centers on the Tokyo Olympics where a housing shortage forces two men and a woman to share living quarters in a single apartment. The older man, played by Cary Grant, attempts to play matchmaker between the younger man and woman. Jones shared his memorable experience:

> I remember when I had just started the musical score for a movie entitled "Walk, Don't Run," starring Cary Grant. This incidentally was Grant's last film. There was a special screening scheduled for an afternoon and the person who had been slated to drive me to the studio had forgotten about the date. At 3:15 I was at home literally on pins and needles, worrying about how I was going to get to Columbia Pictures by 3:30. . . .
>
> The laundry truck driver was at the house, and I thought he might be my saving grace. I asked him if he would give me a lift to the studio. He was more than happy to oblige. The laundry truck had only a driver's seat, so I also had to stand for the ride with attaché case in hand.
>
> When we got about two blocks from Columbia Pictures, I asked him to let me off at the newsstand so I could walk through the gates. But he . . . insisted on taking me all the way. I argued with him gently, but [h]e insisted on taking me to the gate. . . .
>
> I was dressed for the screening and I suppose I didn't want to be seen getting out of a laundry truck at the gates of the studio. . . . [A]s I was getting out of the truck; who should come by but Cary Grant and Sol Seigel who headed up Columbia at that time.
>
> We joked about my choice of limousine services, and I wound up scoring about a dozen films for Columbia. I finally got tired of not being able to drive and decided that I would rectify the matter by learning to drive a car.[28]

Some of the selections on the *Walk, Don't Run* score seem to reflect this experience: "Happy Feet," "Stay with Me," and "Abso Bleedin' Lutely."

In the film *Banning* (1967), Robert Wagner plays a golf pro who is having a run of bad luck. He uses his charm and skill to hustle golf and women while attempting to escape from a loan shark. Jones cleverly interweaves into the storyline a song titled "The Eyes of Love: Carol's Theme," performed by Gil Bernal. Jones received an Academy Award nomination for this song, the same year he was nominated for the film score of *In Cold Blood*.

In the Heat of the Night (1967) is about Virgil Tibbs (played by Sidney Poitier), an African American police detective from Philadelphia who becomes involved in a murder investigation in a racist small town in Mississippi. The police detective helps the sheriff, played by Rod Steiger, solve the murder. Alan and Marilyn Bergman wrote the lyrics of the theme song, also titled "In the Heat of the Night." The music and lyrics of the song and the soulful, blues, gospel singing and piano rendition provided by Ray Charles capture an image of the Deep South. Charles is accompanied by the Raelettes on background vocals and a deep bass played by Ray Brown. A bluesy texture is also provided by an instrumental part written for Hammond B-3 organ (performed by Billy Preston).[29]

"Who Needs Forever" is the theme song from *The Deadly Affair* (1967), a film about a British agent investigating an apparent suicide of a Foreign Office official.[30] Astrud Gilberto sings the theme song.[31] Violins and harps are interwoven with the melody and supported by the pulsation of a *clave* rhythm.[32] The song also incorporates a tenor saxophone solo by Zoot Sims.

For Love of Ivy (1968) is a film about an African American maid named Ivy Moore (played by Abbey Lincoln) who is employed by an upper-class white family. Ivy announces to her employers (played by Carroll O'Connor and Nan Martin) that she intends to leave her job to attend a secretarial school. In an attempt to keep Ivy in the household, the teenage children (played by Beau Bridges and Lauri Peters) hatch a scheme to set Ivy up with a trucking-company executive (played by Sidney Poitier). Initially the meetings of the couple are awkward, but eventually develop into a budding romance.[33]

In this film score Jones integrates several styles using strings, symphonic sounds, trumpet/horn melodies, electric guitar improvisations, and blues. The song "You Put It On Me," with lyrics by Maya Angelou written in a distinct poetic scheme that follows a twelve-bar blues harmonic progression, as performed by B. B. King captures the mood, complex love, and courtship themes of the film: "ain't no woman that a man can trust / because they all use joo-joo and goofy dust." The song is given true essence through King's blues singing style, phrasing, and improvisational skill on electric guitar. The main title song is performed by jazz vocalist Shirley Horn in a more subdued tempo that contrasts with the lyrical and dynamic coloration. Jones received an Academy Award nomination for his work on *For Love of Ivy*.

Shirley Horn also sings the song "The Spell You Spin—The Web You Weave" in *A Dandy in Aspic* (1968), a film starring Laurence Harvey and Mia Farrow about a double agent who attempts to avoid danger. Jones's arrangement combines influences of jazz with light funk and symphonic fusion styles. Jones integrates a technique of overlapping the vocal solo parts into what sounds similar to semi-sung and spoken passages, producing an echoing effect that conveys in the textural symmetry of Horn's voice a sense of intrigue and mystery.

An orchestra of strings is incorporated in the arrangement of "The Time for Love Is Anytime" the theme song from the film *Cactus Flower* (1969), a comedic love story starring Walter Matthau, Ingrid Bergman, and Goldie Hawn. This song is sung with the rich textural interpretations and vocal style of Sarah Vaughan and includes a flügelhorn solo performed by Bobby Bryant.

$ [*Dollars*] (1971) follows the perils of several characters played by Warren Beatty, Golden Hawn, and others who use safe deposit boxes in a German bank to store a large amount of stolen cash. For the film score, Jones integrated elements of rock 'n' roll, funk, and gospel music, highlighted by the shouting vocal style of Little Richard on the song "Money Is." The song also features steady riff-like improvisational passages played by the bass, keyboards, percussion, drums, and synthesizers. The use of sound effects is a very important aspect of this arrangement. Other performers include Dave Grusin (electric bass and synthesizer) and Billy Preston (keyboards).

Jones incorporated interesting sound techniques on "Money Runner" by using the Don Elliott Voices as backup singers whose soft, continual singing of the word "money" begins slowly and gradually increases in tempo, which along with the supporting background instruments results in what sounds similar to the wheels and steam engine of a locomotive. The song ends abruptly with the musical instruments engaged in what sounds like a sudden crash of broken glass.

The Wiz (1978), directed by Sidney Lumet based on the Broadway musical, is an adaptation of *The Wizard of Oz* (1939) re-cast with African Americans playing the leading roles and characters. Diana Ross plays the lead character of Dorothy, a 24-year-old Harlem kindergarten teacher brought by snowstorm to a mysterious Land of Oz that resembles New York City. Michael Jackson, Lena Horne, Richard Pryor, Mabel King, and others play other characters. Jones makes a cameo appearance in the "Gold" segment from Emerald City.

Jones and Charlie Smalls prepared the film score. For the soundtrack Jones served as a producer, adaptation, and score and musical supervisor. The score includes such notable selections as "Ease On Down the Road," "What Would I Do If I Could Feel," and "Believe in Yourself."

The Wiz took approximately two years to complete and was a box office failure. Jones was bitter about the failure and blamed it largely on the way the film was marketed and distributed: "With *The Wiz* I saw how color-conscious the studios can be . . . and the exhibitors and distributors. I heard some priceless lines—'The picture's all black? Mm humm. We don't want to turn our theater into a combat zone.' Those are the realities today—that's what's going on. The movie game is very tough, you know, for everybody."[34]

For Jones, working as composer, arranger, and music supervisor, and producer on *The Color Purple* (1985) represented a pedagogical and historical validation of his exploration of African American cultural and music history. In the score, Jones incorporated many different styles that represented African American musical expression from blues to gospel. His use of particular themes and melodies to personify specific characters includes the Academy Award–nominated original blues/ragtime style song "Miss Celie's Blues (Sister)," and the riveting gospel song "God Is Trying to Tell Me Something."

On many occasions Jones worked on primetime television scores at the same time he was composing for films. Between the mid-1960s and 1980s Jones prepared scores for TV movies, drama and comedy series, and special programming on all three major broadcasting networks, CBS, ABC, and NBC.

Writing for television was even more demanding in that Jones had to constantly prepare music scores in days and weeks. From his experience writing for films, Jones was accustomed to writing an excessive amount of music in detail; but for television he had to learn how to edit his music to fit much smaller time limitations. Part of the learning process involved mentorship from composers like Henry Mancini and Benny Carter. Jones has said: "Henry Mancini and/or Benny Carter would sometime drop by [the studio] and look over my scores and say, 'Are you crazy? You're writing forty-four minutes of music weekly, like it's for a feature film. . . . Don't try to write Stravinsky's *Firebird Suite* for every episode, or you'll never live through the year.'"[35] Jones did learn how to condense scores and change things at the last minute to reduce or heighten the intensity according to the editing cuts.

Similar to his work on films, some of Jones's television scores combine fusion styles. The main theme from the series *Ironside* (1967–75), one of the most innovative themes in television history, is an example of jazz/funk fusion at its best. The series was centered on a wheelchair-bound former police officer, Robert T. Ironside (played by Raymond Burr), who after having survived an assassination attempt sets out to battle crime with several of his associates.

Jones's work on *Ironside* is an example of a big band sound that incorporates jazz techniques like walking bass lines, ride rhythms[36] and intensive drumming, and electric bass funk music improvisations. The instrumentation for this score included five trumpets and flügelhorns, five trombones, keyboards, organ, soprano saxophone, flute, two synthesizers, two guitars, string bass, electric bass, drums, vibraphone, percussion, and whistling performed by Toots Thielemans.

Jones used sound as a type of simulacrum in the orchestration to represent the feeling of a police chase or an ambulance: a siren effect by incorporating ascending and descending tones; the manipulation of synthesizers; slides of brass instruments; and constant rhythmic momentum of the percussion. A flute solo accompanied by horns follows, and there is much contrasting motion as the horns support the different melodies.

Another section of the score includes a funk style with a transition to a faster tempo, followed by a soprano saxophone improvisation and string bass accompaniment. There is also a swing jazz rhythm introduced with a distinct increase in tempo, improvisation, and a combination of instruments—trumpets, flügelhorns, and soprano saxophone—playing in high ranges, all with constant rhythmic movements of the drums and string bass.

For the NBC-TV comedy series *The Bill Cosby Show* (1969–71), Jones co-wrote with Bill Cosby the theme song "Hikky Burr." This song is both representative of the playfulness and improvisational comedic personality of Bill Cosby and an example of Jones's jazz-funk fusion and big band styles. It has the improvisational characteristics of jazz but it is also arranged with the rhythmic flow and instrumentation of a big band sound integrated within a funk style and danceable tempo. The lyrical content is based upon a few words that are sung by Cosby as he sings and engages in vocal and rhythmic improvisations of variations of the words "Hoo," "Lawd," "Hikky," "Burr," and so forth.

The theme music "The Street Beater" from *Sanford and Son* (1972–77), a series about a trash collector named Fred Sanford played by Redd Foxx, is musically whimsical, especially the wailing sounds and special techniques provided by the instruments Jones incorporated in the arrangement. In many ways this score is a type of leitmotif—a recurring melody associated with the major character of Fred Sanford. The orchestration includes both electric and acoustic instruments: Hammond B-3 organ, clavinet, Fender bass, soprano saxophone, drums, bass harmonica, cowbell, and shaker.

In the score a constant propelling movement of sounds similar to clicks and snaps is played on percussion instruments. On top of these percussive sounds Jones included an elaborate soprano saxophone and a funk Fender bass guitar improvisation.

In *Roots* (1977), the television mini-series, the author Alex Haley attempted to capture the experience of how in American society, race played a significant role. Slavery was based on a two-tiered system of the colonizer and the colonized. The social, political, and cultural interaction between African slaves (the colonized) and whites (the colonizers) were master/slave relationships. Haley showed how slavery became synonymous with race, perceived inferiority, and powerlessness. Haley also characterized slavery as a type of caste system: for African slaves, there was no social mobility. The slave status was for your lifetime and was passed on to any offspring.

Working on *Roots* also had a special significance for Jones, not only to comprehend the complexities of the African/African American experience but also to understand how music related to the historical experience of displaced Africans. With the score and soundtrack album, Jones desired to capture the essence of Alex Haley's book and the African American experience. He felt a great bond with Haley's representation of experiences as depicted in *Roots*:

> One of the greatest challenges I have undertaken is the scoring of David Wolper Productions' ABC Television mini-series on a novel for T.V. entitled "Roots." Roots was one of those projects that hit so close to home that I had to be part of it. Aside from being a great admirer of Haley's literary prowess, the social magnitude of the book was something that reached inside me and grabbed me where I lived. I've spent a great deal of time and money studying, researching, and tracing the history of black music as well as the social significance that our music has had on society. Haley's work and my work share a strong kinship.[37]

Jones regarded the social significance of music in American society as one of the best resources for comprehending the history of the African American experience. In the score he attempted musically to chronicle various aspects of the African American experience. As part of his work on the score, he delved deeply into researching the legacy of drums and drumming, religion, and how in American society African Americans created innovative and alternative ways for maintaining many African musical traditions. After his research Jones concluded the following about the history of the African/African American experience and the significant role that music played in African music preservation:

The drum was banned in the United States . . . because it was a communications device and it was dangerous in slavery times. . . . After it was banned, what remained of the African heritage went into the field hollers and spirituals. The vocal inflections and rhythms were held onto by handclaps or makeshift percussion instruments. As a result, the whole 12/8 African polyrhythmic impulse (pattern) was reconceived. . . . It's all linked to religion. The Africans could identify with the French and Catholic influences in America because they had a ritualistic, multi-god kind of worship. The Protestants, who banned the drum, didn't want passion involved in praising God. The more I've studied this thing, the more I'm convinced that the best social history we have of the United States is in the music. The chronicling happened more in the music than in anything else.[38]

When Jones began working on the film score, his main objective in writing was to chronicle the social history of music through the authentic sounds, instrumentation, rhythms, and textures as key elements in conveying and capturing the true essence of the African/African American experience and storyline. Jones's primary writing task was to convey the story of African music origins; that is, how Africans brought to the Americas traditions of complex musical systems where music making was an ingrained tradition centered on community participation. In daily life, music informed religious expression as well as secular activities. Many Africans transported into slavery in the Americas were taken from communities socialized in communal music making that involved the integration of music and dance, meshed with complex drumming. African musicians often served in many capacities as master musicians, oral historians, and court musicians. Also, African musicians were often linked through ancestry and guilds that mastered their craft through many years of study and performance.

In recreating some of these scenarios of the African music origins and heritage, Jones divided the music score into two thematic sections: *The Motherland* (Africa), the land where the music began, and *The Promised Land* (America), the land where the music was maintained and reinvented. In the score the instrumentation involved incorporating polyrhythmic parts written for some traditional African and African diaspora instruments into the orchestration and score:

Shekere—West Africa/Yoruba and Cuba
Conga, Tumba (rumba drums)—Cuba
Kagan drum—Ghana
Itole (Bata)—West Africa/Yoruba and Cuba
Iya I'lu (mother drum)—West Africa/Yoruba
Sansa, mbira, kalimba (thumb piano)—West Africa
Donno (or Dundun)—West Africa
Log drum—West Africa
Omele or Okontolo/Bata—Cuba
Duembe or (Djembe)—West Africa
Gakoqui (Bell)—Ghana

Jones incorporated various percussive techniques such as clicking of the tongue and mouth and finger snaps performed by singers and musicians. He also collaborated with musicians with backgrounds in African and African American experiences—Bill Summers, Caiphus Semenya, vocalist Letta Mbulu, Reverend James Cleveland, and the Wattsline Choir.

In some sections Jones incorporated Western orchestral techniques and a classical symphonic feel. For example, "Many Rains Ago (Oluwa)" one of the most inspiring song arrangements in the score, shows Jones attempting to capture the true essence of the African/African American experience through lyrical and musical contents—but is also an example of his mastery and maturity in integrating Western classical ideas in his works. Choir, violins, violas, cellos, string bass, keyboards, guitar, woodwinds, percussion, trumpets, French horn, trombone, and guitar support a poetic/lyrical vocal (sung by Letta Mbulu). The lyrics reflect the historical legacy of ancestral roots, struggles, and hope for people of African descent.

Many of Jones's film and television scores continue to be recognized as innovative music of the time and have been included in different types of international albums and compilations.[39] Over the years Jones has been recognized by his peers in the Hollywood film industry by becoming the first African American to hold the positions of musical director and executive producer of the 43rd (1971) and 68th (1996) annual Academy Award ceremonies. He is among Hollywood's most highly regarded film composers and has paved the way for many contemporary artists. In addition, Jones is highly regarded as an executive producer of special programs, including *Duke Ellington . . . We Love You Madly* (1973), *The Fresh Prince of Bel-Air* (1990–96), *In the House* (1995–99), *The History of Rock 'n' Roll* series (1995), *Say It Loud: A Celebration of Black Music in America* (2001), and many others.

Jones represents a prime example of what can be accomplished with hard work and persistence. By refusing to be labeled or stereotyped as an African American musician possessing the ability only to perform or write in one style, Jones proved that he could create a film score with many sounds, textures, instruments, and musical ideas. In this way he opened doors for other aspiring film composers of all races. He also proved that passion and ambition could lead to a successful career in the competitive Hollywood film industry.

FINALE

How Does Quincy Jones Keep the Music Playing?

When concluding a book about the life, music, and career of Quincy Jones, one of the most appropriate songs to point out and discuss from his body of work is "How Do You Keep the Music Playing?" written by Michel Legrand with lyrical content by Alan and Marilyn Bergman. An arrangement performed by vocalists James Ingram and Patti Austin and was included on Ingram's album *It's Your Night* (Qwest, 1983), produced by Quincy Jones and Johnny Mandel. The song conveys the idea of beautiful music that never ends. The lyrics also provide implications of love and meaningful relationships imagined as unending sounds of flowing music.

Jones's life has proceeded like constant rhythm in motion, and flowing music. Jones's life and musical experiences are representative of and similar to migrating narratives, talking books, and speakerly texts, telling stories of his experiences as an African American musician who excelled, overcame many obstacles, and succeeded at the highest levels of the music industry in both American and international settings. His body of work can also be regarded as a matrix of inventiveness and aesthetic impulses that has allowed him to reinvent himself creatively in jazz, popular music, film, recording, and humanitarian work. For Jones, music has been symbolic of his personal identity and self-definition. Throughout his life he has been involved in giving meaning to American popular music. He has continued to absorb the American popular music lexicon in many different ways.

Music has always been a type of artistic, kinetic agency that has kept his creativity invigorated. This invigoration has stimulated an inquiry of new technologies, contemporary music, and musicians. Jones has kept himself current not just with the artistic side of music-making processes, but also the technical aspects such as the control, operation, and business of the recording studio.

Jones has also learned how to keep his music projects and ideas vibrant to meet the demanding changes of commercial and global markets. He states of starting a new music project:

> it's [synergistic] like I sketch a physical thing in my mind—like colors, contours, and shapes. I literally see pictures and colors. These undefined shapes come through first, then the secondary colors. Then I have to be patient; I have to sit and wait until it becomes clearer and clearer. I may formulate eighteen ideas of different things that I feel, that I really want to do and, in the end, I may use nine of them. Maybe in the last part of the project, I'll find two other things that'll divert you. But I just let it flow, let whatever happens happen, then I start boilin' and get specific.[1]

In starting new projects Jones has always been a risk-taker, totally committed and concentrated. He commented, "young producers and musicians coming up always ask me how I got going in so many different enterprises. I never knew what producing was per se: I just threw myself into everything involved with making the song or the album work."[2]

The creative spirit that Jones integrates in making his songs and albums successful is often infectious and similar to a cyclic process in that many aspiring musicians that work with him on these projects are inspired to dream. For example, popular musicians Patti Austin and James Ingram noted that "Quincy dreams very large dreams and makes them happen. . . . [Quincy] treated me as if I were a real singer, so I started thinking of myself as one. . . . Music is a spiritual force. Everybody who works with Quincy loves him and respects him, so the feeling just flows."[3]

Music has been a type of all-knowing language to express his feelings, emotions, and ideas. He has constantly attempted to encourage people of different races, ideas, beliefs, religions, and creeds to explore the possibilities, beauty, and complexity of different musical traditions. In this type of exploration, one often acquires more knowledge about ethnic diversity.

Jones is without a doubt a man that values people, places, and cultures. Since his early 1950s international experiences, Jones has constantly been engaged in performing, traveling, and experiencing different cultures firsthand. His indoctrination of cultures has involved the integration of different types of experiences with listening to the music, reading, researching, and enjoying diversity in artistic expression. In this way, Jones's career also demonstrates how he has continued to abstain from musical, social, racial, and cultural prejudices to view all music as vital sources of inspiration in the world.

In his career Jones has continually been involved in cultural exchanges through music. These types of exchanges have indeed kept the music playing as a viable part of his life. In 2011 he attempted to create open borders and connections with international musicians. He recently aligned with United Arab Emirates businessman Badr Jafar to form what is known as the Global Gumbo Group. The goal of this organization is to cultivate entertainers across multiple outlets in the Middle East and North Africa. This organization's major agenda is to produce live entertainment opportunities in the Middle East for Western artists in collaboration with Middle Eastern artists in an effort to nurture new regional talent, and also to content from the region to introduce in the West. Through this organization Jones also offers aid to various types of educational, social, and cultural organizations. A major recent project of the Global Gumbo organization was a collaborative recording of the song "Tomorrow/Bokra" (2011), performed by a group of distinguished Middle Eastern artists that Jones organized with the proceeds to aid children and various arts, cultural, and humanitarian organizations in the region. With these types of collaborations, Jones's work in popular music continues to be active.

Jones has not only excelled as a performer, composer, arranger, and producer but has used his success and fame in the music profession to involve himself in humanitarian work, attempting to make the world a better place for people of all races, creeds, and ages with special emphasis on empowering and preserving a bright future for children. In his career, Jones has demonstrated how people in the world can use knowledge to help make the world a better place. This type of exploration is not limited to musicians but can be made by people in all walks of life, backgrounds, and interests. And of course, he has stimulated in people a desire to listen to and appreciate music.

Jones recently partnered with the National Association for Music Education (NAfME) to establish music education programs in schools across the United States. In conjunction with this partnership, in 2010 he established the Quincy Jones Musiq Consortium,[4] an educational program, along with the organizations Jazz Roots, A. Larry Rosen Jazz Series, and Sony Masterworks. The major goal of this program is to implement the Quincy Jones American Popular Music Curriculum in schools throughout the country. As part of the program, Sony Masterworks will produce a two-disc compilation package tracing the history of African drums and their influence on music of the Americas.[5]

In addition Jones has published a series of sheet music, books, and study materials titled *Quincy Jones & Sammy Nestico Premier Jazz Series* and *Be A Star! Quincy Jones, Complete Pack Music Express Series for Students and Teachers* (Hal Leonard Publishing, 2011). With all of his efforts in music education, Jones continues his active engagement in music by attempting to instill in the younger generation an admiration for music.

Throughout his career Jones has constantly inspired individuals and communities. His experiences in the popular music/entertainment industry give real meaning to the song and a theme, "We Are the World." From his childhood experiences in Chicago and Seattle to the cities of New York, Paris, and Los Angeles, Jones has carved out a distinguished and significant place in American music history, society, and the world at large. His music will never end.

APPENDIX I

Albums, Singles, Film Scores and
Soundtracks, and Television Scores

Albums:

Adderley, Julian "Cannonball." *Julian "Cannonball" Adderley*. 1955. EmArcy
MG-36043.

Alpert, Herb. *You Smile, the Song Begins*. 1974. A&M 3620.

Ann-Margret. *Songs from "The Swinger" and Other Swingin' Songs*. 1966. New York
RCA Victor, LPM 3710.

Anthony, Ray. *Standards*. 1954. Capitol T663.

Armstrong, Louis. *Louis*. 1964. Mercury SR-61081/MG 21081.

Arnold, Harry, Big Band and the Quincetet. *The Music of Quincy Jones Played by the
Quincetet and the Harry Arnold Big Band*. 1959–1961. Lone Hill Jazz 10139.

Arnold, Harry. *Harry Arnold + Big Band + Quincy Jones=Jazz!* 1958. Metronome
MLP-15010.

*Arranger's Touch, The: A History of the Jazz Arrangement from Jelly Roll Morton to
Quincy Jones*. Various artists. 2004. Proper P-1401-P1404.

Austin, Patti. *Every Home Should Have One*. 1981. Qwest QWS-3591.

Austin, Patti. *Patti Austin*. 1984. Qwest 1-23974.

Barclay, Eddie. *Americans in Paris*. 1959. New York United Artists.

Barclay, Eddie. *Confetti*. 1959. Barclay B.B. 10 X BLY X 2368 (Stereo).

Barclay, Eddie. *Eddie Barclay présente Swing & Sweet Vol. 2*. 1958. EP 72180.

Barclay, Eddie. *Eddie Barclay présente Swing & Sweet*. 1958. EP Barclay 72133.

Barclay, Eddie. *Eddie Barclay*. 1959. EP Barclay 72634.

Barclay, Eddie. *Et Voilà*. 1957. Barclay 82-138.

Barclay, Eddie. *Surprise Party Caniche Vol. 1*. 1959. LP Barclay 82. 169.

Barclay, Eddie. *Surprise Party Caniche Vol. 2*. 1960[1959]. Barclay BCE 28161.

Barclay, Eddie. *Twilight Time*. 1959. Mercury SR-60167 (1960 Barclay).

Basie, Count, and Billy Eckstine. *Basie-Eckstine, Inc.* 1959. Roulette SR-52029.

Basie, Count. *Basie—One More Time: Music from the Pen of Quincy Jones*. 1958. Roulette SR-52024.

Basie, Count. *Li'l Ol' Groovemaker. . . . . Basie!* Count Basie. 1963. New York Verve
V6-8549.

Basie, Count. *String Along with Basie*. 1959. Roulette SR 52051.

Basie, Count. *This Time by Basie: Hits of the 50s and 60s*. 1963. Reprise R-6070.

Bennett, Tony. *The Movie Song Album*. 1966. Columbia CS-9272.

Benson, George. *Give Me the Night*. 1980. Qwest HS-3453.

Benton, Brook. *There Comes [Goes] That Song Again*. 1961. Mercury MG-20673.

Brothers Johnson. *Blam*. 1978. A&M SP-4685.

Brothers Johnson. *Light Up the Night*. 1980. A&M SP-3716.

Brothers Johnson. *Look Out for #1*. 1976. A&M SP-4567.

Brothers Johnson. *Right on Time*. 1977. A&M SP-4644.

Brothers Johnson. *The Best of the Brothers Johnson: 20th Century Masters Millennium Collection*. 2007. A&M.

Brown, Clifford, and Art Farmer. *Clifford Brown-Art Farmer [Stockholm Sweetnin']*. 1953. Metronome MEP18 & 19 (10").

Brown, Clifford. *The Clifford Brown Big Band in Paris*. 1953. Prestige.

Brown, Oscar. *Between Heaven and Hell*. 1962. Columbia CS 8574.

Brown, Ray. *Harold Robbins Presents Music from The Adventurers*. 1970. Symbolic SYS-9000.

Byers, Billy, with the Quincy Jones Orchestra. *Impressions of Duke Ellington*. 1961. Mercury PPS 2028.

Cain, Jackie, and Roy Kral. *Bits and Pieces—The Glory of Love*. 1957. ABC Paramount ABC-163.

Carroll, David. *Happy Feet*. 1964. Mercury SR-60846.

Carroll, Diahann. *Diahann Carroll Sings Harold Arlen's Songs*. 1956. Victor LPM-1467.

Carter, Betty, and Ray Bryant. *Meet Betty Carter and Ray Bryant*. 1955. Epic LN-3202.

Charles, Ray. *A Message from the People*. 1972. Tangerine ABCX-755/TRC.

Charles, Ray. *Genius + Soul = Jazz*. 1961. Impulse AS-2.

Charles, Ray. *The Genius of Ray Charles*. Ray Charles. 1959. Atlantic 1312.

Charles, Ray. *The Great Ray Charles*. 1956. Atlantic SD-1259.

Clayton, Jeff and John. *Expressions/The Clayton Brothers*. 1997. Qwest 946351-1.

Cleveland, Jimmy. *Introducing Jimmy Cleveland and His All-Stars*. 1955. EmArcy MG-36066.

Cosby, Bill, and Quincy Jones. *The Original Jam Session 1969* (Live). 2004. Concord CCD 2257-2.

D'Amico, Hank. *Holiday with Hank/We Brought Out Axes*. 1954. Bethlehem LP 10" BCP 1006; Bethlehem LP 12" BCP 7.

Davis, Miles. *Live at Montreux*. 1991. Warner Bros. 45221.

Davis, Sammy, Jr., and Count Basie. *Our Shining Hour*. 1964. Verve V6-8605.

Double Six of Paris. *The Double Six Meet Quincy Jones*. 1960. Columbia (import) FPX188.

Eckstine, Billy. *Billy Eckstine and Quincy Jones at Basin Street East*. 1962. Mercury SR-60674.

Eckstine, Billy. *Don't Worry 'Bout Me*. 1962. Mercury MG-20736.

Eckstine, Billy. *Mr. B. in Paris with the Bobby Tucker Orchestra*. 1957. Barclay.

Eckstine, Billy. *The Golden Hits of Billy Eckstine*. Billy Eckstine. 1963. Mercury SR-60796.

Eckstine, Billy. *The Modern Sound of Mr. B.* 1964. Mercury SR-60916.

Edelhagen, Kurt. *Kurt Edelhagen Plays Jim Webb.* 1972. Polydor 2371-077-2414-067.

Elliot, Don. *A Musical Offering by Don Elliot.* 1955. ABC-Paramount ABC-106.

Farmer, Art, Jimmy Cleveland, Oscar Estelle, Clifford Solomon, Monk Montgomery, and Sonny Johnson. *Work of Art.* 1953. Prestige PrLP-162 (10").

Farmer, Art. *A. Farmer Septet Plays Arrangements of Gigi Gryce and Quincy Jones.* 1953. Prestige P-7031.

Farmer, Art. *Last Night When We Were Young.* 1957. ABC Paramount ABC-200.

Farnon, Robert. *Captain from Castile and other Themes.* 1964. Philips PHM-200-098.

Farnon, Robert. *The Sensuous Strings of Robert Farnon.* 1962. Philips 200-038.

Fitzgerald, Ella, and Count Basie. *Ella and Basie.* 1963. Verve 2304 049.

Fonda, Jane. *Jane Fonda's Workout Record.* 1984. Columbia CX239287.

Franklin, Aretha. *Hey Now Hey (The Other Side of the Sky).* Aretha Franklin. 1973. Atlantic SD-7265.

Gibbs, Terry. *Terry Gibbs Plays Jewish Melodies in Jazztime.* 1963. Mercury MG-20812.

Gillespie, Dizzy, Benny Carter, and Lalo Schifrin. *The New Continent.* 1962. Limelight LJ-86022.

Gillespie, Dizzy. *Afro.* 1954. Norgran MG N-1003.

Gillespie, Dizzy. *Diz Big Band.* 1954. Verve MGV-8178 (EP).

Gillespie, Dizzy. *Dizzy Gillespie: World Statesman.* 1956. Norgran MG N-1084.

Gillespie, Dizzy. *Dizzy in Greece.* 1956. Verve MGV-8017.

Gillespie, Dizzy. *Dizzy on the French Riviera.* 1962. Philips PHM-200-048.

Gillespie, Dizzy. *New Wave!* 1962. Philips PHM-200-070.

Gillespie, Dizzy, Goodwill Tour Band. *Dizzy in South America Official U.S. State Department Tour, vol. 1, 1956.* 1999. Red Anchor CAP 933.

Gillespie, Dizzy, Goodwill Tour Band. *Dizzy in South America Official U.S. State Department Tour, vol. 2, 1956.* 1999. Red Anchor CAP 934.

Gillespie, Dizzy, Goodwill Tour Band. *Dizzy in South America: Tangos, Sambas, Interviews and More Big Band Bebop, Vol. 3, 1956.* 2001. Consolidated Artists/ Red Anchor CAP 935.

Gordon, Joe. *Introducing Joe Gordon.* 1954. EmArcy MG-26046 (10").

Gore, Lesley. *Boys, Boys, Boys.* 1964. Mercury MG-20901.

Gore, Lesley. *California Nights.* 1967. Mercury MG-61120.

Gore, Lesley. *Girl Talk.* 1964. Mercury MG-20943.

Gore, Lesley. *I'll Cry If I Want To.* 1963. Mercury MG-20805.

Gore, Lesley. *Love Me By Name.* 1976. A&M SP-4564.

Grice, Gigi, and Clifford Brown. *Gigi Gryce/Clifford Brown—Gigi Gryce and His Little Band,* Vols. 1 & 2. 1953. Blue Note BLP 5049.

Gryce, Gigi. *Jazz Time Paris, Vol. 10.* 1953. Vogue LD173.

Hampton, Lionel. *Lionel Hampton and His Orchestra 1950–1951.* 2002. Classic #1262.

Hampton, Lionel, and His Orchestra. *Lionel Hampton—European Concert.* 1953. IAJRC 31.

Hampton, Lionel, and His Orchestra. *Lionel Hampton Orchestra, Part 2, Mustermesse, Basel, 1953*. 2008. TCB 021.

Handel's Messiah: A Soulful Celebration. Various artists. 1992. Reprise B0000ZLUJ.

Hodeir, André. *Jazz et Jazz*. 1963. Philips PHS 600-073.

Horn, Shirley. *Shirley Horn with Horns*. 1963. Mercury MG-20835.

Horne, Lena. *The Lady and Her Music—Live on Broadway*. 1981. Qwest 2QW-3597.

Hunter, Lurlene. *Lonesome Gal*. 1955. RCA Victor LPM-1151.

Ingram, James. *It's Your Night*. 1983. Qwest 1-23970.

Ingram, James. *Never Felt So Good*. 1986. Qwest 1-225424.

Jackson, Michael. *Bad*. Epic OE-40600.

Jackson, Michael. *Off The Wall*. 1979. Epic FE-35745.

Jackson, Michael. *Thriller*. 1982. Epic QE-40600.

Jackson, Milt. *Plenty, Plenty Soul*. 1957. Atlantic 1269.

Jackson, Milt. *The Ballad Artistry of Milt Jackson*. Milt Jackson. 1959. Atlantic SD-1342.

Jacquet, Illinois. *Illinois Jacquet Flies Again*. 1959. Roulette 97272.

James, Bob, Trio. *Bold Conceptions*. 1962. Verve SR-60768.

Jo, Damita. *This One's for Me*. 1964. Mercury MG-20818.

Jones Boys. *The Jones Boys—Quincy, Thad, Jimmy, Jo, Eddie, and Elvin*. 1956. Period SPL-1210; Everest FS 270.

Jones, Quincy, and Herbie Hancock. *Walk on the Wild Side: Quincy Jones and Herbie Hancock*. 2001. Mojo Music B0017X1ZQM.

Jones, Quincy, and His Orchestra. *Around the World: Quincy Jones and His Orchestra*. 1961. Mercury PPS-6014.

Jones, Quincy, and His Orchestra. *Big Band Bossa Nova*. 1962. Mercury MG-20751.

Jones, Quincy, and His Orchestra. *Go West, Man*. 1957. ABC Paramount ABC-186.

Jones, Quincy, and His Orchestra. *Golden Boy*. 1964. Mercury MG-20938.

Jones, Quincy, and His Orchestra. *I Dig Dancers*. 1960. Mercury SR-60612.

Jones, Quincy, and His Orchestra. *I Had a Ball*. 1964. Mercury MG-21002.

Jones, Quincy, and His Orchestra. *Quincy Jones and His Orchestra at Newport '61*. 1961. Mercury SR-60653.

Jones, Quincy, and His Orchestra. *Quincy Jones Explores the Music of Henry Mancini*. 1964. Mercury MG-20863.

Jones, Quincy, and His Orchestra. *Quincy Jones Plays for Pussycats*. 1965. Mercury MG-21050.

Jones, Quincy, and His Orchestra. *Quincy Jones Plays the Hip Hits*. 1963. Mercury SR-60799.

Jones, Quincy, and His Orchestra. *Quincy's Got a Brand New-Bag*. 1965. Mercury MG-21063.

Jones, Quincy, and His Orchestra. *The Great Wide World of Quincy Jones*. 1959. Mercury SR-60221.

Jones, Quincy, and His Orchestra. *The Great Wide World of Quincy Jones—Live in Zurich!* 1961. Mercury 195J-32.

Jones, Quincy, and His Orchestra. The *Quintessence*. 1961. Impulse AS-11.

Jones, Quincy, and His Orchestra. *This Is How I Feel About Jazz.* 1956. ABC Paramount ABC-149.

Jones, Quincy, and His Swedish-American All-Stars. *Quincy Jones and His Swedish-American All-Stars.* 1953. Prestige PrLP-172.

Jones, Quincy, and Sammy Nestico Orchestra. *Basie and Beyond* (by Quincy Jones and Sammy Nestico). 2000. Qwest 47792.

Jones, Quincy, and the Jones Boys. *Quincy Jones and the Jones Boys: Jump for Jones.* 2001. SRI B002HIES5Q.

Jones, Quincy, Big Band. *Free and Easy Live in Stockholm 1960.* 1994. Ancha Trading ANC 9500.

Jones, Quincy, Big Band. *Lausanne 1960/Swiss Radio Days, Jazz Series, Vol. 1.* 1995. TCB Music SA.

Jones, Quincy, Big Band. *Live at the Alhambre '60.* 1994. Jmy B000019C2.

Jones, Quincy, featuring Toots Thielemans. *I Never Told You.* 2005[1999]. Universal B0006GAWYW.

Jones, Quincy. *20th Century Masters Millennium Collection: Ultimate Collection.* 2002. Hip-O 314585902-2/31458 5902-2.

Jones, Quincy. *A&M 25th Anniversary Classic Volume 3 Quincy Jones.* 1987. A&M B000008BFF.

Jones, Quincy. *Abstractions.* 1999. ABM B0000025A4C (United Kingdom).

Jones, Quincy. *Back on the Block.* 1989. Qwest 26020-1.

Jones, Quincy. *Body Heat.* 1974. A&M SP-3617.

Jones, Quincy. *Exodus.* 2003. Prism Platinum B000088E6V.

Jones, Quincy. *Forever Gold: Quincy Jones.* 2007. St. Clair Entertainment B000QXDJBI.

Jones, Quincy. *From Q With Love.* 1999. Qwest 46490.

Jones, Quincy. *Gula Matari.* 1970. A&M SP-3030.

Jones, Quincy. *I Heard That!* 1976. A&M SP-3705.

Jones, Quincy. *Ironside.* 1975. A&M AMLP.

Jones, Quincy. *Jazz 'Round Midnight: Quincy Jones.* 1997. Verve 314537702-2.

Jones, Quincy. *Jazz Manifesto.* 2009. Distribution B002810IDS [import].

Jones, Quincy. *Listen Up: The Lives of Quincy Jones.* 1990. Warner Bros./WEA, B000008HS0.

Jones, Quincy. *Live at the Budokan.* 1981. A&M AMP-28045.

Jones, Quincy. *Love, Q.* 2004. Hip-O B00016MT0C.

Jones, Quincy. *Lullaby of Birdland.* 1955. RCA Victor LPM-1146.

Jones, Quincy. *Mastercuts.* 2007. Mastercuts Artists B000MMMU50.

Jones, Quincy. *Mellow Madness.* 1975. A&M SP-4526.

Jones, Quincy. *Moanin': Quincy Jones Big Band Vol. 2.* 1977. Mercury 45S-11.

Jones, Quincy. *Mode.* 1974. ABC ABCX-782/2.

Jones, Quincy. *Ndeda.* 1972. Mercury SRM 263.

Jones, Quincy. *Pure Delight: The Essence of Quincy Jones and His Orchestra (1953–1964).* 1995. Razor & Tie B000002Z9P.

Jones, Quincy. *Q Digs Dancers*. 2006. Universal B000FPWXGY.

Jones, Quincy. *Q Live in Paris Circa 1960*. 1996. Qwest 46190 and WEA International B000002N50.

Jones, Quincy. *Q: The Musical Biography of Quincy Jones* (Box Set) 4 vols. 2001. Rhino R2-74363.

Jones, Quincy. Q: *Soul Bossa Nova Nostra*. Qwest/Interscope B001429402.

Jones, Quincy. *Q's Jook Joint*. 1995. Qwest 45875.

Jones, Quincy. *Quincy Jones [ARC Album]*. 2000. The Magic Collection.

Jones, Quincy. *Quincy Jones Finest Hour*. 2000. Polygram B00004TWRP.

Jones, Quincy. *Quincy Jones-Swinging the Band*. 2006. Verve 06024- 9841791.

Jones, Quincy. *Quincy Jones—Greatest Hits*. 1986. A&M B000002G5S.

Jones, Quincy. *Quincy Jones—Music Is My Life*. 1983. Pickwick SHM 3126 (United Kingdom).

Jones, Quincy. *Quincy Jones*. 1977. AMGA 855531.

Jones, Quincy. *Smackwater Jack*. 1971. A&M SP-3037.

Jones, Quincy. *Sounds . . . And Stuff Like That!!* 1978. A&M SP-4685.

Jones, Quincy. *Spanish Fly*. 1964. Mercury 134 602 MFY (Netherlands).

Jones, Quincy. *Strike Up the Band*. [1987]1988. Verve 538459-2.

Jones, Quincy. *Summer in the City*. 2009. Verve/Eur/Zoom B000UXEYIQ.

Jones, Quincy. *Take Five*. 1983. Century Vista B000005NRY.

Jones, Quincy. *The Best of Quincy Jones, Vol. 2*. 1970. Rebound B0000047QS.

Jones, Quincy. *The Best of Quincy Jones*. 1998. Polygram International B00000DB4O.

Jones, Quincy. *The Best of Quincy Jones*. 2001. Interscope B000047879.

Jones, Quincy. *The Best*. 1990. A&M B000002GAT.

Jones, Quincy. *The Birth of a Band Vol. 2*. 1984. Mercury 1995J-30.

Jones, Quincy. *The Birth of a Band*. 1959. Mercury MG-204444.

Jones, Quincy. *The Dude*. 1981. A&M SP-3721.

Jones, Quincy. *The Genius of Quincy Jones*. 1999. Hallmark 306202.

Jones, Quincy. *The Giants of Jazz: Quincy Jones and the All-Stars*. 1955. Columbia CL-1970.

Jones, Quincy. *The Music of Quincy Jones*. 2001. Rhino R2-74363.

Jones, Quincy. *The Q in Jazz*. 2007. Golden Stars (Netherlands) B000W8FYKQ.

Jones, Quincy. *The Quincy Jones ABC/Mercury Big Band Jazz Sessions*. 2007. Mosaic B0015MHXYI (box set).

Jones, Quincy. *The Reel Quincy Jones*. 1999. Hip-O B00000JC9S.

Jones, Quincy. *Thousand Yen Jazz by Quincy Jones*. Universal B000BR20U6.

Jones, Quincy. *Walking in Space*. 1969. A&M SP-3023.

Jones, Quincy. *You've Got It Bad, Girl*. 1972. A&M SP-3041.

Jordan, Louis. *Somebody Up There Digs Me (Greatest Hits)*. 1956. Mercury MG-20242.

Krupa, Gene, featuring Roy Eldridge and Anita O'Day. *Drummer Man*. 1956. Verve MGV-2008.

Laws, Hubert, Quincy Jones, and Chick Corea. *Hubert Laws-Quincy Jones-Chick Corea [New Earth Sonata/Telemann Suite in A minor]*. 1985. CBS Masterworks M-39858.

Lee, Peggy. *Blues Cross Country.* 1961. Capitol ST-1671.

Lee, Peggy. *If You Go.* 1961. Capitol T-1630.

Little Richard. *It's Real.* 1961. Mercury MG-20656.

Lookofsky, Harry. *Miracle in Strings.* 1954. Epic EG-7081 (EP).

Lookofsky, Harry. *The Hash Brown Sounds and His Ignunt Strings.* 1962. Philips PHM-200-018.

Madigan, Art, and Joe Gordon, Paul Gonsalves, and Clark Terry. *The Jazz School.* 1954. Wing MGW-60002.

Mandel, Johnny. *The Sandpiper.* 1965. Mercury MG 21032/SR 61032.

Mathis, Johnny. *The Sweetheart Tree/Mirage.* 1965. Mercury 61041.

McRae, Carmen. *Carmen/Carmen McRae.* 1972. Temponic TB-29562.

Merrill, Helen, and Clifford Brown. *Helen Merrill with Clifford Brown.* 1954. EmArcy MG-36006.

Merrill, Helen. *You've Got a Date with the Blues.* 1959. Metrojazz E-1010.

Moody, James. *James Moody's Mood for Blues.* 1954. Prestige PrLP-198.

Moody, James. *Moody's Mood.* 1954. Prestige PrLP-192.

Moody, James. *Wail, Moody Wail.* 1955. Prestige LP-7036.

Most, Sam. *Sam Most Sextet.* 1955. Vanguard LP 12" VRS 8014.

Mouskouri, Nana. *Mouskouri in New York—The Girl from Greece Sings.* 1999. Mercury 546 232-1.

Newman, Joe. *Joe Newman Quintet at Count Basie's.* 1961. Mercury SR-60696.

Newman, Joe. *Soft Swingin' Jazz and the Happy Cats.* 1957. Coral 57121.

Official Music of the 23rd Olympiad in Los Angeles. Various artists. 1984. Columbia BJS-39322.

Pettiford, Oscar. *Basically Duke.* 1954. Bethlehem BCP-1019.

Pettiford, Oscar. *Oscar Pettiford* [Modern Quintet]. 1954. Bethlehem BCP-1003.

Pettiford, Oscar. *The Finest of Oscar Pettiford.* 1955. Bethlehem BCP-6007.

Pettiford, Oscar. *The New Oscar Pettiford Sextet.* 1951. Debut DLP-8.

Pleasure, King. *King Pleasure Sings.* 1954. Prestige # 208 [913/908 (78 RPM) EPs].

Preston, Billy. *I Wrote a Simple Song.* 1971. A&M SP-3507.

Quincy Jones/The Isley Brothers—The Artists Vol. 4. Various artists. 1986. Street Sounds ARTIS4.

Quinichette, Paul. *Moods.* 1954. EmArcy MG-36003.

Roy Haynes/Quincy Jones–Jazz Abroad. 1954. EmArcy MG 36083.

Rufus and Chaka Khan. *Masterjam.* 1979. MCA MCA-5103.

Sachs, Aaron. *Aaron Sachs Quintette/Sextet.* 1954. Bethlehem BCP-1008 (10").

Sasson, Jean-Pierre. *Jean-Pierre Sasson & the Muskrats-Dixie Downbeat.* 1958. Wing MGW12144/SRW12503 (Barclay Hoche Studio Paris).

Save the Children. Various artists. 1973. Motown M800-R2.

Scott, Bobby. *Joyful Noises.* 1962. Mercury MG-20701.

Scott, Bobby. *When the Feeling Hits You.* 1962. Mercury SR-60767.

Simon, Paul. *There Goes Rhymin' Simon.* 1973. CBS 32280.

Sinatra, Frank, with the Count Basie Orchestra. *Sinatra at the Sands with the Count Basie Orchestra.* 1966[1998]. Reprise 1019.

Sinatra, Frank, with the Count Basie Orchestra. *Sinatra, Basie, and Friends.* 1965. Retrospect 509.

Sinatra, Frank. *L.A. Is My Lady.* 1984. Qwest 25145-1.

Sinatra, Frank. *My Way—The Best of Frank Sinatra.* 1997. Reprise 9362-46710-2.

Sinatra, Frank. *It Might as Well Be Swing.* 1964. Reprise FS-1012.

Starr, Ringo. *Sentimental Journey.* 1970. Apple SW-3365.

Stitt, Sonny. *Sonny Stitt Plays Arrangements from the Pen of Quincy Jones.* 1955. Roost LP-2204.

Summer, Donna. *Donna Summer.* 1982. Geffen GHS-2005.

Talkin' Verve Groovy. Various artists. 1998. Verve 314557081-2.

Talkin' Verve with a Twist. Various artists. 1997. Polygram B0000047FP.

Talkin' Verve. Various artists. 2001. Polygram B000059QCY.

Taylor, Billy. *My Fair Lady Loves Jazz.* 1957. ABC Paramount ABC-177.

Terry, Clark. *Clark Terry in the P.M.* 1955. EmArcy EP-1-6108 (EP).

Terry, Clark. *Clark Terry.* 1955. EmArcy MG-36007.

Terry, Clark. *Swahili.* 1955. Trip Jazz TLP-5528.

Three Sounds, The. *Live at the Living Room.* 1964. Mercury MG-20921.

Three Sounds, The. *Some Like It Modern.* 1963. Mercury SR-60839.

Three Sounds, The. *The Three Sounds Play Jazz on Broadway.* 1962. Mercury MG-20776.

Vaughan, Sarah. *Sarah Vaughan Sings the Mancini Songbook.* 1965. Mercury MG-21009.

Vaughan, Sarah. *Sarah Vaughan—Vol. 1—Night Song.* 1964. Philips 6336 224.

Vaughan, Sarah. *Sassy Swings the Tivoli.* 1963. Mercury SR-60831.

Vaughan, Sarah. *Vaughan and Violins.* 1958. Mercury MG-203370.

Vaughan, Sarah. *Vaughan with Voices.* 1963. Mercury MG-20882.

Vaughan, Sarah. *Viva! Vaughan.* 1964. Mercury MG-20941.

Vaughan, Sarah. *You're Mine, You.* 1962. Roulette R-52082.

Wallington, George. *George Wallington and His Swedish All-Stars.* 1953. EmArcy MG-36121.

Wallington, George. *George Wallington Showcase.* 1954. Blue Note BLP-5045.

Washington, Dinah. *Dinah Washington Golden Hits, Volume Two.* 1963. Mercury 60789.

Washington, Dinah. *For Those in Love.* 1955. Mercury[EmArcy] MG-36011.

Washington, Dinah. *I Wanna Be Loved.* 1961. Mercury MG-20729.

Washington, Dinah. *Tears & Laughter.* 1961. Mercury SR-60661.

Washington, Dinah. *The Queen and Quincy.* 1956. Mercury SR-60928.

Washington, Dinah. *The Swingin' Miss D.* 1956. EmArcy MG-36104.

Washington, Dinah. *This Is My Story* (Vols. 1 & 2). 1962. Mercury SR-60765/60769.

Watkins, Julius. *French Horns for My Lady.* 1960. Philips PHM-200-001.

Watts, Ernie. *Chariots of Fire.* 1981. Qwest QWS-3637.

White, Josh. *At Town Hall.* 1961. Mercury MG-20672.

Williams, Andy. *Under Paris Skies.* 1960. Cadence CLP-3047.

Yuro, Timi. *The Amazing Timi Yuro.* 1964. Wing MG-20963.

Singles:

Anderson, Ernestine. After the Lights Go Down. 1962. Mercury.
Anderson, Ernestine. Hurry, Hurry. 1962. Mercury.
Baker, LaVern. Game of Love. 1957. Atlantic.
Baker, LaVern. Humpty Dumpty Heart. 1957. Atlantic.
Baker, LaVern. Jim Dandy Got Married. 1957. Atlantic.
Baker, LaVern. Learning to Love. 1957. Atlantic.
Baker, LaVern. Love Me Right. 1957. Atlantic.
Baker, LaVern. Substitute. 1957. Atlantic.
Benton, Brook. Can I Help It. 1955. Okeh.
Benton, Brook. The Kentuckian. 1955. Okeh.
Big Maybelle. Ocean of Tears. 1955. Okeh.
Big Maybelle. Such a Cutie. 1955. Okeh.
Big Maybelle. The Other Night. 1955. Okeh.
Big Maybelle. Whole Lot of Shakin' Goin' On. 1955. Okeh.
Cardinals, The. Let the Sunshine Shine on You. 1956. Okeh.
Cardinals, The. Near You. 1956. Atlantic.
Cardinals, The. One Love. 1956. Atlantic.
Cardinals, The. Sunshine. 1956. Atlantic.
Carol, Lily Ann. Everybody. 1956. Mercury.
Carol, Lily Ann. Oh No! 1956. Mercury.
Carol, Lily Ann. Ooh Poppa Doo. 1956. Mercury.
Carol, Lily Ann. So Used to You. 1956. Mercury.
Clovers, The. Baby Darling. 1957. Atlantic.
Clovers, The. I-I-I Love You. 1957. Atlantic.
Clovers, The. Pretty, Pretty, Eyes. 1957. Atlantic.
Clovers, The. Shakin'. 1957. Atlantic.
Clovers, The. So Young. 1957. Atlantic.
Davis, "Wild" Bill, Trio. Belle of the Ball. 1955. Okeh.
Davis, "Wild" Bill, Trio. Serenade to Benny. 1955. Okeh.
Davis, "Wild" Bill, Trio. Syncopated Clock. 1955. Okeh.
Farmer, Art. Elephant Walk. 1954. Prestige.
Farmer, Art. Evening in Paris. 1954. Prestige.
Franklin, Aretha. Master of Eyes. 1973. Atlantic.
Gore, Lesley. You Don't Own Me. 1963. Mercury.
Hamlisch, Marvin. If You Hadn't Left Me (Crying). 1976. A&M.
Hamlisch, Marvin. One. 1976. A&M.
Hampton, Lionel, and His Orchestra. Kingfish. 1951. M.G.M.
Hampton, Lionel. Don't Flee the Scene Salty. 1951. M.G.M.
Hendricks, Jon. Cloud Burst. 1955. Decca.
Hendricks, Jon. Flyin' Home. 1955. Decca.
Hendricks, Jon. Happy Feet. 1955. Decca.
Horn, Shirley. For Love of Ivy. 1968. ABC.

Horn, Shirley. If You Want to Love. 1968. Bell.

Horn, Shirley. The Spell You Spin (The Web You Weave). 1968. Bell.

Jacquet, Russell. Port of Rico. 1953. Network.

Jacquet, Russell. They Tried. 1953. Network.

Jones, Quincy, and His Orchestra. Soul Bossa Nova. 1962. Mercury.

Jones, Quincy, Henri Salvador, and Darcas Cochran. Soleil de minuit (The Midnight Sun Will Never Set). 1960. Barclay.

Jones, Quincy, Septet. Be My Guest. 1957. Impulse.

Jones, Quincy, Septet. Dancin' Pants. 1957. Impulse.

Jones, Quincy, Septet. King Road Blues. 1957. Impulse.

Pleasure, King. Don't Get Scared. 1954. Prestige.

Pleasure, King. Funk Junction. 1954. Prestige.

Pleasure, King. I'm Gone. 1954. Prestige.

Pleasure, King. You're Crying. 1954. Prestige.

Renaud, Henri. Dillon. 1954. Vogue.

Renaud, Henri. Meet Quincy Jones. 1954. Vogue.

Renaud, Henri. Wallington Special. 1954. Vogue.

Richmond, June. Between the Devil and the Deep Blue Sea. 1957. Barclay.

Richmond, June. Devil and Deep Blue Sea. 1957. Barclay.

Richmond, June. Everybody's Doin' It. 1957. Barclay.

Richmond, June. Sleep. 1957. Barclay.

Ross, Annie. Jackie. 1953. Metronome.

Ross, Annie. The Song is You. 1953. Metronome.

Salvador, Henri. Blouse du Dentiste. 1958. Barclay.

Salvador, Henri. Moi J'Prefere La Marche à Pied. 1958. Barclay.

Salvador, Henri. Tous Les Saints. 1958. Barclay.

Salvador, Henri. Trompette D'Occasion. 1958. Barclay.

Sandmen, The, featuring Brook Benton. Bring Me Love. 1955. Okeh.

Sandmen, The, featuring Brook Benton. Ooh, Fool Enough to Love You. 1955. Okeh.

Treniers, The, with Willie Mays. Go! Go! Go! 1954. Okeh.

Treniers, The, with Willie Mays. Say Hey (The Willie Mays Song). 1954. Okeh.

Treniers, The. Oh, Oh. 1955. Okeh.

Treniers, The. Who Put the Ungh in the Mambo. 1955. Okeh.

USA for Africa. We Are The World. 1985. Columbia.

Vaughan, Sarah. Misty. 1959. Mercury.

Willis, Chuck. Come On Home. 1955. Okeh.

Willis, Chuck. Give Me a Break. 1955. Okeh.

Willis, Chuck. I Can Tell. 1955. Okeh.

Willis, Chuck. Ring-Ding-Doo. 1955. Okeh.

Willis, Chuck. Search My Heart. 1955. Okeh.

Film Scores and Soundtracks:

A Dandy in Aspic. 1968. Columbia.
Banning. 1967. Universal.
Bob & Carol & Ted & Alice (Soundtrack). 1969. Bell 1200.
Brother John. 1971. Columbia.
Cactus Flower (Soundtrack). 1970. Bell 1201.
Come Back Charleston Blue. 1972. Warner Bros.
Dig. 1972. Paramount/Hubley Studios [CINE Golden Eagle].
$ [Dollars] (Soundtrack). 1971. Reprise MS-2051.
Eggs. 1970. Paramount /Hubley Studios.
Enter Laughing (Soundtrack). 1967. Liberty LOM-16004.
E.T. The Extra-Terrestrial (Soundtrack). 1982. MCA MCA-70000.
For Love of Ivy (Soundtrack). 1968. Cinerama. ABC ABCS-OC-7.
Get Rich or Die Tryin'. 2006. Paramount.
Honky. 1971. Getty & Fromkess.
In Cold Blood (Soundtrack). 1967. Colgems COM-107.
In the Heat of the Night (Soundtrack). 1967. United Artists UAL-160.
John and Mary (Soundtrack). 1969. A&M SP-4230.
Last of the Mobile Hot-Shots. 1970. Warner Bros.
Listen Up: The Lives of Quincy Jones. 1990. Warner Bros.
MacKenna's Gold (Soundtrack). 1969. RCA Victor LSP-4096.
Man and Boy (Soundtrack). 1972. Sussex/Buddah SXBS 7011.
Mirage (Soundtrack). 1965. Mercury MG-21025.
Of Men and Demons. 1969. Paramount/Hubley Studios.
The Anderson Tapes. 1971. Columbia.
The Boy in the Tree (*Pojken i trädet*) (Soundtrack). 1961. Mercury (Sweden)
    EP-60338.
The Color Purple (Soundtrack). 1985. Qwest 25389-1.
The Deadly Affair (Soundtrack). 1967. Verve V-8679-ST.
The Getaway. 1972. First Artists/Warner Bros.
The Hell with Heroes. 1968. Universal.
The Hot Rock (Soundtrack). 1972. Prophesy SD-6055.
The Italian Job (Soundtrack). 1969. Paramount PAS-5007.
The Lost Man (Soundtrack). 1969. Uni 73060.
The New Centurions. 1972. Columbia.
The Out-of-Towners. 1970. Paramount.
The Pawnbroker (Soundtrack). 1964. Mercury SR-61011.
The Slender Thread (Soundtrack). 1966. Mercury MG-21070.
The Split. 1968. MGM/United Artists.
The Wiz (Soundtrack). 1978. MCA MCA2-14000.
They Call Me Mister Tibbs! (Soundtrack). 1970. United Artists UAS-5241.
Walk, Don't Run (Soundtrack). 1966. Mainstream S-6080.

Television Scores:

Banacek. 1972. Wednesday Mystery Movie theme; 8 episodes. NBC.
Cool Million. 1972. Wednesday Mystery Movie theme; 4 episodes. NBC.
Hey, Landlord. 1966. NBC.
In the Heat of the Night. 1988–94. ABC.
Ironside. 1967–75. NBC.
Jigsaw. 1968. Universal Pictures.
Killer by Night. 1972. CBS-Television/Cinema Center 100 Productions.
Madigan. 1972. Wednesday Mystery Movie theme; 6 episodes. NBC.
Now You See It. 1989. CBS.
Oprah Winfrey Show. 1986. ABC.
Roots miniseries-Episode 1. 1977. ABC. A&M SP-4626.
Sanford and Son. 1972–77. NBC.
Split Second to an Epitaph. 1967. NBC.
The Bill Cosby Show. 1969–71. NBC.
The Counterfeit Killer. 1968. Morpics.
The NBC Mystery Movie of the Week. 1971. NBC.
The New Bill Cosby Show. 1972. CBS.
Up Your Teddy Bear. 1970. Joslyn Films.

APPENDIX II

Awards, Honors, and Special Recognition

I. Grammy Awards—The National Academy of Recording Arts and Sciences

1963   Best Instrumental Arrangement: "I Can't Stop Loving You" (featuring the Count Basie Band)

1969   Best Instrumental Jazz Performance, Large Group or Soloist with Large Group: "Walking in Space"

1971   Best Pop Instrumental Performance: *Smackwater Jack* (album)

1973   Best Instrumental Arrangement: "Summer in the City"

1978   Best Instrumental Arrangement: "Main Title-Overture Part One," from *The Wiz Original Soundtrack* (with Robert Freedman)

1980   Best Instrumental Arrangement: "Dinorah, Dinorah" (George Benson) (cowinner with Jerry Hey)

1981   Best R&B Performance by Duo or Group with Vocal: "The Dude," from the album *Quincy Jones*

1981   Best Cast Show Album: *Lena Horne: The Lady and Her Music-Live on Broadway* (album); Quincy Jones, Producer

1981   Best Arrangement on an Instrumental Recording: "Velas," from the album *The Dude*; Quincy Jones, arranger

1981   Best Instrumental Arrangement Accompanying Vocal: "Ai No Corrida," from the album *The Dude* [cowinner with Jerry Hey, instrument arrangement]

1981   Producer of the Year

1983   Record of the Year: "Beat It" by Michael Jackson; Quincy Jones, Producer (cowinner with Michael Jackson)

1983   Album of the Year: *Thriller* by Michael Jackson; Quincy Jones, Producer (cowinner with Michael Jackson)

1983   Best Recording for Children: *E.T. The Extra-Terrestrial*; Quincy Jones, Producer (cowinner with Michael Jackson)

1983   Producer of the Year: *Thriller* by Michael Jackson; Quincy Jones (cowinner with Michael Jackson)

1984   Best Arrangement of an Instrumental: "Grace (Gymnastics Theme)," from *The Official Music of the 23rd Olympiad in Los Angeles*; Quincy Jones with Jerry Lubbock

1985   Record of the Year: "We Are the World," USA for Africa

1985   Best Pop Performance by a Duo or Group with Vocal: "We Are the World" (single), USA for Africa

1985   Best Music Video, Short Form: *We Are the World—The Video Event*, USA for Africa [cowinner with Tom Trbovich, video director)

1988   Trustees Award: Presented to Quincy Jones for his contribution to the recording industry as a composer, arranger, producer, and conductor

1990   Album of the Year: *Back on the Block;* Quincy Jones, Producer

1990   Best Rap Performance by a Duo or a Group: "Back on the Block" from the album *Back on the Block* [cowinners: Ice-T, Melle Mel, Big Daddy Kane, Kool Moe Dee, Quincy D III)

1990   Best Jazz Fusion Performance: "Birdland," from the album *Back on the Block* (Qwest)

1990   Best Arrangement of an Instrumental: "Birdland," from the album *Back on the Block*

1990   Best Instrumental Arrangement Accompanying Vocals: "The Places You Find Love," from the album *Back on the Block* (Qwest)

1990   Producer of the Year

1990   Grammy Living Legend Award: Quincy Jones for lifetime achievement

1993   Best Large Jazz Ensemble Performance: *Miles and Quincy Live at Montreux*

1996   MusiCares Person of the Year: Awarded to Quincy Jones as a humanitarian award

II. Grammy Award Nominations—The National Academy of Recording Arts and Sciences

1960   Best Arrangement: "Let the Good Times Roll," Ray Charles

1960   Best Jazz Performance, Large Group: *The Great Wide World of Quincy Jones*

1961   Best Performance by an Orchestra for Dancing: *I Dig Dancers*

1962   Best Performance by an Orchestra for Dancing: *Big Band Bossa Nova*

1962   Best Instrumental Arrangement: "Quintessence"

1962   Best Original Jazz Composition: "Quintessence"

1963   Best Instrumental Arrangement: "I Can't Stop Loving You," Count Basie

1963   Best Instrumental Jazz Performance, Large Group: *Quincy Jones Plays the Hip Hits*

1963   Best Performance by an Orchestra for Dancing: *Quincy Jones Plays the Hip Hits*

1964   Best Instrumental Arrangement: "Golden Boy (String Version)"

1964   Best Instrumental Performance, Non-Jazz: "Golden Boy (String Version)"

1964   Best Jazz Performance, Large Group or Soloist with Large Group: *Quincy Jones Explores the Music of Henry Mancini*

1964 Best Original Jazz Composition: "The Witching Hour," from the album
      Golden Boy
1967 Best Original Score Written for a Motion Picture or a Television Show:
      In the Heat of the Night
1969 Best Instrumental Jazz Performance, Large Group or Soloist with Large
      Group: *Walking in Space*
1969 Best Original Score for a Motion Picture or a Television Show: *MacKenna's
      Gold*
1969 Best Instrumental Theme: *MacKenna's Gold*—Main Title
1969 Best Original Score for a Motion Picture or a Television Show: *The Lost
      Man*
1969 Best Instrumental Arrangement: Walking in Space
1970 Best Instrumental Arrangement: "Gula Matari"
1970 Best Instrumental Composition: "Gula Matari"
1970 Best Jazz Performance, Large Group or Soloist with Large Group: *Gula
      Matari*
1971 Best Contemporary Instrumental Performance: "Soul Flower," from the
      soundtrack of *They Call Me Mister Tibbs!*
1972 Best Pop Instrumental Performance: *Smackwater Jack*
1972 Best Original Score Written for a Motion Picture: *$ [Dollars]* Soundtrack
1972 Best Instrumental Arrangement: "Money Runner," from the soundtrack
      of *$ [Dollars]*
1972 Best Pop Instrumental by Arranger, Composer, Orchestra: "Money Run-
      ner," from the soundtrack of *$ [Dollars]*
1973 Best Instrumental Arrangement: "Summer in the City"
1973 Best Pop Instrumental Performance: *You've Got It Bad, Girl*
1974 Best Pop Instrumental Performance: "Along Came Betty," from the album
      Body Heat
1974 Best Pop Vocal Performance by a Duo or Group or Chorus: *Body Heat*
1976 Best Instrumental Composition: "Midnight Soul Patrol," from the album *I
      Heard That*
1977 Best Arrangement for Voices: "Oh Lord, Come by Here," from the
      soundtrack of *Roots*
1977 Best Inspirational Performance: "Oh Lord, Come by Here" (Reverend
      James Cleveland), from the soundtrack of *Roots*
1977 Best Instrumental Composition: "Roots Medley (Motherland, *Roots*, Mural
      Theme)," from the soundtrack of *Roots*
1978 Best Instrumental Arrangement: "Main Title: Overture Part One,: from
      the soundtrack of *The Wiz* [cowinner with Robert Freedman]
1978 Best Instrumental Composition: "End of the Yellow Brick Road" (Nicholas
      Ashford and Valerie Simpson), from soundtrack of *The Wiz*
1978 Best Arrangement for Voices: "Stuff Like That," from the album *Sounds . . .
      And Stuff Like That!!*

1978   Producer of the Year

1979   Best Disco Recording: "Don't Stop 'Til You Get Enough" Michael Jackson, from the album *Off The Wall*; Quincy Jones, producer

1979   Producer of the Year

1980   Best Instrumental Arrangement: "Dinorah, Dinorah," George Benson; producer, Quincy Jones [cowinner with Jerry Hey]

1980   Producer of the Year

1981   Best R&B Performance by Duo or Group with Vocal: *The Dude—Quincy Jones*

1981   Best Cast Show Album: *Lena Horne: The Lady and Her Music—Live on Broadway*; Quincy Jones, producer

1981   Best Arrangement on an Instrumental Recording: "Velas," from the album *The Dude*; Quincy Jones, arranger (Johnny Mandel synthesizer and string arranger)

1981   Best Instrumental Arrangement Accompanying Vocal: "Ai No Corrida," from the album *The Dude* [cowinner with Jerry Hey]

1981   Producer of the Year

1981   Album of the Year: *The Dude* (album)

1981   Best Pop Instrumental Performance: "Velas," from the album *The Dude*

1982   Producer of the Year

1983   Record of the Year: "Beat It," Michael Jackson; Quincy Jones, producer [cowinner with Michael Jackson)

1983   Album of the Year: *Thriller*, Michael Jackson; Quincy Jones, producer (cowinner with Michael Jackson)

1983   Best Recording for Children: *E.T. The Extra-Terrestrial;* Quincy Jones, producer (cowinner with Michael Jackson, Narrator, Vocals)

1983   Producer of the Year: *Thriller* (cowinner with Michael Jackson)

1983   Best R&B Instrumental Performance: "Billie Jean (Instrumental version)," Michael Jackson, from the album *Thriller;* Quincy Jones, producer

1983   New R&B Song: "P.Y.T. (Pretty Young Thing)," Michael Jackson, from the album *Thriller;* Quincy Jones, producer

1983   Producer of the Year

1984   Best Arrangement of an Instrumental: "Grace (Gymnastics Theme)," from *The Official Music of the 23rd Olympiad in Los Angeles*; Quincy Jones with Jerry Lubbock

1984   Best R&B Song: "Yah Mo B There," James Ingram and Michael McDonald; Quincy Jones, producer

1985   Album of the Year: *We Are the World—USA for Africa/The Album* (Various artists)

1985   Record of the Year: "We Are the World," USA for Africa; Quincy Jones, producer

1985   Best Pop Performance by a Duo or Group with Vocal: "We Are the World," USA for Africa; Quincy Jones, producer

1985   Best Music Video, Short Form: *We Are the World—The Video Event*, USA
        for Africa (cowinner with Tom Trbovich, video director)
1987   Album of the Year: *Bad*, Michael Jackson
1987   Producer of the Year
1988   Record of the Year: "Man in the Mirror," Michael Jackson, from the album
        Bad
1990   Best Rap Performance by a Duo or a Group: "Back on the Block," from the
        album *Back on the Block* [with Ice-T, Melle Mel, Big Daddy Kane, Kool
        Moe Dee, Quincy D III)
1990   Best Jazz Fusion Performance: "Birdland," from the album *Back on the Block*
1990   Best Arrangement of an Instrumental: "Birdland," from the album *Back on
        the Block*
1990   Best Instrumental Arrangement Accompanying Vocals: "The Places You
        Find Love," from the album *Back on the Block*
1990   Best Pop Instrumental Performance: "Septembro (Brazilian Wedding
        Song)," Quincy Jones and various artists, from the album *Back on the
        Block*
1990   Producer of the Year
1990   Album of the Year: *Back on the Block*
1993   Best Large Jazz Ensemble Performance: *Miles and Quincy Live at
        Montreux*
1993   Best Music Video, Long Form: *Miles and Quincy Live at Montreux*, Miles
        Davis and Quincy Jones
1996   Best Instrumental Arrangement with Accompanying Vocals: "Do Nothin'
        Till You Hear from Me," Phil Collins, from the album *Q's Jook Joint*

III. Grammy Award Official Certificates and Special Recognition— The National Academy of Recording Arts and Sciences

1960   Best R&B Performance: "Let the Good Times Roll" Ray Charles, from the
        album *The Genius of Ray Charles*; Quincy Jones, Arranger/Conductor
1963   Best Performance by an Orchestra for Dancing: *This Time by Basie! Hits of
        the '50s and '60s*, Count Basie; Quincy Jones, Arranger/Conductor
1965   Song of the Year: "The Shadow of Your Smile–Love Theme," from the
        soundtrack of *The Sandpiper* (composed by Johnny Mandel and Paul
        Francis Webster); Quincy Jones, Producer
1965   Best Original Score Written for a Motion Picture or Television Show: *The
        Sandpiper*; Quincy Jones, Producer
1973   Best R&B Vocal Performance by a Female: "Master of Eyes," Aretha
        Franklin; Quincy Jones, Coproducer with Aretha Franklin
1973   Best R&B Instrumental Performance: "Q," Brothers Johnson, from the
        album *Right on Time*; Quincy Jones, Producer

1979   Best R&B Performance by a Male: "Don't Stop 'Till You Get Enough,
       Michael Jackson, from the album *Off The Wall*; Quincy Jones, Producer

1980   Best R&B Performance by a Male: *Give Me the Night*, George Benson;
       Quincy Jones, Arranger/Producer

1980   Best R&B Instrumental Performance: "Off Broadway," George Benson,
       from the album *Give Me the Night*; Quincy Jones, Producer

1980   Best Jazz Vocal Performance by a Male: "Moody's Mood," George
       Benson, from the album *Give Me the Night*; Quincy Jones, Arranger/
       Producer

1981   Best Pop Vocal Performance by a Female: *Lena Horne: The Lady and Her
       Music—Live on Broadway*, Lena Horne; Quincy Jones, Producer

1981   Best R&B Vocal Performance by a Male: "One Hundred Ways," James
       Ingram, from the album *The Dude*; Quincy Jones, Artist/Producer

1982   Best Pop Instrumental Performance: "Chariots of Fire-Theme/Dance
       Version," Ernie Watts, from the album *Chariots of Fire*; Quincy Jones,
       Producer

1983   Best Pop Vocal Performance by a Male: *Thriller*, Michael Jackson; Quincy
       Jones, Producer

1983   Best Rock Vocal Performance by a Male: "Beat It," Michael Jackson, from
       the album *Thriller*; Quincy Jones, Producer

1983   Best R&B Vocal Performance by a Male: "Billie Jean," Michael Jackson,
       from the album *Thriller*; Quincy Jones, Producer

1983   Best New R&B Song: "Billie Jean," Michael Jackson, from the album
       Thriller; Quincy Jones, Producer

1983   Best Engineered Recording (nonclassical): *Thriller*, (Michael Jackson
       (Bruce Swedien, engineer); Quincy Jones, Producer

1984   Best R&B Performance by a Duo or Group with Vocal: "Yah Mo Be
       There," James Ingram and Michael McDonald, from the album *It's Your
       Night*; Quincy Jones, Cocomposer, Arranger, Producer

1984   Best Video Album: *Making Michael Jackson's Thriller*, Michael Jackson
       (Vestron Music Video); Quincy Jones, Producer

1985   Song of the Year: "We Are the World," Michael Jackson and Lionel Richie;
       Quincy Jones, Producer/Conductor

1987   Best Engineered Recording (nonclassical): *Bad*, Michael Jackson (Bruce
       Swedien and Humberto Gatica); Quincy Jones, Producer

1990   Best R&B Performance by a Duo or Group with Vocal: "I'll Be Good to
       You," Ray Charles and Chaka Khan, from the album *Back on the Block*;
       Quincy Jones, Arranger, Artist, Producer

1990   Best Engineered Recording (nonclassical): *Back on the Block*, Quincy Jones
       (Bruce Swedien, engineer); Quincy Jones, Artist/Producer

1992   Best Contemporary Soul Gospel Album: *Handel's Messiah—A Soulful
       Celebration*, Various artists (Mervyn Warren, Producer); Quincy Jones,
       Conductor

IV. Music and Recording Awards and Special Recognition

1960   Best New Arranger of the Year—International Critics' Poll, *Down Beat* Magazine

1960   Best New Big Band of the Year—International Critics' Poll, *Down Beat* Magazine

1960   Readers' Choice Award, Jazz Arranger, Composer of the Year, *Jet* Magazine

1964   Edison International Music Award, Edison Foundation, The Netherlands

1970   Edison International Music Award, Edison Foundation, The Netherlands

1971   Arranger of the Year—Readers' Poll, *Down Beat* Magazine

1972   Big Band Album of the Year—*Smackwater Jack*, NAACP Image Awards

1972   Edison International Music Award, Edison Foundation, The Netherlands

1972   Arranger of the Year—Readers' Poll, *Down Beat* Magazine

1972   Trendsetters Award, *Billboard* Magazine

1973   Arranger of the Year—Readers' Poll, *Down Beat* Magazine

1974   Best Jazz Artist—*You've Got It Bad, Girl*, NAACP Image Awards

1974   Arranger of the Year—Readers' Poll, *Down Beat* Magazine

1975   Best Jazz Artist—*Body Heat*, NAACP Image Awards

1976   Best Composer, Jazz—*I Heard That*, *Ebony* Magazine Music Award

1976   Musician of the Year, Jazz—*I Heard That*, *Ebony* Magazine Music Award

1976   Big Band Leader, Jazz—*I Heard That*, *Ebony* Magazine Music Award

1976   Arranger of the Year, Jazz—*I Heard That*, *Ebony* Magazine Music Award

1978   American Black Achievement Award for Music—*Sounds . . . And Stuff Like That!!*, *Ebony* Magazine Music Award

1978   Edison International Music Award, Edison Foundation, The Netherlands

1979   Edison International Music Award, Edison Foundation, The Netherlands

1979   Most Popular Arranger, Producer, Composer, Black College Radio Convention

1980   Best Musical Score for a Motion Picture—*The Wiz*, NAACP Image Awards

1980   Producer of the Year, *Billboard* Magazine

1981   Best Jazz Album—*The Dude*, NAACP Image Awards

1981   Album of the Year—*The Dude*, NAACP Image Awards

1982   American Black Achievement Award for Music—*Thriller*, *Ebony* Magazine Music Award

1982   Golden Note Award, American Society of Composers, Authors, and Publishers (ASCAP)

1982   Trendsetters Award, *Billboard* Magazine

1983   Producer of the Decade, NAACP Image Awards

1983   Producer of the Year, *Billboard* Magazine

1983   Jazz Composer/Songwriter of the Year, *Playboy* Music Award

1984   Special Recognition, MTV Video Award

1984   Jazz Composer/Songwriter of the Year, *Playboy* Music Award

1985   American Black Achievement Award for Music—"We Are the World,"
       Ebony Magazine Music Award
1985   Jazz Composer/Songwriter of the Year, *Playboy* Music Award
1986   Special Recognition for "We Are the World," American Music Award
1986   Best Motion Picture—*The Color Purple*, NAACP Image Awards
1986   Record of the Year, *Playboy* Music Award
1986   Jazz Composer/Songwriter of the Year, *Playboy* Music Award
1988   Luminary Award, American Society of Young Musicians
1990   Best Album—*Back on the Block*, NAACP Image Awards
1990   Hall of Fame Award, NAACP Image Awards
1990   Nesuhi Ertegun—Cartier Man of the Year, International Music Market
       Conference—Cannes, France
1990   Entrepreneur of the Year, *USA Today*/Financial News Network
1994   Golden Score Award, American Society of Composers, Authors, and Pub-
       lishers (ASCAP)
1996   Outstanding Jazz Artist—*Q's Jook Joint*, NAACP Image Awards
1996   Entertainer of the Year, NAACP Image Awards
1996   Entertainer of the Year, *Weekly Variety*
1997   Outstanding Jazz Artist—*Q Live in Paris Circa 1960*, NAACP Image Awards
2000   Outstanding Jazz Artist—*From Q, With Love*, NAACP Image Awards

V. Film and Television Awards

1967   Academy Award Nomination, Best Original Music Score: *In Cold Blood*
1967   Academy Award Nomination, Best Original Song: "The Eyes of Love"
       from the film *Banning* (music by Quincy Jones and lyrics by Bob
       Russell)
1968   Academy Award Nomination, Best Original Song: "For Love of Ivy" from
       For Love of Ivy (music by Quincy Jones and lyrics by Bob Russell)
1970   Golden Globe Nomination, Best Original Song from a Motion Picture:
       "The Time for Love Is Anytime" from *Cactus Flower*
1970   Emmy Award Nomination, Outstanding Achievement in Music Composi-
       tion: *The Bill Cosby Show* (NBC)
1973   Golden Globe Nomination, Best Original Score for a Motion Picture: *The
       Getaway*
1977   Emmy Award, Outstanding Achievement in Music Composition for a
       Series or a Single Program of a Series: *Roots—Episode I* (ABC) (co-
       winner with Gerald Fried)
1978   Academy Award Nomination, Best Adaptation Score: *The Wiz*
1985   Academy Award Nomination, Best Original Song: "Miss Celie's Blues
       (Sister)" from *The Color Purple* (music by Quincy Jones and Rod Temper-
       ton, lyrics by Quincy Jones, Rod Temperton, and Lionel Richie)

1985   Academy Award Nomination, Best Original Score: *The Color Purple*
1985   Academy Award Nomination, Best Picture: *The Color Purple* (Quincy Jones, Producer)
1986   Golden Globe Nomination, Best Original Score for a Motion Picture: *The Color Purple*
1995   Emmy Award Nomination, Outstanding Informational Series: *The History of Rock 'n' Roll: Punk*
1996   Winner of the distinguished Oscar, The Jean Hersholt Humanitarian Award, from the Academy of Motion Picture Arts and Sciences, for humanitarian efforts that have brought credit to the motion picture industry
1996   Emmy Award Nomination, Outstanding Variety, Music or Comedy Special: *The 68th Annual Academy Awards*

VI. Lifetime Achievement Awards

1984   American Academy of Achievement Golden Plate, American Academy
1989   Lifetime Achievement, National Academy of Songwriters
1990   American Black Achievement Lifetime Award, *Ebony* Magazine
1990   Heritage Award for Lifetime Achievement, *Soul Train* Music Awards
1991   Lifetime Achievement Award, Rose d'Or, Montreux, France
1993   Trumpet "Living Legend" Award for Outstanding Career Achievement, Turner Broadcasting Systems
1994   Lifetime Achievement, *Essence* Magazine
1996   Pioneer in Black Achievement Lifetime Achievement Award, The Brotherhood Crusade
1996   Lifetime Achievement Award, The Thelonious Monk Institute of Jazz
1996   Thurgood Marshall Lifetime Achievement Award, NAACP Legal Defense Fund
1997   Vanguard Award for Lifetime Achievement, National Academy of Songwriters
1999   Henry Mancini Lifetime Achievement Award, American Society of Composers, Authors, and Publishers (ASCAP)
1999   Oscar Micheaux Award for Outstanding Career as a Film and Television Producer, Producers Guild of America
1999   Influential Jazz Artist of the Century (shared with Louis Armstrong, Duke Ellington, Charlie Parker, Miles Davis, and Wynton Marsalis), *Time* Magazine
1999   Media Spotlight Award for Lifetime Achievement, Amnesty International
2007   George and Ira Gershwin Award for Lifetime Achievement, University of California, Los Angeles
2008   Lifetime Achievement, BET (Black Entertainment Television)

2008   Lifetime Achievement Award, NAACP (National Association for the
         Advancement of Colored People)
2009   Lifetime Achievement Award, AARP (American Association of Retired
         Persons)
2009   Lifetime Achievement Award, Seattle City of Music Outstanding
         Achievement Award

VII. Humanitarian, Arts, and Humanities Awards

1971   Distinguished Service Award, The Brotherhood Crusade (Socioeconomic
         and America's Urban Communities)
1982   Spirit of Life "Man of the Year", City of Hope (Cancer Research)
1986   Norma Zarsky Humanitarian Crystal Award, Women In Film (efforts to
         improve human condition)
1986   Whitney Young Jr. Award, National Urban League
1986   Humanitarian of the Year, T. J. Martell Foundation (Leukemia, Cancer and
         AIDS Research)
1990   Honors Award, Los Angeles Arts Council
1991   Angel Award, Center for Population Options
1992   Spirit of Liberty Award, People for the American Way
1993   Entertainment and Community Achievement Award, NAACP Legal
         Defense Fund
1994   Distinguished Service Award, Northside Center for Child Development
1994   Equal Opportunity Award, National Urban League
1994   President's Committee on the Arts & Humanities, Office of the President,
         Washington, D.C.
1995   Horatio Alger Award, Horatio Alger Association
1996   Time Warner Ambassador of Good Will, Time Warner, Inc.
1996   International Committee Award, Intercambios Culturales
1996   Distinguished Honoree, Young Audiences of America
1996   Humanitarian Award, The H.E.L.P Group
1998   Spirit Award, Children's Defense Fund
1999   Ellis Island Medal of Honor, National Ethnic Coalition of Organizations
1999   Seasons of Hope, AMFAR (The Foundation for AIDS Research)
2000   Lena Horne Legend Award, Citizens Committee for New York
2001   Ted Arison Award, National Foundation for Advancement in the Arts
2001   Inductee, American Academy of Arts and Sciences
2001   Honoree, Kennedy Center, Washington, D.C.
2005   Honoree, Evening of Stars, United Negro College Fund
2005   Inducted for outstanding achievement as a producer, Dance Music Hall
         of Fame
2008   California Hall of Fame, California Museum, Sacramento, California

2008   Humanitarian Award, BET
2008   Unity Through Music, Thank Q: A World Music Tribute to the Humanitarian Works of Quincy Jones
2008   The Quincy Jones Performing Arts Center, Seattle, Washington
2009   Humanitarian Award, African Diaspora Heritage Trail Award
2009   Be Beautiful to Yourself Jet Fashion Show in Support of Down Syndrome Research and Care, Quincy Jones Exceptional Advocate Award
2009   Humanitarian Award, Ludacris Foundation Commitment to Community Service Award
2009   Humanitarian Award, Global Down Syndrome Foundation, Quincy Jones Exceptional Advocacy Award

VIII. International and Domestic Distinguished Awards, Citations, and Special Recognitions

1973   Citation of Excellence, Texas House of Representatives
1973   Citation of Excellence, Canadian National Exhibition
1974   Special Recognition, California State Assembly
1976   In Special Recognition of the 20th Anniversary in Music, City of Philadelphia, PA
1980   Hollywood Walk of Fame, Hollywood, CA
1982   Key to the City, Indianapolis, IN
1985   Centennial Hall of Honor, State of Washington
1990   Living Treasure Governor's Arts Award, State of California
1990   Officier de la Legion d' Honneur, Republic of France
1990   Japan Grand Prix Album of the Year, Jazz Fusion: *Back on the Block*
1991   Alexander Pushkin Award, Union of Soviet Socialist Republics
1991   Lifetime Achievement Award, Rose d'Or, Montreux, France
1994   Polar Music Prize, Royal Swedish Academy of Music
1995   Rudolph Valentino Award, Republic of Italy
1996   Distinguished Arts & Letters Award, French Ministry of Culture, U.S. Ambassador Pamela Harriman
1999   Trophée des Arts, French Institute Alliance Française
2000   Crystal Award, World Economic Forum, Davos, Switzerland
2000   Key to the City, Paris, France
2000   National Medal of the Humanities, National Endowment of the Humanities, awarded by President Bill Clinton
2001   Commandeur de la Legion d' Honneur, Republic of France
2001   Marion Anderson Award, City of Philadelphia
2009   Distinguished Fellow, Royal Welsh College of Music and Drama, Cardiff, Wales
2009   Global Contribution, Clinton Global Citizen Award
2010   National Medal of the Arts, awarded by President Barack Obama

IX. Honorary Academic Degrees, Awards, Medals, and Special Recognition

1983   Honorary Doctor of Arts, Berklee College of Music
1985   Honorary Doctor of Arts and Letters, Howard University
1990   Honorary Doctor of Philosophy, Seattle University
1991   Honorary Doctor of Arts, Wesleyan University
1991   Scopus Award, Hebrew University
1992   Honorary Doctor of Arts, Loyola University
1992   Honorary Doctor of Arts and Letters, Brandeis University
1993   Honorary Doctor of Philosophy, Clark University
1994   Legend in Leadership Award, Emory University
1995   Honorary Doctor of Letters, Claremont University Graduate School
1995   Chancellor's Medal, University of California, Los Angeles
1996   Honorary Doctor of Fine Arts, University of Connecticut
1996   Magnum Opus Award for Lifetime Achievement, University of Southern
        California School of Music
1996   Lifetime Achievement Award, Thelonious Monk Jazz Institute
1996   Harvard Foundation Medal for Intercultural and Race Relations, Harvard
        University
1997   Honorary Doctor of Fine Arts, Harvard University
1997   Honorary Doctor of Fine Arts, American Film Institute
1998   Honorary Doctor of Music, University of Southern California
1999   Honorary Doctor of Fine Arts, Tuskegee University
1999   Honorary Doctor of Fine Arts, New York University
1999   Honorary Doctor of Fine Arts, University of Miami
1999   Frederick D. Patterson Award, United Negro College Fund
1999   Candle of Light Award, Morehouse College
2000   Quincy Jones Professorship of African American Music-Endowed Chair,
        Harvard University/AOL Time Warner, Inc.
2000   W. E. B. Du Bois Medal, Harvard University
2001   Inductee, American Academy of Arts and Sciences
2007   Honorary Doctor of Humanities, Morehouse College
2007   Q Prize named and instituted in honor of Quincy Jones, Harvard Univer-
        sity School of Public Health
2007   Mentor of the Year, Harvard University School of Public Health
2008   Honorary Doctor of Music, Princeton University
2008   Honorary Doctor of Arts, University of Washington
2008   Honorary Doctor of Arts, Washington University (St. Louis, Missouri)
2009   Distinguished Fellow, Royal Welsh College of Music and Drama, Cardiff,
        Wales
2010   Honorary Doctor of Music, Indiana University

NOTES

Introduction

1. Feather 1975: 74.
2. Amiri Baraka was one of the major innovators of the Black Arts Movements of the mid-1960s. A major focus of this artistic movement was centered on the influences of popular music. One of the major arguments was that jazz and other African American music styles were the language that developed to give African Americans uncensored accounts of their experiences. Baraka and other civil activists also believed that African American music could promote a distinct black identity and encourage a sense of pride that was vital to the civil rights struggle.
3. See Floyd (1995).
4. Small (1998[1987]): 50.
5. Wilson 1995: 26–34. There are other works that examine African American music and culture that employ W. E. B. Du Bois's paradigms of double consciousness such as the works of Monson 1999: 31–65 and Gilroy (1993).
6. Rose 1994: 5.
7. See the works of O'Meally (1998), Gates (1988), Gates and McKay (1997), and Baker (1984).
8. The Harlem Renaissance greatly influenced African American music, literary, and artistic production. It emerged in the early 1920s as an interdisciplinary movement—arts, literature, politics, and music—that sought to define African Americans as strong, articulate, educated, empowered, and possessing an appreciation of African and African American history and heritage. For readings that focus on the Harlem Renaissance see Smith and Jones 2000: 2, 163–66, Watson (1995), Kellner (1984), Bontemps (1972), and Huggins (1971).
9. See Locke (1936) and (1925).
10. Smith and Jones 2000: 165.
11. W. E. B. Du Bois was a leading writer, social activist, scholar, professor, and administrator that assisted in shaping the intellectual life of the Harlem Renaissance era. His book *The Souls of Black Folk* (1903) focuses on race relations in American society.
12. The topic of migrating narratives is presented in a work by Griffin (1995); talking books and speakerly texts are discussed in a work by Gates (1988). Griffin and Gates use these topics as literary symbolism and metaphoric tropes to vividly demonstrate the historical significance and preservation of writing, music, and other artistic forms as communicative devices relaying the African American experience in American society.

13. See Floyd (1995), Berry 1988: 3–12, Stuckey (1987), Raboteau (1978), Levine (1977), and Herskovits 1958[1941].

14. Jones 2001: 285.

15. See *New York Times*, March 28, 1956, p. 33.

16. See *New York Times* March 30, 1956, p. 27.

17. Quincy Jones quote from "Arts Education in America," *Huffington Post*, May 9, 2009. www.huffingtonpost.com.

18. See Dvořák 1895: 428–34, and Burkholder, Grout, and Palisca 2006: 744. Dvořák composed his Symphony No. 9 during an extended appointment in the United States as artistic director of the National Conservatory of Music in New York. He had been hired with the expectation of demonstrating to his students how to create a new national style of classical/art music for the United States. However, Dvořák believed that a truly national music could only be derived from folk (ethnic) traditions. As a result, Dvořák looked to the music of Native Americans and African Americans. After studying Native American melodies and hearing Harry T. Burleigh (1866–1949), one of his African American students at the Conservatory, sing plantation songs and spirituals, Dvořák incorporated elements of those idioms into this symphony.

19. Sergei Diaghilev (1872–1929) was a producer and director of the Ballets Russes who assembled a team of artists that included painters, dancers, choreographers, conductors, and composers.

20. See Chilton 1996: 289.

21. Burkholder, Grout, and Palisca 2006: 825 and Bonds 2006: 559–61. Stravinsky became interested in the use of ragtime in his works during World War I. Because of the wartime economy Stravinsky was forced to turn away from composing large orchestra pieces of his early ballets toward writing for smaller staged works employing small combinations of instruments. *L' histoire du soldat* (The Soldier's Tale, 1918) called for six solo instruments in pairs (violin and double bass, clarinet and bassoon, cornet and trombone) and one percussionist to play interludes in a spoken narration and dialogue. Although Stravinsky had originally composed the work *Ragtime for Eleven Instruments* (1917–18), he continued to be influenced by the style and later composed a piano arrangement also titled *Ragtime*.

22. Hajdu (1996) and Gridley 2005: 104–21. From 1939 until 1967 Duke Ellington worked closely with Billy Strayhorn (1915–1967) on numerous compositions. Several compositions are credited to Strayhorn, including "Take the A Train," which replaced "East St. Louis Toodle-oo" as the Duke Ellington band's theme.

23. Burkholder, Grout, and Palisca 2006: 862. Also see Ellington (1976).

24. Jones 1976: D15 and Holden 1980: D23.

25. See *The Official Music of the 23rd Olympiad in Los Angeles*, Columbia: BJS-39322 (1984).

26. Most of the music for *Fantasia 2000* was performed by the Chicago Symphony Orchestra with James Levine conducting all works except George

Gershwin's composition *Rhapsody in Blue* (1924), which was performed by the Philharmonic Orchestra.

27. See Barnet, Nemerov, and Taylor 2004: 232–33.

28. Some of the reference sources on Jones include Gates (2009) and (2004), Jones (2008) and (2001), Young (2008), Bayer (2001), Kavanaugh (1998), and Horricks (1985).

Chapter 1

1. Lawn 2007: 107.

2. Stride is a type of piano style that developed out of ragtime. The style often required the pianist to have fast, virtuosic technique. Stride pianists placed heavy emphasis on the left hand, employing bass notes on the first and third beats of each measure and chords on the second and fourth beats while the right hand played elaborate scale and melodic passages. Innovators of the stride style include James P. Johnson and Willie "The Lion" Smith. See Silvester (1988).

3. Territorial bands were basically dance bands that performed in various regions of the United States from approximately the 1920s through the 1960s. Many of these bands helped disseminate popular music such as jazz to many areas. Some of the most popular territorial bands include the Cab Calloway band, Jimmy Lunceford Orchestra, and Bennie Moten's Kansas City Orchestra.

4. Jones 2001: 30–31.

5. Terry 1990: 25.

6. De Barros 1993: 102.

7. Clark Terry was also a member of what was known as "The Count Basie Seven" that included musicians such as Marshall Gray and Wendell Gray. For references and biographical sources on Clark Terry, see Terry (2011), Lees (2001), and Jimmy Owens's interview titled, *Oral History interview with Clark Terry, 15 September 1993* (video recording) produced by the New York Public Library, Schomburg Center Video Oral History (part of the Louis Armstrong Oral History project).

8. Early 2001: 22.

9. See Paynter 2000: B1–3. This article also includes a photo of the 1948 Garfield High School Military Band with Jones and Calvo.

10. After leaving Seattle in the 1950s, Robert "Bumps" Blackwell (1918–1985) became a successful rock 'n' roll producer and songwriter. He produced several songs for Little Richard, Sam Cooke, and other artists. Blackwell also wrote or co-wrote several hits songs that include "All Shook Up," "Rip It Up," "Good Golly Miss Molly," "Tutti Frutti," and "Long Tall Sally."

11. See Buddy Catlett's interview with Peter Monaghan and Lola Pedrini 2001: 4, 6, 12.

12. Hampton 1989: 94–95.

13. De Barros 1993: 109.

14. Jones 2001: 66–70.

15. Stewart 1985: 17.

16. A video copy of "Slide Hamp Slide," is located at the Archive Center, National Museum of American History, the Ernie Smith Jazz Film Collection, 1894–1979 #491. Willie Bryant (1908–1964) was a jazz bandleader, vocalist, and disc jockey. In the mid-1930s he formed his first band that included Teddy Wilson, Benny Carter, Ben Webster and others. In the late 1940s he was the host of *Uptown Jubilee* (also known as *Harlem Jubilee* and *Sugar Hill Times*), an African American variety show that aired for a short time on CBS-TV.

17. Tiegel 2001: 26.

18. During the European tour Monk Montgomery used a prototype of the Fender bass. The Fender Guitar Company wanted to feature the new bass with one of the most dynamic bands they could find; Hampton's band was selected.

19. Hampton 1989: 100.

20. Big Maybelle's version of "Whole Lot of Shakin' Goin' On" was recorded before Jerry Lee Lewis's 1957 hit version of the song.

21. Adam Clayton Powell Jr. (1908–1972) was an American politician and pastor who represented the Harlem section of Manhattan in New York City in the U.S. House of Representatives from 1945 through 1971. Powell was the first African American elected to Congress in New York. In 1961 he became chairman of the Education and Labor Commission.

22. See Davenport (2009) and Harker 2005: 180–81.

23. Gillespie 1979: 413. As early as 1954 Jones assisted in organizing and performing with the Gillespie bands, and he appears as a trumpeter on several of Gillespie's albums. See the albums *Afro*, Norgan MG N-1003 (1954), and *Diz Big Band*, Verve MGV-8178 (EP) (1954).

24. Feather 1956: 2.

25. Monson 2007: 118–19.

26. *Ibid.*

27. Porter 1997: 202–3. Also see Taylor (1957).

28. Her American students included Aaron Copland, Virgil Thompson, Roy Harris, Walter Piston, Ross Lee Finney, Philip Glass, and Elliott Carter.

29. *Daphnis et Chloé* (1909–12) is a ballet with music by Maurice Ravel. *The Firebird* (1910) is a ballet with music by Igor Stravinsky. For Readings on Ravel and Stravinsky see Zank (2005), Joseph (2001), Ivry (2000), Mawer (2000), and Taruskin (1996).

30. Parnell 1960: 9.

31. Jones 2001: 133, 306.

32. The Bibliothèque Nationale de France (National Library of France) has archival holdings of correspondence between Jones and Boulanger titled *Deux lettres de Quincy Jones à Nadia Boulanger, 1958, 1960*, cataloged as FRBNF 39833429. Jones narrated the documentary *Mademoiselle: A Portrait of Nadia Boulanger* (1987). There are several reference sources that examine the career and life of Nadia Boulanger. Also see books by Marsack (1988), Spycket (1992), and Campbell (1984).

33. See Campbell (1975). Also see Stewart 1985: 18.

34. See Fisk University, Nashville, TN, *Institute for Research in Black American Music Collection, 1920–1985.* This organizational Development and Infrastructure series consist of records documenting the Institute for Research in Black American Music and the framework created to implement its objectives. This extensive collection include correspondence from notable artists and scholars such as Quincy Jones, Charley Pride, Albert J. Raboteau, Bernice Johnson-Reagon, Max Roach, and Samuel A. Floyd.

35. For discussion of *The Black Requiem* see Lyndon 1998: 294–95. *The Black Requiem* was composed and conducted by Quincy Jones for the celebration of Ray Charles's twenty-fifth anniversary in the entertainment industry, premiering in February 1971 Houston with the city's Symphony Orchestra and the Prairie View College Chorale. The music blended slave songs, spirituals, and jazz. *The Black Requiem* has never been released in recorded form.

36. Aldore 1990: 74.

37. See "Quincy Jones Urges Rappers to Drop the 'N' Word." World Entertainment News Network, November 8, 2005.

38. See "Quincy Jones: Rappers Need to Learn About Their Forefathers." World Entertainment News Network, November 4, 2005.

39. See articles by Blair 2002: 80; Fagien 2002: 10; De Barros 2001: 4–7, 11–15, 24; Jisi 2001: 50–52, 54, 56; Nai 1998: 15–27; Uszler 1997: 40–43; Voce 1996: 8–9.

40. See "Smithsonian Program Preserves Our Rich Jazz Heritage," *International Musician* 102(4): 24 (2004), and "Jazz Appreciation Month, April 2002," *Music Educators Journal* 88(5): 15.

41. See Randolph (2007), Wild (2007), Houston and Bagert (2006), Turner (2006), Cogan and Clark (2003), Swedien (2003), Hasse (2000), Levy (2000), Boston (1998), and Percelay (1994).

42. Jones 1997: 19.

43. Jones 2008(c): 60.

44. Jones 2008(d): 44.

45. See "Honoring Quincy Jones," *Congressional Records*, Vol. 149 (June 23, 2003), Page S7376-S7377.

46. The Q Prize is supported by Time Warner and individual donors. In 2008, the prize was awarded to El Sistema, a groundbreaking organization in Venezuela that has continually demonstrated the power of music in transforming the lives of at-risk children. José Antonio Abreu founded El Sistema in 1975, mostly from improvised circumstances, through a combination of early music education and an extensive network of youth orchestras of Venezuela. The program counts among its alumni maestro Gustavo Dudamel, a young and charismatic classical music director of the Los Angeles Philharmonic. The press release of the Q Prize award to Abreu can be found at hsph.harvard.edu/news/press-release/2008-releases.

47. See "LAUSD Honors Quincy Jones with a school in the music producer's name," written by Jason Lewis on December 22, 2010, lasentinel.net.

48. Nicholson 1998: 106.
49. Siders 1969: 13.

Chapter 2

1. In 1954 Jones also organized an ensemble for his collaboration with Clifford Brown and Helen Merrill on the album *Helen Merrill with Clifford Brown*, EmArcy MG-36006 (1954).

2. In 1954 Brown and drummer Max Roach organized a group that became known as the Clifford Brown–Max Roach Quintet, which recorded the album *Brown and Roach, Inc.* (1954). One of Brown's historic recordings is *The Complete Sessions Vols. 1, 2, and 3* (1953).

3. Quincy Jones served as a composer, arranger, and instrumentalist on several of Art Farmer's albums.

4. For a compilation of Jones's early work in Europe see the album *Quincy Jones Swedish All Stars*, Prestige PrLp-172 (1953).

5. Also see the album *Sonny Stitt Plays Arrangements from the Pen of Quincy Jones*, Roost LP-2204 (1955).

6. Hentoff 1954(a): 35 and 1954(b): 12.

7. See "Jones Forming Band," *Down Beat* 26(9): 12 (April 30, 1959).

8. In Europe, one of the big band musicians with whom Quincy Jones collaborated was Harry Arnold (1920–1971), a Swedish saxophonist and bandleader. From 1956 to 1965 Arnold led the Swedish Radio Big Band that featured many of Sweden's best-known jazz musicians—Arne Domnérus, Bengt Hallberg, and Åke Persson. Jones also served as a conductor, composer, and arranger for the album, *Harry Arnold + Big Band + Quincy Jones = Jazz!*, Metronome MLP-15010 (1958).

9. See Jones 1959: 16–17.

10. *Ibid.*

11. Parnell 1960: 8.

12. Harold Arlen is regarded as one of the foremost jazz-oriented contributors to the Great American Songbook from the 1920s through the 1960s. Some of his popular music standards include "Over the Rainbow," "Let's Fall in Love," "Stormy Weather," and "Blues in the Night." For a complete biographical and reference source on Arlen, see Jablonski (1996).

13. The Martin Beck Theatre, located at 302 West 45th Street, was opened in 1924 by vaudeville promoter Martin Beck (1967–1960). In 2003 the theater was renamed the Al Hirschfeld Theatre in honor of the famous caricaturist Al Hirschfeld (1903–2003), who was famous for his satirical black-and-white portraits of Broadway celebrities.

14. Because of negative criticism of the musical *St. Louis Woman*, actress Lena Horne refused the starring role. When the show premiered there were several

protests by African Americans outside the theatre, which initially negatively affected ticket sales.

15. *Porgy & Bess* is an opera with music by George Gershwin, libretto by DuBose Heywood, and lyrics by Ira Gershwin and DuBose Heywood. It featured an African American cast, and was first performed in 1935. *Porgy & Bess* incorporated blues and jazz idioms into the classical form of opera; Gershwin considered it one of his finest works.

16. See "Quincy Scoring Show," *Down Beat* 26(21): 12 (October 15, 1959).

17. *Ibid.*

18. *Ibid.*

19. Funke 1959: X1, *New York Times* (October 18).

20. Jones 2001: 135.

21. *New York Times* 1959: 39 (November 17).

22. Jones also served as a composer and arranger for several of Terry's recordings: *Clark Terry*, EmArcy MG-36007 (1955); *Clark Terry in the P.M.*, EmArcy EP-1-6108 (EP) (1955); *Swahili*, Trip Jazz TLP-5528 (1955).

23. Jones also served as a conductor, composer and arranger for the album *Introducing Jimmy Cleveland and His All-Stars*, EmArcy MG-36066 (1955).

24. In recent years Woods recorded many of Jones's compositions and arrangements in a compilation titled *This Is How I Feel About Quincy*, Jazzed Media B000TPVRHG (2004).

25. The album *Patti Bown Plays Big Piano* is catalogued on Columbia Records as CL 1379 (1958).

26. Liston is also featured on several Dizzy Gillespie and Quincy Jones album recordings: *Dizzy in South America*, Vol. 1 and 2, Cap Records ASIN: B00000JSOJ (1956); *Newport '61*, Mercury SR-60653 (1961); *The Birth of a Band*, Mercury MG-20444 (1956); *Q Live in Paris Circa 1960*, Qwest 46190 (1996).

27. Many of Melba Liston's compositions and arrangements are located in the Center for Black Music Research Library and Archives in Chicago. In addition to her work as a composer and arranger in jazz, Liston served as an arranger for recording companies—especially Motown—and for performers such as Marvin Gaye, Ruth Brown, and Gloria Lynne.

28. Jones also served as a producer and arranger on Julius Watkins's album *French Horns for My Lady*, Philips PHM-200-001 (1960).

29. Jones 2001: 141.

30. See Nai (1998), a biographical profile of jazz saxophonist and trumpeter Floyd Standifer. In this article Standifer discusses his work with the Quincy Jones band and his early experiences in hearing and playing jazz in the 1930s through the 1960s. Also see Buddy Catlett's interview with Peter Monaghan and Lola Pedrini 2001: 4, 6, 12.

31. See Waggoner, *New York Times* 1959: X3 (December 20).

32. *Ibid.*

33. The Algerian war crisis lasted from 1954–1962. There are numerous historical sources that examine the crisis in Algeria such as Renaud (2008), Shepard (2006), and Alexander, Evans, and Keiger (2002).

34. Frantz Fanon was a psychiatrist, philosopher, revolutionary, and author from Martinique. He was influential in studying the effects of colonialism. Fanon wrote other important books such as *Peau noire, masques blancs* (*Black skin, white mask*) 1971[1952].

35. Tiegel 2001: 28.

36. Dance 1974: 298–99.

37. Jones 2001: 302.

38. *Q Live in Paris Circa 1960*, Qwest Records 46490 (1996).

39. See *New York Amsterdam News* 1960: 19 (December 17).

40. Feather 1975: 74.

41. Also see *Free and Easy Live in Stockholm* 1960, Ancha Trading ANC 9500; *Pure Delight: The Essence of Quincy Jones and His Orchestra (1953–1964)*, Razor & Tie B000002Z9P (1995); *Quincy Jones and His Orchestra at Newport '61*, Mercury SR-60653 (1961); *The Great Wide World of Quincy Jones—Live in Zurich*, Mercury 195J-32 (1961); *The Quincy Jones Big Band, Lausanne 1960/Swiss Radio Days, Jazz Series, Vol. 1*, TCB SA (1995).

Chapter 3

1. Jones 2001: 99.

2. The American Society of Composers, Authors, and Publishers (ASCAP), a not-for-profit organization to protect members' musical copyrights, was founded in 1914 in New York City.

3. King Pleasure first achieved fame by singing the Eddie Jefferson vocalese classic "Moody's Mood for Love," based on James Moody's saxophone solo to the song "I'm in the Mood for Love." In his career Pleasure performed and recorded with several female jazz vocalists, including Annie Ross and Betty Carter. The song "I'm Gone" is in the album *King Pleasure Sings*, Prestige 208 (1955).

4. See the album *Julian "Cannonball" Adderley*, EmArcy MG-36043 (1955). In the mid-1950s Adderley relocated from Tampa, Florida, to New York City. Upon his arrival he and his brother Nat Adderley visited the Café Bohemia in Greenwich Village, where Oscar Pettiford was leading a small combo in which Jerome Richardson (tenor saxophone) was absent from the performance that night. Pettiford allowed Adderley, then an unknown, to perform with the combo. Adderley's musical and technical virtuosity left both the musicians and audience astonished.

5. Washington was a vocalist very much influenced by jazz, blues, and gospel music. Similar to Jones, Washington had also performed in Hampton's band (from 1943 to 1945) and recorded with Hampton on the Decca label several recordings: *Flyin' Home (1942–1945)*, MCA 42349; and re-releases *Hamp: The Legendary Decca*

Recordings, GRP 652, and *Lionel Hampton and His Orchestra 1945–1946*, Classics 922. Jones's arrangement of "Makin' Whoopee" is on the album *The Swingin' Miss "D,"* EmArcy 36104 (1957).

6. A koto is a traditional Japanese stringed musical instrument with thirteen strings strung over thirteen moveable bridges along the width of the instrument. Players of the koto can adjust the string pitches by moving these bridges before playing and pluck the strings using three finger picks placed on the thumb, index, and middle fingers. Also see *Blues for Trumpet and Koto* (1963), a one-hour Japanese television drama that Jones scored and acted in with soap opera actor Anthony George. Marvin Hamlisch also composed some of the music.

7. The song "Faith" is on the album *Louis*, Mercury 61081 (1964).

8. Eldridge is often considered a link between swing and modern jazz, with a trumpet style that some saw as a bridge between those of Louis Armstrong and Dizzy Gillespie. Drummer Gene Krupa (1909–1973) and vocalist Anita O'Day (1919–2006) are two important figures in jazz history. Krupa's drumming can be heard on several popular recordings, including "Sing, Sing, Sing (with a Swing)" (1937) with Benny Goodman and His Orchestra and "Drum Boogie" (1941). O'Day was a white jazz singer who performed in the bands of Gene Krupa, Woody Herman, and Stan Kenton. She also recorded popular albums on the Verve label, such as *Anita Sings the Most* (1957) with jazz pianist Oscar Peterson.

9. "Let Me Off Uptown" is recorded on *Drummer Man*, Verve 2008 (1956).

10. See MacDonald 1974: 1.

11. Bebop musicians such as Charlie Parker, Dizzy Gillespie, and Thelonious Monk elevated jazz to a new level not only with high standards of performance. Although not entirely new in jazz, one of the most significant technical devices among the bebop musicians was developing improvisational themes ranging from classical music, blues, pop tunes, children's songs, and folk ditties. A prime example is Charlie Parker's rendition of "Salt Peanuts" in Paris in 1949, during which he began improvising on Stravinsky's *The Rite of Spring*. Also, in the 1950s during a television performance of an arrangement of Tadd Dameron's composition "Hot House," Dizzy Gillespie improvised on a theme from Bizet's opera *Carmen*.

12. MacDonald 1974: 1.

13. Jones 2001: 76.

14. A walking bass is a style of bass line in which each beat of each measure of music receives a separate tone. Normally, when a bass players plays a walking line the tones follow an ascending and descending (or vice versa) motions on scale-like passages.

15. Some of Jones's early arrangements with the Hampton orchestra are located at University of Idaho, in the Lionel Hampton Library Collection, International Jazz Collections. Copies of these arrangements are also available online. Some of Jones's compositions and arrangements are located at the University of California, Los Angeles Performing Arts Special Collections Folios of Printed Music Scores.

16. In two historical sessions in 1949 and 1950, Miles Davis collaborated with white arranger Gil Evans on a recording session of a nine-piece band that most jazz historians identify as Miles Davis's Nonet or "Birth of the Cool" band. This unique jazz session, comprised of some of the best musicians, performed complex arrangements with high levels of lyricism.

17. Heckman 2001: 56.

18. Jones recently contributed a commentary on arranging and traveling on a State Department tour. See "The Power of Jazz" by Quincy Jones; Jam Sessions: America's Jazz Ambassadors Embrace the World, meridian.org/jazzambassadors. Jones's commentary is included as part of an exhibition organized in 2008 at the Meridian International Center's White-Meyer Cafritz Galleries in Washington, D.C. The exhibition uses photographs and documents to chronicle the State Department's sponsored travels of American jazz artists around the globe from the 1950s through the 1970s, serving as cultural diplomats.

19. For recording of Jones's arrangement of "Moanin'," see the album *Q Live in Paris Circa 1960*, recorded at the Alhambra Theatre, Qwest 46190 (1996).

20. The Brill Building, located at 1619 Broadway in New York City near Times Square, was erected in the early part of the 1930s. Popular music songwriters and producers that have been associated with the Brill Building include Burt Bacharach, Paul Anka, Neil Diamond, Gerry Goffin, Carole King, Barry Mann, Cynthia Weil, Howard Greenfield, Neil Sedaka, Jerry Leiber, Mike Stoller, and many others.

21. Jones 2001: 99.

22. Hentoff 1954(b): 12.

23. In his career, John Lewis (1920–2001) composed numerous works ranging from ballet to film music with instrumentation ranging from jazz combos to symphony orchestras. Lewis was also a member of the Modern Jazz Quartet with Milt Jackson (vibraphone), Percy Heath (bass), and Connie Kay (drums). The Modern Jazz Quartet was known not only for improvisation but also for sophisticated arrangements and compositions.

24. See Horricks 1955: 10, 28–29. This biographical profile includes excerpts from Quincy Jones's letters about several musicians (Gigi Gryce, Clifford Brown, and Thelonious Monk) and his comments on jazz and classical music. Also see Horricks 1957: 9–10.

25. See *Vaughan and Violins*, Mercury MG-203370 (1958).

26. For a complete biographical sketch of Sarah Vaughan, see Gourse (1993).

27. See Jones 1963: 12.

28. See Lee (1989); Fry 2002: 372–73.

29. Boogie-woogie is a rhythmically charged and blues-inspired solo piano style that emerged in the late 1920s. The styles featured a repetitive left hand pattern. The term was first used in 1928 in the title of a recording by Clarence "Pinetop" Smith, "Pinetop's Boogie-Woogie." Some of the major exponents of the style after 1930 included Meade Lux Lewis, Albert Ammons, and Pete Johnson. For readings on boogie-woogie see Silvester (1988).

30. Count Basie led what is regarded as the first rhythm section in jazz history that consistently played fast swing jazz in a smooth and relaxed way. This section consisted of Basie (piano), Freddie Green (rhythm guitar), Walter Page (bass), and Jo Jones (drummer). There are many biographical sources on the life and career of Count Basie; for example, see Basie (1985) and Dance (1980).

31. Ella Fitzgerald possessed a distinct ability of scat singing, a type of jazz improvisation using voice as an instrument singing nonsense syllables instead of words. For more readings on the life and career of Ella Fitzgerald, see Gourse (1998) and Fidelman (1994).

32. Fidelman 1994: 156.

33. There are many biographical works on Frank Sinatra. For example, see Fuchs and Prigozy (2007), Jacobs (2003), Freeland (1997), and Sinatra (1995).

34. "Fly Me to the Moon" is recorded on the album *It Might as Well Be Swing*, Reprise FS-1012 (1964).

35. The Theatre Owners' Booking Association (T.O.B.A.) was in essence an entertainment circuit for theatrical acts and popular music performances located in different venues of the United States. The "chitlin' circuit" was similar to the T.O.B.A. This circuit was the name given to a number of performance venues throughout the eastern and southern United States that were regarded as safe and acceptable for African American musicians, comedians, and other entertainers to perform for African American audiences during the period of racial segregation in the United States. Some of the noted theaters on the chitlin' circuit included the Cotton Club and the Apollo Theater in New York City, and the Uptown Theater in Philadelphia.

36. For references on Louis Jordan see Garrod (1994), Chilton (1992), and Copeland (1992).

37. Cage 1955: 42.

38. Astor Piazzolla (1921–1992) was an Argentine *bandoneón* virtuoso who developed unique style for composing and arranging contemporary urban Argentine tangos. The *bandoneón* is an accordion that is associated with traditional Argentine tango music and dance.

39. See Schifrin 2008: 79–82.

40. Gillespie was very impressed with Schifrin and invited him to write an extended work for the Gillespie Big Band. In 1958 Schifrin completed *Gillespiana*. See *Gillespiana*, Verve (1960) also recorded on Polygram B0000046R7.

41. See liner notes from Jones's album *Big Band Bossa Nova*.

42. *Big Band Bossa Nova* (1962), Mercury MG-20751.

43. Surdos, cuícas, and pandeiros are important Brazilian percussion instruments. Surdos are low-sounding samba drums that are played with sticks. Cuíca is a small friction drum with a thin stick inside of the instrument attached to the drum head; the drummer rubs the stick with a moistened cloth while applying pressure to the head to produce squeaking sounds. Pandeiros are similar to tambourines.

44. See Stewart 1985: 49.

45. The *Walking in Space* (1969) album also became symbolic with the U.S. space walk on the moon.

46. In the late 1960s there was an integration of soul and gospel music as cross-overs to the pop charts for the first time, with recordings such as "Oh Happy Day" (1969) by the Edwin Hawkins Singers. It was the first gospel song to cross over to the soul [popular music] charts.

47. Nicholson 1998: 279.

48. The arrangements of "Tell Me a Bedtime Story" and "Takin' It to the Streets" are on *Sounds . . . And Stuff Like That!!*, A&M 4685.

49. The Watts Poets employed music and rapping techniques similar to Black Nationalist artists such as the Last Poets and Gil-Scott Heron.

50. Rap music or rapping began in the Bronx, New York in the early 1970s, with African American disc jockeys called "mobile disc jockeys" (deejays) who would mix pre-recorded hits alternately on two turntables while reciting party phrases to the crowd in a microphone.

51. For references and sources on rap music, see Keyes (2002) and 1996: 223–48, Perkins (1996), Rose (1994), Dyson (1993), Baker (1993), George (1992), Nelson and Gonzales (1991), and Toop (1991).

52. The African hindehoo is a wooden flute played by different ethnic groups in the Central African Republic.

53. See Andrews (1995). Jones also developed a CD-ROM project titled *Q's Jook Joint* as a multimedia history of African American music.

54. James Moody plays various saxophones (tenor and alto) and flute. He is also a vocalist. In the mid-1940s Moody performed with the Dizzy Gillespie band. He later relocated to Europe and performed with many of the noted jazz musicians and bands. Moody is best known for his hit "Moody's Mood for Love," a solo instrumental improvisation based on "I'm in the Mood for Love" (composed by Jimmie McHugh and Dorothy Fields). Later Eddie Jefferson wrote lyrics to Moody's improvisation. The song attained popularity with the release of King Pleasure's vocal version (1952).

55. See liner notes from Jones's album *Q's Jook Joint*.

56. Benny Golson is a tenor saxophonist, composer, and arranger. Over the years he has composed many jazz standards that include "Killer Joe," "Whisper Not," and "Along Came Betty." In the 1950s both Jones and Golson were members of the Lionel Hampton European tour band.

57. "The Quintessence" is recorded on *The Quintessence*, Impulse A-11 (1961).

58. Wilson 1962: 156.

59. Quincy Jones also produced Lena Horne's Grammy Award–winning album, *The Lady and Her Music—Live on Broadway*, Qwest 2QW-3597 (1981).

60. Carmen McRae (1920–1994) was a jazz vocalist noted for her style and range. She gained fame for her phrasing and interpretation of lyrics. Her career in jazz spanned over sixty years. In the 1940s McRae performed as a vocalist with

Benny Carter, Count Basie, and Mercer Ellington. In the 1950s McRae performed as a vocalist and pianist at the famous Minton's Playhouse in Harlem, New York City. In her career she recorded on Decca, Bethlehem, Columbia, and Atlantic record labels.

61. "A Tribute to Benny Carter" is recorded on the album, *Carmen/Carmen McRae*, Temponic TB-29562 (1972).

Chapter 4

1. See the album, *Quincy Jones: Music Is My Life*, Pickwick SHM 3126 (1983) (United Kingdom).

2. See the albums *The Q in Jazz*, Golden Stars B000W8FYKQ (2007) (Holland); and *Moanin': Quincy Jones Big Band Vol. 2*, Mercury 45S-11 (1977) (Japan).

3. *Brown v. Board of Education of Topeka* (1954) overturned state laws that established separate but equal schools for African American and white students. This particular case paved the way for racial integration and the Civil Rights movement in American society.

4. Meadows 1983: 176–82.

5. *Lullaby of Birdland* (1955) is a unique album that features twelve interpretations of the song "Lullaby of Birdland" performed by twelve different modern arrangers.

6. The Jones Boys session was originally recorded for the Period label and reissued as part of Fantasy's original Jazz Classic limited edition series.

7. Leonard Feather (1914–1994) was a British-born jazz pianist, composer, and producer who was well known for his music journalism and other writings. Feather wrote for many years for *Down Beat* jazz magazine. He is also the co-author with Ira Gitler of *The Encyclopedia of Jazz in the Seventies, with introduction by Quincy Jones*. New York: Da Capo Press [originally published New York: Horizon Press, 1976].

8. The Okeh record label was created by Otto Heineman, who had connections with a group of companies owned by Carl Lindstrom in Berlin, Germany. Heineman was sent to New York in 1914, where at first he set up the manufacture of phonograph motors, later moving into recording and then mass producing records. The first Okeh disc appeared in 1918 and contained the pop and light classical music that was popular on records at that time.

9. Members of the group included Brook Benton (Benjamin Peavy) (leader), Thurmon Haynes (baritone), Walter Springer (baritone), and Adriel McDonald (bass, formerly of the Ink Spots).

10. Many doowop groups were influenced by male gospel music quartet singing (e.g., Sam Cooke and the Soul Stirrers). Many of these groups were noted not only for their singing style but also for incorporating stylized choreography and special attire to accompany musical performances. The Platters, the Coasters, and Ray

Charles were also influenced by the doowop tradition. In the 1940s and 1950s the Treniers performed a combination of swing jazz and rock 'n' roll.

11. In 1957 Ahmet Ertegun, the son of a Turkish ambassador to the United States, and Herb Abramson formed Atlantic Records, a small independent company dedicated to African American rhythm & blues.

12. During the 1950s and 1960s other singing groups that took the names of birds included the Ravens, the Orioles, the Larks, and the Robins.

13. Ray Charles also recorded a heartfelt song about Quincy Jones, "My Buddy," at the 1991 Montreux Jazz Festival. This spontaneous tribute to Jones was performed thirty-two years after Ray Charles submitted the song to Quincy Jones. He was to arrange it for the *Genius of Ray Charles* in 1959, but it never made the record.

14. Milt Jackson (1923–1999) is most often remembered as a distinguished member of the Modern Jazz Quartet. In the 1940s and 1950s, Jackson performed with Dizzy Gillespie, Thelonious Monk, Tadd Dameron, Woody Herman, Charlie Parker, and Ben Webster. In the 1950s and 1960s he recorded and performed with Quincy Jones on several albums.

15. This album on the Prestige label features Clifford Brown, Art Farmer, Quincy Jones (trumpets), Jimmy Cleveland (trombone), Gigi Gryce (alto saxophone), Clifford Simmons (tenor saxophone), Henri Renaud (piano), and Alan Dawson (drums).

16. Henri Renaud is a French jazz pianist who style was highly influenced by swing, bebop, and cool jazz. From late 1940s to the 1950s he performed with Don Byas, James Moody, Clifford Brown, Lester Young, and Sarah Vaughan.

17. Billy Eckstine (1914–1993), also known as "Mr. B," was a vocalist, bandleader, and an innovator of bebop. During the 1930s Eckstine performed in Chicago and New York. He became a member of the Earl Hines (1939–1943) band. Eckstine introduced songs such as "Skylark" (1942) over network radio. Eckstine was one of the musicians who influenced a young Quincy Jones.

18. Mimi Perrin who was also one of the major arrangers for the group the Double Six of Paris formed in 1959. The name Double Six stems from the practice and technique of superimposing two separate recordings that give the impression that twelve voices are singing at the same time.

19. André Hodeir is an early proponent of bebop and the styles of Charlie Parker and Dizzy Gillespie. In the 1950s he was one of the major composers and arrangers in France. Hodeir also arranged jazz tunes by Thelonious Monk, Tadd Dameron, Miles Davis, Milt Jackson, Benny Carter, Duke Ellington and others. He was the editor-in-chief of *Jazz Hot*, the French magazine that has often featured articles on and biographical profiles of Quincy Jones. Hodeir has written several books of jazz criticism. See Hodeir (2006).

20. Irving Green, Berle Adams, and Arthur Talmadge originally founded Mercury Records in 1945 in Chicago.

21. See the album *I Dig Dancers* (1960), Mercury SR-60612.

22. Holden 1980: 104.

23. Stewart 1985: 49.

24. See the album *Impressions of Duke Ellington*, Mercury PPS 2028 (1961). Billy Byers (1927–1996) was a trombonist, arranger, and bandleader. In the mid-1940s Byers served as an arranger and performer in the bands of George Auld, Buddy Rich, Benny Goodman, Charlie Venture, and Teddy Powell. In the 1950s he performed with Harold Arnold (1959–60).

25. Klezmers are musicians who perform a style of music known as klezmer music, a genre that originated from the Ashkenazi Jews of Eastern Europe. This type of music consists mainly of dance tunes and instrumental pieces for weddings and other celebrations. Although klezmer has its origins in Eastern Europe, it also greatly developed in the United States among Yiddish-speaking Jewish immigrants who arrived between 1880 and 1924.

26. Gibbs 2003: 229. Terry Gibbs is a vibraphonist, drummer, and bandleader. In the 1940s and 1950s Gibbs performed in the bands of Tommy Dorsey, Chubby Jackson, Buddy Rich, Woody Herman, Charlie Shavers–Louis Belson and Benny Goodman. In the 1960s Gibbs was a regular performer on *The Steve Allen Show*.

27. For readings on Josh White see Shelton (1963). White was a product of the Jim Crow South who recorded during the 1920s and 1930s the height of the race record era and later relocated to New York and expanded his repertoire to urban blues, Tin Pan Alley, cabaret, folk songs from around the world, and political protest songs.

28. Jones 1972: 19.

29. Nana Mouskouri recorded in many different languages including, Greek, English, Spanish, German, and Italian. Mouskouri's vocal style is a combination of classical music and jazz. She was highly influenced by Frank Sinatra, Ella Fitzgerald, Billie Holiday, and Édith Piaf.

30. Norman Granz (1918–2001) also managed the extensive career of Ella Fitzgerald. He constantly advocated against racism in jazz and in the recording industry by not allowing his performers to appear in segregated venues. He also coordinated African American and white performances in a series of concerts called Jazz at the Philharmonic (JATP).

31. See Jones tribute to Sammy Davis Jr. in *Rolling Stone* 1990: 35.

32. A&M is currently owned by the Universal Music Group and operates under the Interscope-Geffen-A&M Division. Herb Alpert, like Jones, is an American popular music icon. Alpert is highly regarded as an innovator of a trumpet style influenced by Mexican mariachi brass bands and is most associated with the group variously known as Herb Alpert & the Tijuana Brass, Herb Alpert's Tijuana Brass, or simply as T.J.B. Alpert's 1974 A&M album titled *You Smile, the Song Begins* includes a string arrangement by Jones of Gato Barbieri's "Last Tango in Paris."

33. As high school students in Los Angeles, George, a guitarist/vocalist, and Louis, a bassist/vocalist, formed the band Johnson Three Plus One, with their older brother Tommy and a cousin Alex Weir. They backed such artists as the Dells,

David Ruffin, Bill Medley, and Bobby Womack. George and Louis later joined Billy Preston's band and wrote the songs "Music in My Life" and "The Kids and Me." Quincy Jones also hired George and Louis (as the Brothers Johnson) for a tour in Japan.

34. The Brothers Johnson also wrote the song "Q," a tribute to Quincy Jones that was awarded the 1977 Grammy for best instrumental.

35. In the late 1960s Preston performed and recorded in London with the Beatles. Some of his work with the Beatles is included on *The Beatles Anthology III* (1996).

36. Jones 2001: 228–29.

37. Jones 2001: 231.

38. Holden 1980: 104.

39. Quincy Jones has written several articles about working with Jackson and producing *Thriller*. See Jones 2008(a), 2008(b): 37, and 1999: 74. Also see Monroe 2007: 94–109.

40. Rodney L. ("Rod") Temperton worked with Quincy Jones on several recordings and with many other popular musicians.

41. In addition to *Thriller*, Landis also directed Jackson's *Black & White* music video.

42. MTV went on the air in 1981. Initially, MTV pursued a policy of mainly featuring white performers. But MTV proved a perfect medium for a performer like Michael Jackson, whose talent as a dancer more than matched his singing ability. Jackson's dancing was crucial to his success, because his medium of expression was the music video.

43. Vincent Price (1911–1993) was a Hollywood actor well known for his distinctive voice and dramatic performances in a series of horror films that include *The House of Wax* (1953), *The Fly* (1958), *The Pit and the Pendulum* (1961), *The Masque of the Red Death* (1964), and many others.

44. Rod Temperton wrote the music and lyrics.

45. The songwriters of "Man in the Mirror" include Glen Ballard and Siedah Garrett.

46. See the story behind "We Are the World" in Barnet, Nemerov, and Taylor 2004: 228–29.

47. Also see Swedien 2009. In this book Grammy Award–winning music engineer Bruce Swedien shares his experiences of working in the popular music industry with Quincy Jones and Michael Jackson.

48. See Stewart 1985: 18.

49. Jones continues to represent a network of communication and unlimited boundaries because many of his albums are currently available as electronic resources through Naxos Music Library and the Alexander Street Music Online Jazz and American Song Series.

50. In the album *There Goes Rhymin' Simon* (1973), Jones arranged a lyrical string accompaniment to Paul Simon's song "Something So Right."

51. See the album *Live at Montreux* 1993[1991], Warner Bros. 45221.

52. Georg Philipp Telemann (1681–1767) was a major German composer during the eighteenth century. He is credited with over three thousand compositions in various genres.

53. Hubert Laws has recorded with both classical and popular music artists including Jessye Norman, Kathleen Battle, Mongo Santamaria, and Ashford and Simpson. Laws appears with Quincy Jones on numerous arrangements and recordings, such as *Ironside* (soundtrack) (1967–75), "Killer Joe" (1970), and "Tell Me a Bedtime Story" (1978), *Walking in Space* (1969), and *Sounds . . . And Stuff Like That!!* (1978).

54. Chick Corea followed Herbie Hancock as pianist in the Miles Davis Quintet (1968–70). He also appeared as an instrumentalist on several of Davis's albums: *In a Silent Way* (1969), *Bitches Brew* (1969), *At the Fillmore: Live at the Fillmore East* (1970), and *Black Beauty* (1970). His repertoire has ranged from jazz and Latin American music to the music of twentieth-century composers (e.g., John Cage, Karlheinz Stockhausen).

55. For readings on the album *A Soulful Celebration*, see Fermor 2000: 98–127 and Stetson 1992: 5.

56. George Frideric Handel (1685–1759) was a classical composer who worked in Germany and Italy, but it was in England where he matured as a highly regarded composer. The English came to regard Handel as a national institution. He wrote all of his major works for British audiences. In his career he composed numerous operas, oratorios, concertos, suites, sonatas, and instrumental works. *The Messiah*, a sacred work, is one of Handel's greatest contributions to the Western classical music repertoire.

Chapter 5

1. For filmographies that include a list of some of Jones's music scores, see McCarthy (2000), Craggs (1998), Limbacher, Wright, and Wright (1991), Darby and Du Bois (1990), and Limbacher (1981).

2. For readings on the history of African Americans in the Hollywood film industry, see Locke (2009), Mapp (2008), Bogle (2005) and (1988), Gabbard (2004), Donaldson (2003), Torriano (2001), Ross (1996), and Siders 1972: 12–15.

3. Many of the early films made featuring African Americans were musicals. In 1929 *Hearts in Dixie* was released, a full-length Hollywood musical with an all–African American cast. Other African American musicals include *The Green Pastures* (1936), *Cabin in the Sky* (1943), *Stormy Weather* (1943), *Carmen Jones* (1954), *St. Louis Blues* (1958), and *Porgy & Bess* (1959).

4. See Phil Moore's interview in *Down Beat*, May 15, 1943: 1, 8; and "Exclusion of Blacks from Staff Orchestras," *Down Beat*, August 1, 1944: 2. Also see Berger, Berger, and Patrick 2002: 282–87.

5. See Berger, Berger, and Patrick 2002: 258–99.

6. Benny Carter (1907–2003) played alto saxophone, trumpet, and other instruments. He was one of the most diverse composers and arrangers in jazz history. Early in his career Carter performed with Earl Hines in the mid-1920s and with Fletcher Henderson from 1930–1931. He wrote several arrangements for Henderson such as "Keep a Song in Your Soul" (1930). Carter formed his own band in 1932 that helped influence the swing style of the 1930s. He worked in London as a staff arranger for the BBC from 1936–38 and returned to New York to form a new orchestra at the Savoy Ballroom in 1939.

7. J. J. Johnson (1924–1977) was a trombonist, composer, and arranger who was very much influenced by jazz, classical music, and film. In the 1940s he performed with Benny Carter, Count Basie, Illinois Jacquet, and was very active with the Jazz at the Philharmonic concerts in New York City. In the 1950s Johnson was a member of the Gillespie big band. In the mid-1950s Johnson led his own small ensembles. Johnson wrote music for several films such as *Across 110th Street* (1972), *Man and Boy* (1972), and *Cleopatra Jones* (1973).

8. Oliver Nelson (1932–1975) was a jazz saxophonist. He composed and arranged many television series that include *Columbo*, *The Six Million Dollar Man*, and *The Bionic Woman*. In his scores, Lalo Schifrin often included elements of jazz and other popular music styles. Schifrin's film scores include *The Cincinnati Kid* (1965), *Bullitt* (1969) staring Steve McQueen, and the Clint Eastwood films *Dirty Harry* (1971), *Magnum Force* (1973), and *Sudden Impact* (1983). Schifrin is probably best known for his television score for the intriguing 1960s spy series *Mission Impossible*.

9. MacDonald 1974: 1.

10. Siders 1969: 31.

11. Feather 1968: 8.

12. In some early Hollywood films jazz was played and sung by both white and African American performers. For example, Al Jolson starred in the film *The Jazz Singer* (1927), and he appeared in blackface makeup. This was one of the first films to introduce jazz/African American music to white audiences. As early as 1929 authentic jazz was presented in short films such as *After Seven* with the Chick Webb Orchestra and *Black and Tan* with the Duke Ellington Orchestra.

13. For references on the art and history of Hollywood film scoring, see Bellis (2007); Burkholder, Grout, and Palisca 2006: 765–67, 862–64, 905, 945–50; Timm (2003); Dickinson (2003); Davis (2000); Buhler, Flinn, and Neumeyer (2000); Marmoestein (1997); McDonald (1998); Chion (1994); Burt (1994); Prendergast (1992); Darby and Du Bois (1990); and Gorbman (1987).

14. Some of Johnny Mandel's most famous compositions include "Suicide is Painless" (theme from *M*A*S*H*) and the film score *The Sandpiper* (1965), for which he received an Academy Award for Best Song for "The Shadow of Your Smile," co-written with Paul Francis Webster. Also, in 1981 Mandel received a Grammy Award for Best Instrumental Arrangement Accompanying Vocal(s) for his work on "Velas" from Quincy Jones's album *The Dude*.

15. In *Anatomy of a Murder*, Ellington made a cameo appearance; for the score he received a Grammy Award (1959) in the category of Best Soundtrack Album, Background Score from Motion Picture or Television.

16. The film *Paris Blues* starred Paul Newman, Joanne Woodward, Sidney Poitier, Diahann Carroll, and Louis Armstrong. Ellington received Academy Award and Grammy Award nominations in the category Best Score from a Motion Picture.

17. See Pollack (1999). Copland was highly influenced by jazz and this is reflected in some of his early works that include *Music for Theatre* (1925) and the *Piano Concerto* (1927). For his score of *The Heiress* (1949), a film directed by William Wyler and starring Montgomery Cliff and Olivia de Havilland, Copland won an Academy Award.

18. Lees 1967: 61.

19. See the soundtrack, *The Sandpiper*, Mercury MG 21032 (1965).

20. Holroyd 1968: 8.

21. Jones 2001: 210.

22. See Lees 1967: 59. In the late 1950s a few jazz composers and arrangers attempted a trend of fusing jazz and classical music into a new form. For example, Gunther Schuller, who had played French horn with Miles Davis for the *Birth of the Cool* sessions, saw this fusion as part of an inevitable trend. In a 1957 lecture at Brandeis University he labeled this compositional trend as "third-stream music," representing the merging of the two streams of jazz and classical music into a unique third stream. Along with Schuller one of the major African American proponents of third stream music was jazz pianist and composer John Lewis.

23. *Ibid.*

24. See Rapf (2006) and Lumet (1995).

25. Caps 2003: 44–45.

26. The theme from *The Anderson Tapes* is recorded on the album *Smackwater Jack*, A&M 3037 (1971), and many other compilations.

27. "The Love Theme from The Getaway" is on the album *You've Got it Bad Girl*, A&M 3041 (1972).

28. Jones 1976: D16.

29. The Hammond B-3 organ was popularized and became very much associated with rhythm & blues and gospel music in the mid-1950s.

30. *The Deadly Affair* is based on a story titled *Call for the Dead* (1961[1962]) by John le Carré.

31. Astrud Gilberto is one of the Brazilian vocalists who defined the samba and bossa nova styles. She is most famous for her Grammy Award rendition of the bossa nova song "The Girl from Ipanema" (composed by Antonio Carlos Jobim). This performance established Gilberto as a jazz and popular music performer.

32. A *clave* (which literally means "Key") is often comprised of repeating 3 (beats) + 2 (beats) or reverse 2 (beats) + 3 (beat) rhythmic patterns that are popular in a vast amount of music in Cuba and other Latin American regions. These

rhythms are often played using two wooden sticks that are also called claves that are stuck together to mark the rhythmic pattern.

33. *For Love of Ivy* was written by Sidney Poitier (story) and Robert Alan Arthur (screenplay).

34. Holden 1980: 102.

35. Jones 2001: 193–94.

36. Ride rhythms involved a technique where in jazz performance a drummer uses his/her right hand to play rhythms, which provide a steady pulse and swing feeling. The rhythms are normally played on a cymbal that is suspended on the right side over the drum set. The rhythms that are played on this cymbal are known as "ride rhythms."

37. Jones 1976: D15.

38. Holden 1980: D23.

39. See the following album compilations that include many of Jones's film and television scores and arrangements: *Fly Films and Groovy Music*, Project 3 PMLP 79549-1 (Europe) (1999); and *Great Action Film Themes*, Sunset SLS 500366 (United Kingdom) (1974).

Finale

1. Stewart 1985: 17, and Holden 1980: D23.

2. Jones 2001: 300.

3. See Hackett 1983: 1 and Beers 1983: E3.

4. See Block 2010: 20. This article follows an episode in which Quincy Jones visited his former high school in Seattle, and discovered that few of the students were aware of musicians such as Louis Armstrong and John Coltrane. As a result Jones founded the Quincy Jones Musiq Consortium as an advocacy organization and social network for improving music education for children.

5. For information on Jones recent educational programs see QMUSIQCON-SORITUM on Twitter, twitter.com/QMUSIQCONSORT. Other websites include songmasterworks.com; qmusiqconsortium.ning.com; and jazzroots.com.

BIBLIOGRAPHY

Aldore, Collier. 1990. "After 40 Years, Fame and Fortune, Three Marriages, Brain Surgery and an Emotional Breakdown Quincy Jones Finds Peace." *Ebony* 45(6): 74.

Alexander, Martin S., Martin Evans, and J. F. V. Keiger. 2002. *The Algerian War and the French Army, 1954–62: Experiences, Images, Testimonies.* New York: Palgrave MacMillan.

Baker, David, Lida Belt, and Herman C. Hudson. 1978. *The Black Composer Speaks.* Metuchen, NJ: Scarecrow Press.

Baker, Houston, 1993. *Black Studies, Rap, and the Academy.* Chicago: University of Chicago Press.

———. 1984. *Blues, Ideology, and Afro-American Literature: A Vernacular Theory.* Chicago: University Press of Chicago.

Barnet, Richard D., Bruce Nemerov, and Mayo R. Taylor. 2004. *The Story Behind the Song: 150 Songs that Chronicle the 20th Century.* Westport, CT: Greenwood Press.

Basie, Count. 1985. *Good Morning Blues: The Autobiography—As Told to Albert Murray.* New York: Random House.

Bayer, Linda N. 2001. *Quincy Jones.* Philadelphia: Chelsea House.

Beers, Carole. 1983. "Duo Likes Working with Jones." *Seattle Times*, E3 (February 15).

Bellis, Richard. 2007. *The Emerging Film Composer: An Introduction to People, Problems, and Psychology of the Film Music Business.* Charleston, SC: Booksurge.

Berger, Morroe, Edward Berger, and James Patrick. 2002. *Benny Carter: A Life in American Music, Vols. I & II.* 2nd ed. Lanham, MD: Scarecrow Press and Newark, NJ: Institute of Jazz Studies, Rutgers University.

Berry, Jason. 1988. "African Cultural Memory in New Orleans Music." *Black Music Research Journal* 8(1): 3–12.

Berry, Venise T. 2007. *Historical Dictionary of African American Cinema.* New York: Scarecrow Press.

Blair, Jackson. 2002. "Bruce Swedien on Quincy Jones." *Mix* 31(10): 80.

Block, Debbie Galante. "Popular Music Education Finds Its Q Factor." *Teaching Music* 17 (April 2010): 20.

Bogle, Donald. 2005. *Bright Boulevards, Bold Dreams: The Story of Black Hollywood.* New York: One World/Ballantine.

———. 1988. *Blacks in American Films and Television: An Encyclopedia.* New York: Garland.

Bonds, Mark Evans. 2006. *A History of Music in Western Culture.* 2nd ed. Upper Saddle River, NJ: Prentice Hall.

Bontemps, Arna Wendell, ed. 1972. *The Harlem Renaissance Remembered.* New York: Dodd Mead.

———. 1931. *God Sends Sunday.* New York: Harcourt, Brace.

Boston, Lloyd. 1998. *Men of Color: Fashion, History, Fundamentals.* New York: Artisan.

Buhler, James, Caryl Flinn, and David Neumeyer, eds. 2000. *Music and Cinema.* Hanover, NH: University Press of New England.

Burkholder, J. Peter, Donald J. Grout, and Claude V. Palisca. 2006. *A History of Western Music.* 7th ed. New York and London: W. W. Norton.

Burt, George. 1994. *The Art of Film Music.* Boston: Northeastern University Press.

Cage, R. 1955. "Arranger Quincy Jones Says Quality of R&B Sides Better." *Down Beat* 22: 42.

Campbell, Don G. 1984. *Master Teacher: Nadia Boulanger.* Washington: Pastoral Press.

Campbell, Mary. 1975. "At 42, Quincy Jones Is Just Getting Started." *Seattle Times,* Arts & Entertainment Section (October 5).

Caps, John. 2003. "Soundtracks 101: Movie Score Milestones, 1933–2001—'In Cold Blood.'" *Film Comment Review* 10: 44–45.

Chilton, John. 1996. *Sidney Bechet: The Wizard of Jazz.* New York: Da Capo.

———. 1992. *Let the Good Times Roll: The Story of Louis Jordan and His Music.* London: Quartet.

Chion, Michael. 1994. *Audio-Vision: Sound on Screen.* New York: Columbia University Press.

Cipps, Thomas. 1993. *Making Movies Black: The Hollywood Message Movie from World War II to the Civil Rights Era.* New York: Oxford University Press.

Cogan, Jim, and William Clark. 2003. *Temples of Sound: Inside the Great Recording Studios.* San Francisco: Chronicle.

"Honoring Quincy Jones." 2003. *Congressional Record,* Vol. 149 (June 23): S7376–S7377.

Copeland, David Scot. 1992. *Louis Jordan & His Tympany Five* [video recording]. New York: BMG Video.

Craggs, Stewart R. 1998. *Soundtracks: An International Dictionary of Composers for Film.* Aldershot, UK, and Brookfield, VT: Ashgate.

Dance, Stanley. 1974. *The World of Swing.* New York: C. Scribner's Sons.

———. 1980. *The World of Count Basie.* New York: C. Scribner's Sons.

Darby, William, and Jack Du Bois. 1990. *American Film Music: Major Composers, Techniques, Trends, 1915–1990.* Jefferson, NC: McFarland.

Davenport, Lisa. 2009. *Jazz Diplomacy: Promoting America in the Cold War.* Jackson, MS: University Press of Mississippi.

Davis, Richard. 2000. *Complete Guide to Film Scoring.* Boston: Berklee Press.

De Barros, Paul. 1993. *Jackson Street After Hours: The Roots of Jazz in Seattle.* Seattle: Sasquatch.

———. 2001. "Q's First Joint and Buddy Catlett Reflects on Q and His Music." *Earshot Jazz* [Seattle] 17(11): 4–7, 11–15, 24.

Dickinson, Kaye, ed. 2003. *Movie Music: The Film Reader*. New York: Routledge.

Donaldson, Melvin Burke. 2003. *Black Directors in Hollywood*. Austin: University of Texas Press.

De Bois, W. E. B. 1996 [1903]. *The Souls of Black Folk*. New York: Modern Library.

Dvořák, Antonín. 1895. "Music in America." *Harper's New Monthly Magazine* 90: 428–34.

Dyson, Michael Eric. 1993. "The Culture of Hip-hop, Rap Music, and Black Culture: An Interview." In *Reflecting Black: African American Cultural Criticism.* Minneapolis: University of Minneapolis Press.

Early, Gerald. 2001. "Quincy Jones: The Story of an American Musician." In *Q*, 16–53. Los Angeles: Quincy Jones Productions.

Ellington, Duke [Edward Kennedy]. 1976[1973]. *Music Is My Mistress*. Garden City, NY: Doubleday.

Ellison, Ralph. 1952. *Invisible Man.* New York: Random House.

"Exclusion of Blacks from Staff Orchestras." 1944. *Down Beat* (2): 11.

Fagien, Michael. 2002. "Quincy Jones and Me." *Jazziz* 19(1): 10.

Fanon, Frantz. 2004[1961]. *Damnés de la terre* (*The Wretched of the Earth*). New York: Grove Press.

———. 1971[1952]. *Peau noire, masques blancs* (*Black skin, white mask*). Paris: Éditions de Seuil.

Feather, Leonard. 1975. "Quincy Jones Back From the Shadows." *Los Angeles Times*, 74 (June 1).

———. 1968. "Quincy in Hollywood." *Melody Maker* 43: 8.

———. 1956. "Ambassador Diz Has Made Jazz History." *Melody Maker* 31: 2.

Fermor, Gotthard. 2000. "Georg Friedrich Handels Messias und seine "Soul Celebration": Eine Herausforderung, erneut uber "geist-liche" Musik nachzudenken (Georg Friedrich Handel's Messiah and its "soulful celebration": A Challenge to think about spiritual music anew"). In *Theophonie Grenzgange zwischen Musik und Theologie*, 98–127. Rheinbach, Germany: CMZ-Verlag.

Fidelman, Geoffrey Mark. 1996. *First Lady of Song: Ella Fitzgerald for the Record.* New York: Citadel Press.

Floyd Jr., Samuel A. 1995. *The Power of Black Music: Interpreting Its History from Africa to the United States*. New York: Oxford University Press.

Freeland, Michael. 1997. *All the Way: A Biography of Frank Sinatra*. London: Weiderfeld & Nicolson.

Fry, Stephen. 2002. "Peggy Lee." In *Women and Music in America Since 1900, Vol. 2.* Kristine H. Burns, ed. 373–74. Westport, CT: Greenwood Press.

Fuchs, Jeanne, and Ruth Prigozy. 2007. *Frank Sinatra: The Man, the Music, the Legend*. Rochester, NY: University of Rochester Press, and Hempstead, NY: Hofstra University Press.

Funke, Lewis. 1959. "News and Gossip Gathered on the Rialto." *New York Times*, X1 (October 18).

Gabbard, Krin. 2004. *Black Magic: White Hollywood and African American Culture.* New Brunswick, NJ: Rutgers University Press.

Garrod, Charles. 1994. *Louis Jordan and His Orchestra*. Zehpyrhills, FL: Joyce Records Club.

Gart, Galen. 1989. *The History of Rhythm & Blues*. Milford, NH: Big Nickel.

Gates Jr., Henry Louis. 2009. *In Search of Our Roots: How 19 Extraordinary African Americans Reclaimed their Past*. New York: Crown.

———. 2004. *Celebrating Quincy Jones: A Discussion with the Music Master*. Cambridge, MA: Office for the Arts, Harvard University.

———. 1988. *The Signifying Monkey: A Theory of African American Literary Criticism*. New York: Oxford University Press.

Gates Jr., Henry Louis, and Nellie Y. McKay. 1997. *The Norton Anthology of African American Literature*. New York: W. W. Norton.

George, Nelson. 1992. *Buppies, B-Boys, Baps and Bohos: Notes on Post-Soul Black Culture*. New York: HarperCollins.

Gibbs, Terry, with Cary Ginnell. 2003. *Good Vibes: A Life in Jazz*. Lanham, MD: Scarecrow Press.

Gillespie, John Birks. 1979. *To Be or Not to Bop: Memoirs*. Garden City, NY: Doubleday.

Gilroy, Paul. 1993. *The Black Atlantic: Modernity and Double Consciousness*. Cambridge, MA: Harvard University Press.

Gridley, Mark C. 2005. *Jazz Styles History and Analysis*. 9th ed. Upper Saddle River, NJ: Prentice Hall.

Griffin, Farah Jasmine. 1995. *"Who Set You Flowin'?" The African-American Migration Narrative*. New York: Oxford University Press.

Gorbman, Claudia. 1987. *Unheard Melodies: Narrative Film Music*. Bloomington: Indiana University Press.

Gourse, Leslie. 1998. *The Ella Fitzgerald Companion: Seven Decades of Commentary*. New York: Schirmer.

———. 1993. *Sassy: The Life of Sarah Vaughan*. New York: C. Scribner's Sons.

Hackett, Regina. 1983. "Austin Credits Quincy Jones for Her Success." *Seattle Post-Intelligencer*, P-1 (February 15).

Hajdu, David. 1996. *Lush for Life: A Biography of Billy Strayhorn*. New York: Farrar, Strauss, Giroux.

Hampton, Lionel. 1989. *Hamp: An Autobiography*. New York: Warner Books.

Harker, Brian. 2005. *Jazz: An American Journey*. Upper Saddle River, NJ: Prentice Hall.

Hasse, John Edward, ed. 2000. *Jazz: The First Century*. New York: William Morrow.

Heckman, Don. 2001. "The Tracks: Don Heckman, With Q, Guides You Through." In *Q*, 54–73. Los Angeles: Quincy Jones Productions.

Hentoff, Nat. 1954(a). "Counterpoint Part I." *Down Beat* 21(8): 36.

———. 1954(b). "Counterpoint Part II." *Down Beat* 21(9): 12.

Herskovits, Melville J. 1958[1941]. *The Myth of the Negro Past*. Boston: Beacon.

Holden, Stephen. 1980. "Quincy Jones, Master Synthesist." *High Fidelity/Musical America* 30: 101–4.

———. "Quincy Jones—Now a Record Producer." 1980. *New York Times*, D20, 23 (July 27).

Holyrod, S. 1968. "Soul Brother in Hollywood." *Melody Maker* 48: 8.

Horricks, Raymond. 1985. *Quincy Jones*. Tunbridge Wells, UK: Spellmount.

———. 1957. "Keepin' Up with Jonesy." *Jazz Monthly* 3(8): 9–10.

———1955. "Portrait of Quincy Jones." *Jazz Monthly* 1(6): 10, 28–29.

Houston, David, and Jenny Bagert. 2006. *Jazz, Giants, and Journeys: The Photography of Herman Leonard*. London: Scala, and Easthampton, MA: Antique Collectors' Club.

Huggins, Nathan. 1971. *Harlem Renaissance*. New York: Oxford University Press.

Ivry, Benjamin. 2000. *Maurice Ravel: A Life*. New York: Welcome Rain.

Jablonski, Edward. 1996. *Harold Arlen: Rhythm, Rainbows, and Blues*. Boston: Northeastern University Press.

Jacobs, George. 2003. *Mr. S: My Life with Frank Sinatra*. New York: Harper Entertainment.

"Jazz Appreciation Month, April 2002." 2002. *Music Educators Journal* 88(5): 15.

"Jazz Musical Planned: 'Free and Easy' Rehearsals Begin in Brussels Today." 1959. *New York Times*, 39 (November 17).

Jisi, C. 2001. "The Insider: Studio Great Neil Stubenhaus Tracks the Ups & Downs of L.A. Sessions." *Bass Player* 12(5): 50–52, 54, 56.

Jones, Quincy. 2009. "Arts Education in America." *Huffington Post*, huffingtonpost. com (May 9).

———. 2008. *The Complete Quincy Jones: My Journey & Passions: Photos, Letters, Memories & More From Q's Personal Collection*. San Rafael, CA: Insight Editions.

———. 2008(a). "Thriller Time." *Billboard* 120(2): 37.

———. 2008(b). "Music: Q Notes—Thriller Time: Remembering A Historic Recording 25 Years Later." *Billboard* 120(2): 37.

———. 2008(c). "Teach Your Children Well." *Billboard* 120(4): 60.

———. 2008(d). "Q Notes How to Save the Album." *Billboard* 120(17): 44.

———. 2005. "Quincy Jones: Rappers Need to Learn About their Forefathers." *World Entertainment News Network*, wenn.com (November).

———. 2005. "Quincy Jones Urges Rappers to Drop the 'N' Word." *World Entertainment News Network*, wenn.com (November).

———. 2001. *Q: The Autobiography of Quincy Jones*. New York, New York: Doubleday.

———. 1997. "When Will It End?" *Vibe* 5(4): 19.

———. 1990. "Tribute to Sammy Davis, Jr. 1925–1990." *Rolling Stone* 581: 35.

———. 1976. "The Musical World of Quincy Jones." *New York Amsterdam News*, D16 (August 28).

———. 1976. "Quincy Jones." *New York Amsterdam News*, D15 (August 7).

———. 1972. "The Problems of A & R Work." *Crescendo International* 10: 19.

———. 1963. "Music in the Making: Sarah Makes It All Worth While." *Melody Maker* 38: 12.

———. 1959. "Starting Up a New Band." *Jazz Review* 2(8): 16–17.

"Jones Forming Band." 1959(a). *Down Beat* 26(9): 12.

Joseph, Charles M. 2001. *Stravinsky Inside Out*. New Haven: Yale University Press.

Kavanaugh, Lee Hill. 1998. *Quincy Jones: Musician, Composer, Producer*. Springfield, NJ: Enslow.

Kellner, Bruce, ed. 1984. *The Harlem Renaissance: A Historical Dictionary of the Era*. Westport CT: Greenwood Press.

Kendall, Lukas. 1998. "The Soul of the Seventies: In the Heat of the Night/They Call Me Mr. Tibbs!" *Film Score Monthly* 3(6): 31, 33–34.

Keyes, Cheryl L. 2002. *Rap Music and Street Consciousness*. Urbana: University of Illinois Press.

———. 1996. "At the Crossroads: Rap Music and its African Nexus." *Ethnomusicology* 49(2): 223–48.

Lawn, Richard J. 2007. *Experiencing Jazz*. New York: McGraw Hill.

Lee, Peggy. 1989. *Miss Peggy Lee: An Autobiography*. New York: D. Fine.

Lees, Gene. 2001. *You Can't Steal a Gift: Dizzy, Clark, Milt, and Nat*. New Haven: Yale University Press.

———. 1985. "Adventures of a Black Composer in Hollywood." *New York Times*, Arts & Entertainment Section (March 16).

———. 1967. "The New Sound on the Soundtracks." *High Fidelity/Musical America* 17: 58–61.

Levine, Lawrence. 1977. *Black Culture and Black Consciousness: Afro-American Folk Thought from Slavery to Freedom*. New York: Oxford University Press.

Levy, John (with Devra Hall). 2000. *Men, Women, and Girl Singers: My Life as a Musician Turned Manager*. Silver Springs, MD: Beckham.

Lewis, Jason. 2010. "LAUSD Honors Quincy Jones with a School in the Music Producer's Name." *Los Angeles Sentinel*, lasentinel.net (December 22).

Limbacher, James L. 1981. *Keeping Score: Film Music 1972–1979*. Metuchen, NJ: Scarecrow Press.

Limbacher, James L., and H. Stephen Wright. 1991. *Keeping Score: Film and Television Music, 1980–1988* (with additional coverage of 1921–1979). Metuchen, NJ: Scarecrow Press.

Locke, Alain. 1936. *The Negro and His Music*. Washington: Associates in Negro Folk Education.

———. 1925. *The New Negro: An Interpretation*. New York: A & C. Boni.

Locke, Brian. 2009. *Racial Stigma on the Hollywood Screen from WWII to the Present: The Orientalist Buddy Film*. New York: Palgrave MacMillan.

Lumet, Sidney. 1996. *Making Movies*. New York: Alfred A. Knopf.

Lydon, Michael. 1998. *Ray Charles Man and Music*. New York: Riverhead Books.

MacDonald, Patrick. 1974. "Quincy Jones, Our New Superstar." *Seattle Times*, Arts and Entertainment Section (November 29).

Mapp, Edward. 2008. *African Americans and the Oscar: Decades of Struggle and Achievement*. Lanham, MD: Scarecrow Press.

Marmoestein, Gary. 1997. *Hollywood Rhapsody: Movie Music and Its Makers 1900–1975*. New York: Schirmer.

Marsack, Robyn, transl. 1988. *Mademoiselle: Conversations with Nadia Boulanger.* Boston: Northeastern University Press.

Mawer, Deborah, ed. 2000. *The Cambridge Companion to Ravel.* New York: Cambridge University Press.

McCarthy, Clifford. 2000. *Film Composers in America: A Filmography.* 2nd ed. New York: Oxford University Press.

McDonald, Laurence E. 1998. *The Invisible Art of Film: A Comprehensive History.* New York: Ardsley.

Meadows, Eddie S. 1983. "A Preliminary Analysis of Early Rhythm and Blues Musical Practices." *Western Journal of Black Studies* 7(3): 172–82.

Monaghan, Peter, and Lola Pedrini. 2001. "Buddy Catlett Reflects on Q and his Music." *Earshot Jazz* [Seattle] 17(11): 4, 6, and 12.

Monroe, Bryan. 2007. "Michael Jackson in His Own Words." *Ebony* 63(2): 94–109.

Monson, Ingrid. 2007. *Freedom Sounds: Civil Rights Call Out to Jazz and Africa.* Oxford and New York: Oxford University Press.

———. 1999. "Riffs, Repetition, and Theories of Globalization." *Ethnomusicology* 43(1): 31–65.

Nai, Larry. 1998. "Floyd Standifer Interview." *Cadence—The Review of Jazz & Blues Creative Improvised Music* 29(9)(173): 15–27.

Nelson, Havelock, and Michael A. Gonzales. 1991. *Bring the Noise: A Guide to Rap Music and Hip-hop Culture.* New York: Harmony.

Nicholson, Stuart. 1998. *Jazz-Rock: A History.* New York: Schirmer.

O'Meally, Robert G. 1998. *The Jazz Cadence of American Culture.* New York: Columbia University Press.

Owens, Jimmy. 1993. *Oral History Interview with Clark Terry* [Video recording]. New York: New York Public Library, Schomburg Center Video Oral History Gallery.

Parnell, Colin. 1960. "The Band Business in Europe Is a Headache." *Melody Maker* 35: 8–9.

Paynter, Susan. 2000. "Quincy Jones and Garfield Classmates to Reunite at Last." *Seattle Post-Intelligencer,* B1 (May 5).

Percelay, James, Monteria Ivey, and Stephan Dweck. 1994. *Snaps: The Original Yo' Mama Joke Book.* 1st Quill ed. New York: Morrow.

Perkins, William Eric. 1996. *Droppin' Science: Critical Essays on Rap Music and Hip Hop Culture.* Philadelphia: Temple University Press.

Perlis, Vivian. 1977. "Boulanger—20th Century Music was born in her classroom." *New York Times,* 89 (September 11).

"Phil Moore Interview." 1943. *Down Beat* 1: 8.

Pollack, Howard. 1999. *Aaron Copland: The Life and Work of an Uncommon Man.* New York: Henry Holt.

Porter, Lewis. 1997. *Jazz: A Century of Change: Readings and New Essays.* New York: Schirmer.

Prendergast, Roy M. 1992. *Film Music: A Neglected Art.* 2nd ed. New York: W. W. Norton.

"Quincy Jones Show." 1959(b). *Down Beat* 26: 12.

Raboteau, Albert J. 1978. *Slave Rebellion: The "Invisible Institution" in the Antebellum South*. New York: Oxford University Press.

Randolph, William [Michael Randolph]. 2007. *Popular Music through the Camera Lens of William "PoPsie" Randolph*. Milwaukee, WI: Hal Leonard.

Rapf, Joana E., ed. 2006. *Sidney Lumet: Interviews*. Jackson, MS: University Press of Mississippi.

Renaud, Patrick-Charles. 2008. *Se batter en Algérie*. Paris: Grancher.

Rhinson, E. I. 1940. "Negro Musicians Union, Local 493, AFM Sponsors Trianon 'Colored Night' They Will Do It Every Time." *Northeast Enterprise*, 1, 2 (November 29).

"Rock and Roll Called 'Communicable Disease.'" 1956. *New York Times*, L33 (March 28).

Rose, Tricia. 1994. *Black Noise: Rap Music and Black Culture in Contemporary America*. Hanover, NH: Wesleyan University Press.

Ross, Karen. 1996. *Black and White Media: Black Images in Popular Film and Television*. Cambridge, UK: Polity Press, and Cambridge, MA: Blackwell.

Rowe, Mike. 1975. *Chicago Blues: The City & The Music*. New York: Da Capo.

Schifrin, Lalo. 2008. *Mission Impossible: My Life in Music*. Lanham, MD: Scarecrow Press.

"Segregationist Wants Ban on Rock and Roll." 1956. *New York Times*, 27 (March 30).

Shelton, Robert. 1963. *The Josh White Song Book: Biography and Song Commentaries*. Chicago: Quadrangle.

Shepard, Todd. 2006. *The Invention of Decolonization: The Algerian War and the Remaking of France*. Ithaca, NY: Cornell University Press.

Siders, Harvey. 1972. "The Jazz Composer in Hollywood." *Down Beat* 39: 12–15.

———. 1970. "Quincy's Got a Brand New (Old) Bag." *Down Beat* 37(23): 13.

———. 1969. "Keeping Up with Quincy Jones." *Down Beat* 36(23): 13, 31.

Silvester, Peter J. 1988. *A Left Hand Like God: A History of Boogie-woogie Piano*. New York: Da Capo.

Sinatra, Nancy. 1995. *Frank Sinatra, My Father*. Garden City, NY: Doubleday.

Small, Christopher. 1997. *Music of the Common Tongue: Survival and Celebration in African American Music*. Hanover, NH, and London: Wesleyan University Press.

Smith, Rochelle, and Sharon L. Jones. 2000. *The Prentice Hall Anthology of African American Literature*. Upper Saddle River, NJ: Prentice Hall.

"Smithsonian Program Preserves Our Rich Jazz Heritage." 2004. *International Musician* 102(4): 24.

Spycket, Jerome. 1992. *Nadia Boulanger*. Stuyvesant, NY: Pendragon Press.

Stetson, Nancy. 1992. "Hallelujah! Contemporary Artists Put a Soulful Twist on Handel's Messiah." *Chicago Tribune*, Section 5, 3 (December 24).

Stewart, Zan. 1985. "The Quincy Jones Interview." *Down Beat* 52(4): 16–19.

Stuckey, Sterling. 1987. *Slave Culture: Nationalist Theory and the Foundations of Black America*. New York: Oxford University Press.

Swedien, Bruce. 2009. *In the Studio with Michael Jackson*. New York: Hal Leonard.

———. 2003. *Make Music Mine*. New York: Hal Leonard.

Taruskin, Richard. 1996. *Stravinsky and the Russian Tradition: A Biography of the Works through Marva*. Berkeley: University of California Press.

Taylor, Billy. 1957. "Negroes Don't Know Anything about Jazz." *Duke Magazine* (August).

Terry, Clark, and Gwen Terry. 2011. *Clark/The Autobiography of Clark Terry*. Berkeley: University of California Press.

Terry, Wallace. 1990. "Your Real Home is Within." *Parade Magazine*, 25 (November 18).

Tiegel, Eliot. 2001. "The Touch: Quincy Jones Discusses the Jazz Roots of His Charmed Musical Life." *Down Beat* 68(11): 25–29.

———. 1965. "Quincy at the Movies." *Billboard* 77: 26.

Timm, Larry M. 2003. *The Soul of Cinema: An Appreciation of Film Music*. Upper Saddle River, NJ: Prentice Hall.

Toop, David. 1991. *Rap Attack 2: African Rap to Global Hip Hop*. 2nd ed. London: Serpent's Tail.

Torriano, Berry. 2001. *The 50 Most Influential Black Films: A Celebration of African American Talent, Determination and Creativity*. New York: Citadel.

Turner, Peter. 2006. *The Color of Jazz/Pete Turner Photography*, forward by Quincy Jones. New York: Rizzoli.

Uszler, Marienne. 1997. "Patrice Rushen." *Piano & Keyboard* 197: 40–43.

Voce, Steve. 1996. "Phil Woods Talks to Steve Voce." *Jazz Journal International* 49(10): 8–9.

Waggoner, Walter H. 1959. "Curtain Rises On a Producer-Director Feud." *New York Times*, X3 (December 20).

Watson, Steve. 1995. *The Harlem Renaissance: Hub of African American Culture, 1920–1930*. New York: Pantheon.

Wild, David. 2007. *And the Grammy Goes to . . . : The Official Story of Music's Most Coveted Award*. Ann Arbor, MI: Ann Arbor Media Group.

Wilson, John S. 1962. "Two Recording Jazz Artists Whose Style Has Not Dated." *New York Times*, 156 (May 6).

Wilson, Olly. 1995. "The Black American Composer." *Black Perspectives in Music* 13: 26–34.

Young, Andrew. 2008. *An Easy Burden: The Civil Rights Movement and the Transformation of America*. Waco, TX: Baylor University Press.

Zank, Stephen. 2005. *Maurice Ravel: A Guide to Research*. New York: Routledge.

INDEX

Mouskouri, Nana, 75, 151n29
Movie Song Album, The, 82
Mozart, Wolfgang Amadeus, xvii, xix
Mr. B. in Paris, 72
Mr. Music, 52
MTV, 78, 152n42
Muddy Waters (McKinley Morgan-
  field), 4
Mulligan, Gerry, 57, 94, 98
Muse, Clarence, 86
Music Alive!, 24
Music in America, xvii
Musical choices, 26
Musical freedom, 26
Musical Jim Crowism, xvi–xvii
Musicking, xiii
My Blue Heaven, 87
My Fair Lady, 59
"My Reverie," 44, 50

Napster, 24
National Association for Music Edu-
  cation, 111–12
National Guard Show, 43
National Medal of the Arts, 25
National Museum of History, 24
Navarro, Fats, 30
Ndeda, 82
"Negro Speaks Rivers, The," 83
Nelson, Oliver, 88, 95, 154n8
Nelson, Willie, 81
New Orleans Dixieland jazz band
  style, 46
New Oscar Pettiford Sextet, The, 70
New Urban Entertainment (NUE), 22
New York Times, xvi, 36–37
Newmar, Julie, 97
Newsweek, xx
Nimitz, Jack, 31
"NJR," 46
Noone, Jimmy, 4
Norén, Jack, 30, 31
North, Alex, 90

North by Northwest, 91
"Nothing from Nothing," 77
Nottingham, Jimmy, 31
Nutcracker Suite, xviii

Obama, Barack, 23
O'Connor, Carroll, 100
O'Day, Anita, 47
Of Mice and Men, 91
"Of the Sorrow Songs," xiv
Off The Wall, 78
"Oh Happy Day," 61, 148n46
Okeh records, 71, 149n8. *See also* Race
  records
Olatunji, Babatunde, 43
"Ole Turkey Buzzard," 97
Oliver, Joe King, 4
Oliver, Sy, 39
Omele, Okontolo/Bata, 107
"On Green Dolphin Street," 59
"On the Street Where You Live," 59
"On the Sunny Side of the Street," 49
On the Town, 54
On the Waterfront, 91
"One," 76
Operation PUSH, 21
Ortega, Anthony, 15
Ory, Kid (Edward), 4
Osborne, Jeffery, 81
O'Solomon, Otis, 62
Our Shining Hour, 76
Our Town, 91
"Outa-Space," 77

Palomar Theater, 5, 6, 11
pandeiros, 59, 147n43
Panic in the Streets, 87
Paradigms of double consciousness,
  xiii, 137n5
Paramount Pictures, 88
Paramount Theater, 13
Paris, France (Jazz), 19. *See also* Barclay
  Records